WHERE BAD JOBS
ARE BETTER

WHERE BAD JOBS ARE BETTER

Retail Jobs Across Countries and Companies

Françoise Carré and Chris Tilly

RUSSELL SAGE FOUNDATION / NEW YORK

The Russell Sage Foundation

The Russell Sage Foundation, one of the oldest of America's general purpose foundations, was established in 1907 by Mrs. Margaret Olivia Sage for "the improvement of social and living conditions in the United States." The foundation seeks to fulfill this mandate by fostering the development and dissemination of knowledge about the country's political, social, and economic problems. While the foundation endeavors to assure the accuracy and objectivity of each book it publishes, the conclusions and interpretations in Russell Sage Foundation publications are those of the authors and not of the foundation, its trustees, or its staff. Publication by Russell Sage, therefore, does not imply foundation endorsement.

Library of Congress Cataloging-in-Publication Data

Names: Tilly, Chris, author. | Carré, Françoise J., author.
 Title: Where bad jobs are better : retail jobs across countries and companies / Chris Tilly and Francoise Carre.
 Description: New York : Russell Sage Foundation, [2017] | Includes bibliographical references and index.
 Identifiers: LCCN 2017021366 (print) | LCCN 2017035281 (ebook) | ISBN 9781610448703 (ebook) | ISBN 9780871548610 (pbk. : alk. paper)
 Subjects: LCSH: Retail trade   Employees. | Retail trade.
 Classification: LCC HD8039.M39 (ebook) | LCC HD8039.M39 T55 2017 (print) | DDC 331.7/93   dc23
 LC record available at https://lccn.loc.gov/2017021366

Text design by Suzanne Nichols.

RUSSELL SAGE FOUNDATION
112 East 64th Street, New York, New York 10065

10 9 8 7 6 5 4 3 2 1

Contents

List of Illustrations

About the Authors

Fraçoise Carré is research director at the Center for Social Policy, University of Massachusetts Boston J. W. McCormack Graduate School of Policy and Global Studies.

Chris Tilly is professor in the Department of Urban Planning at the University of California, Los Angeles.

Acknowledgments

In a project this broad, one incurs many debts of gratitude. We start by thanking the National Retail Federation, and in particular Kathy Mance of the NRF Foundation, whose support in reaching out to several U.S. retailers was crucial in our U.S. field research. We also thank the many retail companies, as well as the hundreds of individual headquarter representatives, managers, workers, and union representatives, in the United States and Mexico who shared their knowledge with us. Knowing something about the pace of retail work, we are deeply appreciative to them for not only their time but also their reflections on the future of the industry.

Funding support was critical, and we want to shower unbridled appreciation on the Russell Sage Foundation, which funded our U.S. fieldwork and analysis, the European counterpart projects, the research, writing, and conference collaborations that underlie chapters 5 and 6, and a significant portion of the work of pulling the research together into this book (projects 85-05-03 and 85-10-01). Special heartfelt thanks to program officer Aixa Cintrón-Vélez, former president Eric Wanner, current president Sheldon Danziger, and publications director Suzanne Nichols, who have been extremely supportive and patient throughout this complex process. Big thanks also to the Rockefeller Foundation and then-program officer Katherine McFate for supporting the Mexican cross-sectional study (grant 2003 WC 184), as well as to the Ford Foundation and former program officer Hector Cordero-Guzmán for supporting an important part of the U.S. quantitative data analysis (grant 1085-0487). Author Tilly thanks the Fulbright-García-Robles program (which does not assign grant numbers) for underwriting his 2004 stay in Mexico that made possible the Mexico cross-sectional study and his wife Marie Kennedy's 2007 Mexico stay, thus facilitating the longitudinal study. (Tilly shared Kennedy's Mexico room and board.) As well, we thank the W. E. Upjohn Institute for Employment Research, and Susan Houseman in particular, for support for U.S.-Mexico-Canada comparative research, some of which has found its way into online chapter A1 (http://www.russellsage.org/publications/where-bad-jobs-are-better) and other parts of the book (Grant 2010-126). We also are grateful to the Gould Foundation for the Paris School of Economics for sponsoring our stay at the school, which afforded us the opportunity for collective thinking with French colleagues that resulted in joint analysis and writing (through a grant awarded to our French colleague Philippe Askenazy). Finally, we thank our home institutions, the University of Massachusetts Boston, the University of Massachusetts Lowell, and the University of California, Los Angeles, for direct funding through research grants (UMass Boston Healey Research Grant: 2010–2011 cycle, UMass Lowell Faculty-Student Collaborative Research Grant: 2010–2011 cycle, and UCLA center director research support) and research assistant funding, as well as for more indirect support.

No less appreciated are our numerous collaborators and co-authors. Philip Moss deserves special thanks for taking on an important share of the interviewing duties in a number of the case studies. Dorothea Voss-Dahm and Maarten van Klaveren educated us deeply about retail work in Europe as together we struggled through the six-country comparative analysis that generated much of the analysis in chapter 5 (as well as figure 3.1 and the accompanying conceptual framework). Philippe Askenazy, Jean-Baptiste Berry, and Sophie Prunier-Poulmaire played the same role in the France-U.S. comparison that makes up an even larger proportion of chapter 6 (as well as parts of chapter 5). Brandynn Holgate, José Luis Álvarez-Galván, and Diana Denham were coauthors of other published work that came out of this retail project as well as research assistants, and ideas worked out with them are found especially in chapters 2, 3, 4, and 7 and in the online supplement chapter A1.

Graduate research assistants were our right-hand people throughout this process. Brandynn Holgate, José Luis Álvarez-Galván, and Diana Denham deserve another shout-out here, for all three contributed years of careful toil. Patrick Adler, Iraida Elena Blanco, Amanda

Enrico, Michelle Kahan, Beth O'Donnell, and Fabián Slonimcyk rendered essential help with fieldwork, project management, statistical analysis, and qualitative coding. Many others helped out in more limited capacities: Kyle Arnone, Patricia Jiménez de Greiff, Matt Hopkins, Marc Horne, Xiaoxu Jin, Kristin Kelly, Joe Kennedy, Carolina Martínez Londoño, Jessica McBride, Rob Moreau, Jasmine Mutuku, Ramón Quintero, Gwendelyn Rivera, Ana Tapia, Christina Thompson, Carolyn Vera, and Ariana Vito. Thanks to the UMass Boston Center for Social Policy's former director Donna Haig Friedman for hosting the project during the fieldwork and to colleagues for their encouragement over the years.

We also wish to thank various publications and their mostly anonymous reviewers for enormously helpful feedback. Again, the Russell Sage Foundation and its reviewers lead the list, and Suzanne Nichols has been an editor extraordinaire. The W. E. Upjohn Institute also reviewed and published our work in addition to funding it. Others include editors of edited collections in which we published related work: in chronological order, Nelson Lichtenstein, Stanley Brunn, Enrique de la Garza and Carlos Salas, Jérôme Gautié and John Schmitt, and Patricia Findlay and Chris Warhurst. Journal editors and reviewers also belong on this list—this time in alphabetical order: *Comercio Exterior, Connecticut Law Review, Economía Informa, Global Labour Journal, International Labor and Working Class History, International Labor Brief* (Korea Labor Institute), *Interventions Économiques/Papers in Political Economy, Latin American Research Review, Perspectives on Work, Revista Latinoamericana de Estudios de Trabajo,* and *Work, Employment and Society.* It would be tedious to list the many seminar and conference audiences in a dozen states and an equal number of countries whose comments and questions informed and provoked us, but we proffer thanks to all and special recognition to the Industry Studies Association, the Labor and Employment Relations Association, the Latin American Association of Labor Sociologists, the MIT Institute for Work and Employment Research seminar, and the Latin American Studies Association, all of which hosted multiple papers from this project at their conferences and seminars over the years.

There are also far too many individuals to thank, but we wish to highlight a few who stood out. Marc Maurice, François Sellier, and Jean-Jacques Silvestre are not acquaintances, but their groundbreaking research on comparative, institutionally grounded research on workplaces opened the door (and our minds) for the stream of research in which we place this volume. Eileen Appelbaum, Joel Boone, Larry "Chip" Hunter, Susan Lambert, Richard Murnane, Edward Soja, and David Weil offered particularly provocative and generative reactions to earlier versions of this work. Enrique de la Garza, Alfonso Bouzas, and Matias Bolton provided useful suggestions and insights at a still earlier stage, as we undertook fieldwork. Our spouses, Robert MacLeod and Marie Kennedy, have nourished us with love and support and afforded boundless encouragement, as well as provocative thoughts, for this project. This kind of work would not happen without them.

We dedicate this volume to four highly esteemed mentors we shared while studying at MIT: Eileen Appelbaum, Ben Harrison, Michael Piore, and Martin Rein. Their imprint and influence permeate this book.

1 / Introduction

The United States has a bad jobs problem, and retail jobs are at the heart of it. For those interested in solving the problem, a global shopping trip could prove very instructive. For example, shopping for groceries is a very different experience in France than in the United States. An American shopper in Paris might be surprised to find cashiers seated, to have to do her or his own bagging, and to find stores closed on Sundays and most evenings. Less noticeably, a typical Parisian store is overwhelmingly staffed by adult women, with many fewer workers in their teens or early twenties. Other divergences, equally important, would not be visible to the shopper: perhaps most striking, the average French nonmanagerial retail employee earns almost 90 percent as much per hour as the economy-wide average, far more than the U.S. ratio of just under 70 percent.[1] And though French retail workers are as likely to work part-time as American ones, they are only half as likely to work fewer than twenty hours (see chapter 6). A perceptive shopper might detect signs of one last contrast: underpinning the higher pay, French retail workers are considerably more productive, as reflected in measures like faster item scan rates and larger amounts of sales per hour per employee (see chapter 6).

Crossing into Germany yields even more contrasts. Cashiers sit, customers bag, and stores are closed on Sunday, as in France, but in Germany retailers are required to give notice of work schedules *six months in advance*. This is a luxury that retail workers in San Francisco and Seattle who fought to get two weeks' advance notice (and for that matter their Parisian counterparts) could hardly imagine. The large majority of German frontline workers—cashiers and stockers—have had a two-year specialized apprenticeship and are knowledgeable about everything from troubleshooting cash registers to ordering merchandise. This level of expertise is unheard of among U.S. retail's entry-level workers. At the same time, a growing number of German retail workers hold extra-short "mini-jobs"; often offering lower pay and fewer benefits, mini-jobs converge with some aspects of U.S. retailing (see chapter 5).

If we round out our global shopping spree with a trip to Mexico City, still more differences emerge. At first glance, the scene would look familiar to U.S. shoppers: cashiers stand and are joined by baggers. However, while Wal-Mart, the country's largest retailer, is a low-wage and 100 percent union-free employer in the United States, in Mexico the giant retailer pays more than its competitors and is largely unionized. Instead of a huge cadre of part-timers, as in the United States, Mexican retail workers overwhelmingly work full-time. Instead of complaining about working too few hours, they complain about being made to stay to work extra hours without pay. And Mexican baggers look expectantly at shoppers for tips, since they subsist on tips only (see online supplement chapter A1).

These differences between countries matter not just for the shopping experience but for job quality. Bad jobs, most would agree, are those with low compensation, few promotion opportunities, and difficult schedules and working conditions. Retail, the largest employment sector in the United States—with millions more workers than manufacturing—fits the bill: this industry offers low wages, fluctuating work schedules, and scant opportunities for earnings progression. Conventional retailers insist (usually after reminding us of how many jobs they create) that they must keep wages low and work schedules variable in order to compete with Wal-Mart. Wal-Mart, in turn, maintains that it is simply finding ways to do business more efficiently in order to deliver affordable goods to large numbers of shoppers. But as the French, German, and Mexican examples illustrate, there are other ways to successfully run a store.

It is worth emphasizing here that the evidence is strong that employment in stores is here to stay for a long time to come, in spite of recent predictions of the imminent displacement of store-based retail by online sales. We review the arguments for stores' durability in chapter 8.

Bad jobs in retail are far from exceptional. Retail offers a window into the tens of millions of U.S. jobs that have seen quality stagnate or decline in recent decades, with weak or no compensation growth, decreased employment security, and in many cases ever more unstable schedules. In current debates over job quality, some observers have rightly directed attention to the pulling away of the top—the "1 percent"—as a result of growing inequality, but fundamentally the most pressing concerns involve those falling behind at the bottom, as well as the increasing number of people in the middle who are slipping toward the bottom.[2] Worries about bad jobs have become a hot-button political issue in the United States, cropping up in the debates in each recent election cycle. The clearest manifestation of Americans' concern and even outrage is soaring support for a higher minimum wage. In January 2015, three-quarters of Americans—including 53 percent of Republicans—supported raising the federal minimum wage to $12.50 an hour by 2020. Nearly two-thirds went beyond that to support a federal minimum wage increase to $15 by 2020.[3]

The "bad jobs" crisis reaches well beyond the United States to encompass much of the wealthy world, though the U.S. problem is particularly acute.[4] At the core of the debate, both in the United States and globally, is not just the task of describing or quantifying low-quality jobs, but the need to seek explanations for variation and change in job quality in order to come up with workable improvements. Our goal, and that of other researchers working in this vein, is to develop strategies to improve bad jobs and narrow the gap between bad and good jobs.

Improving retail jobs does not necessarily mean turning them into unambiguously good jobs; retail jobs in our comparison countries are not terrific, but they are better in significant ways. In this book, we examine how and why retail jobs differ—across companies within particular U.S. retail sectors, across two contrasting subsectors within retail, and especially across countries—to determine how the mechanisms behind these differences could be leveraged to make U.S. bad jobs better. Put in the simplest terms, U.S. bad jobs in retail and other low-wage industries will improve when changes are made in the institutional environment—laws, labor relations structures, and broadly held values—followed by changes in managerial approaches.

THE ARGUMENT FOR INEVITABILITY

Casting a long shadow over public and scholarly debate on job quality is the specter of inevitable decline in job quality. If economic and technological developments have structurally narrowed our options to "one best way" at the level of the firm, the nation, and the organization of the global economy, then, in former British prime minister Margaret Thatcher's pithy phrase, "there is no alternative"—or at least, the range of alternatives has been radically narrowed. This perspective is most visible in debates over raising the minimum wage. Business representatives such as the U.S. Chamber of Commerce and the business-backed Employment Policies Institute have led public opposition to boosts in the minimum wage (as well as the opposition on other emerging policy battlefronts, such as required paid sick leave and advance schedule notification), with backing from a number of academic economists.[5] Laws raising the minimum wage have advanced despite these critiques. But as the economist Paul Osterman has pointed out, large numbers of policymakers and intellectuals—especially economists—have continued to take for granted a broader set of myths about the inevitable limits on job quality.[6]

The basic argument for the inevitability of job degradation is that structural changes in the world economy confine businesses and governments to a limited set of viable options—which they ignore at their peril. Recent research on low-wage work has pointed to five structural forces that seem to contribute to the proliferation and further degradation of low-end jobs, both in the United States and globally.[7]

First, *globalization* has "flattened" the world.[8] Workers increasingly compete with one another across countries, and multinational corporations implant their business models around the world.[9] Given retail's relative immobility, global worker competition is less of an issue in this sector, but transnational companies abound. Wal-Mart, itself an increasingly global retailer, is joined in the U.S. food retail market by a long list of global competitors, including Aldi and Lidl (Germany), Ahold (the Netherlands), Delhaize (Belgium), and Chedraui (Mexico), often selling under names like Trader Joe's, Giant Foods, Food Lion, and El Super.

A second structural force is the spread and intensifying implementation of *information and communications technology* that facilitates the automation of routine tasks, the standardization of practices, and the elimination of "slack" in systems of production. Retail boasts numerous applications of this technology, from simplified cash registers and bar code scanners to Wal-Mart's much-vaunted logistical system (now emulated by every large retailer), to scheduling software.

Third, *financialization* has increasingly compelled corporations to wring out costs and boost payouts to financial stakeholders. By financialization, we mean not just direct company takeovers by private equity firms and the like, but also the widespread shift to a "shareholder value" priority that drives companies to focus on quarterly returns and dividend payouts rather than long-term (or even middle-term) investments in the sustainability of the enterprise. Publicly held retailers are on the firing line just like other corporations, and they have been a frequent target for private equity takeovers.[10]

A fourth factor is *neoliberalism*, a package of ideologies and policies that promote deregulating markets, including those for international trade, shrinking the social welfare, labor rights, and employment rights functions of government, and reducing the influence of bottom-up market regulators such as unions.[11] The United States is the acknowledged heartland of neoliberalism, and a number of neoliberal changes have particularly reshaped U.S. retail and its jobs. Prevailing policies and dominant policy thinking have shifted toward relaxed store hour regulation (with long hours leading to worker-unfriendly schedules), lighter restrictions on commercial development and on the growth of huge, market-dominating corporations (fueling retailers' entry into growing numbers of markets and intensifying low-road competition), weaker enforcement of labor and employment laws, and enfeebled unions.

A final transformative force, one that is harder to observe and analyze, is the *shift in business norms* regarding the treatment of workers. For obvious reasons, it is difficult to distinguish the impact of shifting norms (shared values and practices) from that of other changes. Nonetheless, at least some analysts have argued for the importance of norms as an independent factor.[12] In this volume, we report changes in retail that are consistent with this perspective: a shift away from unionized or paternalistic management structures to more stratified, atomized, and low-commitment systems.

One way of summarizing the argument for inevitability—whether locally or globally—starts with the widely shared view that three main types of structures create the context for business strategy in any particular setting. The first, of course, is the *economic environment* in terms of available resources, technologies, and markets. A second is *national institutional structures*, which consist of the ground rules in terms of laws and regulations, labor relations structures, and social norms. The third is *sectoral structures*—the dominant companies and prevailing strategies that to some extent shape the options for other companies and the viability of other strategies.

The inevitability argument posits that the ubiquity of globalization, computer-driven technological change, and financialization has made economic environments more similar around the world. This reality has thus compelled governments to widely adopt neoliberal policies, propelling convergence in national institutional structures. With global convergence in the economic and policy realms, the nature of retail jobs will increasingly be determined by the dominant business models that best adapt to this environment. In an extreme version of this analysis, we should expect the country's and the world's retailers to increasingly act like Wal-Mart (or, if you prefer, fill in your favorite innovative upstart competitor here)—or to get out of Wal-Mart's way as it sweeps the field.

CHALLENGING THE INEVITABILITY ARGUMENT: EVIDENCE FROM FIELD STUDIES AND NATIONAL STATISTICS

The best way to verify or falsify the inevitability argument is to examine variation both *within* countries (seeking evidence about the latitude for divergent company strategies) and *across* countries (seeking evidence about the space for distinct national institutional influences). Although our goal is to come up with explanations and solutions for the bad jobs problem writ large, we have made this enterprise manageable, yet still fruitful, by focusing exclusively on retail, particularly two of its subsectors.[13] In doing so, we build on a rich ongoing research dialogue probing the relationships between industry dynamics, firm strategies, and job characteristics in specific industries, both in the United States and globally.[14] This book incorporates some of our earlier published work on retail jobs, but it goes further by combining a full range of within- and across-country comparisons in a unified argument tied to policy concerns that are particularly salient in the United States. We consider seven countries in some detail: the United States, Denmark, France, Germany, the Netherlands, the United Kingdom, and Mexico.[15] In an analysis of Wal-Mart around the world, we expand the field of view to include information from other countries, adding selected data points to the cross-national analysis. Retail in all the focus countries—and arguably in all the countries in the Wal-Mart analysis as well—is definitely exposed to globalization, computerization, and financialization. All of these countries have shifted in a neoliberal direction in recent decades, though certainly Denmark's "flexicurity"—combining labor flexibility with a broad and strong social safety net—is not neoliberal in the mold of the United States.

But as we document throughout the book, Wal-Mart and other discounters with similar practices are far from marginalizing other business models in retail. Within the United States and the other six countries, there is significant variation among companies in the main traits of jobs. In the United States, for example, Costco and Trader Joe's persist and grow as "high-road" alternatives to Wal-Mart. Likewise, systematic cross-national differences are alive and well, as we saw at the beginning of this chapter.

The cross-company, cross-sector-within-country, and across-country comparisons actually are a bit more complex than we have so far signaled. We spell out this complexity later in the chapter as we lay out the structure of investigation and preview the contents of the chapters. But first, here is a brief introduction to the U.S. retail industry and a description of how we carried out the research.

Retail, the largest employer in the United States, offers promising turf for exploring job quality issues. Retail wages are low and have trended lower—in real dollars and relative to other industries—over the long run. Retail jobs also have a number of other noxious characteristics: high labor turnover, limited upward mobility, and schedules that are variable, often unpredictable, and largely part-time. The sociologists Thomas Bailey and Annette Bernhardt glumly concluded in an influential 1997 article that even U.S. retailers showing high-road productivity and service practices hewed to the low road in job quality. In addition, a majority of retail jobs, especially at lower levels, are held by women; although, as we shall see, women often choose part-time hours, many of them are nonetheless frustrated by insufficient hours, inadequate wages and benefits, and few promotion options. U.S. retail jobs are also disproportionately occupied by younger workers.

A final trait of retail merits special mention: retail jobs are relatively immobile, in the sense that most retail sales take place when consumers visit stores and pick up goods there. The growing "Amazonification" of retail—shifting sales online and in the process greatly shrinking some sectors of retail such as book and record stores—does call this immobility into question. So far consumers have voted with their feet to continue shopping in bricks-and-mortar stores—especially in food retail, the largest retail subsector—but Amazonification may change retail jobs in the future, as we explore in our concluding chapter. In the meantime, retail's relative immobility has important consequences. Standard approaches to improving job quality, such as unionization and labor standards regulation, may simply impel manufacturers to relocate to less costly environs, but immobile industries lack this option. If there is any industry where policy and collective action levers should be able to improve jobs, it is retail.

Our research is primarily grounded in fieldwork carried out in seven countries around the world: the United States, Denmark, France, Germany, the Netherlands, the United Kingdom, and Mexico. We carried out fieldwork in the United States and Mexico ourselves. We collaborated with teams of researchers in the five Western European countries (who are credited in the chapters to which they contributed). The field research touches a limited number of retailers, so to yield a more complete picture we (and in Europe our colleagues) have also analyzed government-collected statistics, coverage of retail in business and general media, and scholarly and consultant research on the sector and its jobs.

In the United States and Europe, the fieldwork followed a uniform plan. From 2005 to 2007, we and our colleagues conducted case studies of large food and consumer electronics retailers—nationwide companies in Europe and a mix of national and regional companies in the United States, which has a larger and more fragmented market.[16] Groceries and consumer electronics present important contrasts: old and new (for example, "big box") retail formats, varying skill demands, and sharply differing gender composition and wage levels (electronics retail employment being more male and better compensated); we lay out these differences for the United States in chapters 2 and 3. In the United States, we visited sixteen retail companies: eight grocery chains, six consumer electronics chains, and two general merchandise retailers that sell both groceries and electronics as well as a range of other goods. (Each general merchandiser thus counts for two cases for a total of eighteen cases.) In each company field study, we interviewed top corporate executives, then visited at least one store where we interviewed managers, supervisors, and a selection of frontline workers (cashiers, baggers, stockers), for a total of 195 interviews. We asked about how work was organized and why, about competitive pressures, about job characteristics and how they fit into workers' lives, and about how and why all these workplace features had changed over time. To the extent possible, we also obtained corporate statistics on jobs in the stores.[17]

In Mexico, we conducted similar company studies in 2003–04, asking about the same topics as in the other countries and conducting 133 interviews in all. Some differences in the study design are described in the chapter devoted to Mexico (chapter A1, http://www.russellsage.org/publications/where-bad-jobs-are-better).

In short, we dug deep into the retail sector in these seven countries, getting the perspectives of everyone from C-suite executives to baggers and street vendors about the retail sector and its jobs. We say more about what the case studies involved in the chapters about the United States (chapter 3), Europe (chapter 5), and Mexico (chapter A1).

WHY FIVE TYPES OF COMPARISON IN SIX EMPIRICAL CHAPTERS?

In the next six chapters, we set out to puncture the myth of inevitably and invariably bad retail jobs and to explain how and why these jobs differ across and even within countries. To the extent that we explain such contrasts, we develop a framework for thinking about how retail jobs could be improved. Our main practical interest is improving U.S. retail jobs, though what we learn also has implications for other high-income countries. We build explanations at two

levels, corresponding to within-country and across-country variation. Within countries, companies follow different paths because of
their own strategies and because of the collective strategies of workers. Companies formulate both *product market strategies*—strategies
to succeed in selling their goods and services—and *labor strategies*—
strategies for compensating and managing their workforce. They
must maintain some level of compatibility between the two types of
strategies. Workers, meanwhile, exercise their ability to act as a
group, termed their *collective agency*. The most obvious form this
takes is unionization, and another form is activity around local regulations—such as the wave of revisions to local minimum wage
laws, driven by coalitions led by unions and worker advocates, that
are under way as we write.

Across countries, we point to both political agency and nationally
differing norms as sources of persistent job quality differences. At
the level of political agency, cross-national differences in public policies and labor relations systems have proven remarkably durable
in the face of economic forces that were predicted to lead to their
demise. Perhaps less surprisingly, differences in norms are also durable. It is beyond the scope of this book to explore the political and
cultural processes that underlie this durability, or the macroeconomic ones that render it sustainable. What we do undertake is an
examination, where possible, that traces differences in job features
back to the institutional divergences that gave rise to them or that
continue to sustain them. In some cases, we can also point to economic patterns that make differing labor practices sustainable
within the retail sector itself: for example, French retail workers are
more highly paid than U.S. retail workers, but they are also more
productive; Mexican retailers do not have the option of "just-in-
time" scheduling of part-timers, as in the United States, but they
routinely press their full-time workers to work extra, unpaid hours.
One consequence of the continued robustness of institutional and
normative differences, termed *national* or *societal effects,* on jobs is
that in a particular sector like retail, national and sectoral effects
combine to create what we and our colleagues have called a *national-
sectoral model.*[18]

As it turns out, one common feature of retail national-sectoral
models is that retailers across all the countries studied, not only in

Table 1.1 / Axes of Comparison in the Book

Comparison	Analytical Focus	Chapter(s)
Compare companies within subsectors (groceries, consumer electronics) within a single country (the United States, Mexico)	Managerial strategies	3, 4, A1
Compare subsectors within one country (groceries versus consumer electronics in the United States)	Product markets, gender, skill	2, 3, 4
Compare retail jobs as a whole across seven countries	Institutions	5, A1
Compare grocery cashier jobs between the United States and France—one job in one subsector in two countries	Institutions	6
Compare jobs in one company (Wal-Mart) across twelve countries	Institutions	7

Source: Authors' summary.

the United States, are pioneers in developing and promoting "exit options"—ways, legal or not, to evade the labor standards in place.[19] Thus, retail workers are not to be found in the aristocracy of labor in any of these countries, nor even at the average in terms of pay and other job traits. Nonetheless, they are sometimes much closer to the average, and each negative feature of retail jobs found in the United States is absent in *at least one* of the comparison countries. Thus, the strong sectoral characteristics of retail still play out differently depending on the national characteristics of each retail industry and its leaders (for instance, Wal-Mart for the United States, Carrefour for France, and Metro for Germany).

We flesh out the various parts of this theoretical framework in the following chapters. Empirically, we implement our within-country and across-country comparisons using five axes of comparison, summarized in table 1.1. Each of these axes holds particular factors constant to analyze distinct aspects of how and why retail jobs differ in different settings. Multiple comparisons are necessary because the factors in question are qualitative, sometimes composite, and not reducible to a single indicator. Throughout, our point of departure is the United States.

The first, narrowest comparison holds constant the country (and therefore large-scale institutional contrasts) and the subsector (large differences in the type of market and service involved), comparing companies one-to-one to search for differences in company strategies. These strategies include how the company engages the *product market*—whether it aims high or low, broad or narrow, in the interface with consumers—and how it engages the *labor market*. The key goal is to analyze how strategic choices translate into job quality outcomes. For example, targeting higher-margin products can make room for better jobs.

A second within-country comparison scales up to our two subsectors, food and consumer electronics retail in the United States. Product markets, skill mixes (technical knowledge in electronics, attention and attitude in groceries), and gender compositions diverge between the two subsectors. What are the consequences for job characteristics, and why?

For the third axis, we zoom out to comparisons between U.S. retailers and their counterparts in Europe and, to some extent, in Mexico. Here we focus on the laws, standards, labor relations systems, reproductive institutions, and norms—in short, the *institutions*. The institutions most consequential for job quality include minimum wages and unionization, but also less obvious ones such as skill development systems, store opening hours (as we saw in our "visits" to French and German grocers), and shopping culture. Secondarily, we draw some electronics–food sector contrasts across countries.

To go deeper into the role of institutions and social norms, the next comparison pits U.S. grocery cashiers—the modal retail job—against their French peers, holding the subsector and the job fixed. We limit our comparison to two countries in order to paint a richer picture of how institutional differences play out for corporate strategies and job outcomes. With this finer-grained comparison, we distinguish a wider range of relevant institutional differences, including those mentioned in describing the previous axis, as well as land use, child care policies, and norms.

In our final axis for empirical analysis, we hold the core corporate model and culture constant across a wide geography. We look at a single retail leader, Wal-Mart, across twelve countries to see how the global retailer responds to varying national institutions. Wal-Mart is particularly interesting precisely because it in some ways sets the pattern for others to follow, yet its jobs vary cross-nationally.

THE PLAN OF THE BOOK

Chapter 2 sets the context for our comparative argument with a review of retail job patterns in the United States from standard statistical sources. Far from dispelling a picture of uniformly bad retail jobs, for the most part the evidence compiled in the chapter is favorable to such a gloomy portrait. The message is clear: the average retail job in the United States is a lousy job. But we also show differences between the average job in food retail/grocery, consumer electronics, and general merchandise. The last category covers warehouses, big-box stores, and small stores that sell a *wide range* of goods and are included in our study because so much food and so many electronic goods are sold through these channels. This portrait of U.S. retail jobs leaves open questions of how job quality varies around the average (though we do document variation in compensation), what explains that variation, and what such patterns might be like when we look beyond this country's borders. In the last section of chapter 2, "Looking Back and Looking Forward," we lay out in more detail the questions that motivate the heart of the book, the primarily qualitative chapters 3 through 7.

Chapters 3 and 4 dig into our study of U.S. retail cases, starting with differences between grocery and consumer electronics jobs, but also comparing companies *within* each retail sector. Chapter 3 introduces the U.S. study in greater detail and already starts to reveal cracks in the façade of inevitability. We distinguish between *cost-cutting strategies,* on the one hand, and two product market strategies—*quality- and service-driven strategies*—on the other. We find that cost-cutting prevails, but that there is substantial variation in the relative mix of the two product market strategies when we compare food retailing (which is more oriented toward quality and variety) and electronics stores (which are more oriented toward adding services). These differences characterize product market strategy in each case, but also shape labor strategy and thus job quality. Even more importantly, we find striking differences in job quality and characteristics *within* each of the two subsectors, reflecting differing managerial strategies within the same market. Since our interviews reveal that difficult work schedules are the most acute issue for U.S. retail workers, we close the chapter with a look at "lived job quality," scrutinizing scheduling practices and part-time jobs through the eyes of job-holders.

Chapter 4 continues to highlight and explain differences in human resource policies and practices between broadly similar retailers. It focuses on the tensions that striate every company's combination of product and labor market strategies. We ask whether current U.S. retail business models are sustainable for the companies implementing them and raise serious doubts about longer-term sustainability and consequences for retail jobs.

Having raised questions about the sustainability of U.S. retail models, we turn in the next three chapters (plus the online supplemental chapter at http://www.russellsage.org/publications/where-bad-jobs-are-better) to cross-national comparisons to inquire about the existence and viability of alternative models. Chapter 5 contrasts U.S. retail jobs broadly with those in five European countries. U.S. retail is an outlier in some regards, such as in having higher labor turnover and in assigning highly fragmented and task-oriented job duties to workers. But the United States sits in the middle of the pack in other regards, such as in the percentage of retail workers who fall below a low-wage threshold and the percentage of part-time workers. Looking at these variations one dimension at a time (compensation, schedules, skills, mobility) elucidates how national-level institutions push different job characteristics in distinct directions. A particularly sharp contrast emerges between, on the one hand, the United States and three other countries where most retail workers are low-wage and, on the other hand, Denmark and France, where few retail workers have low-wage jobs. This divergence motivates a more in-depth U.S.-France comparison in the next chapter.

Chapter 6 puts U.S. and French retail jobs, particularly the cashier job in grocery retailing, under the microscope. As we showed at the outset of this chapter, we find striking differences in the troika of pay, productivity, and posture (whether cashiers stand or sit). We trace the institutional roots of these and other differences in the cashier job between the two countries. Important influences are not just differences in labor regulations but also differences as wide-ranging as zoning and store hours restrictions, the length of the school year, and the system of child care.

For those who are interested, the online chapter A1 takes our cross-national comparisons to the global South (but not very far south) to examine differences between retail jobs in the United States and Mexico.[20] Contrasts emerge, especially between the heavy use of part-time employment in U.S. retail and the overwhelmingly full-time employment of Mexico's retail workers. As before, we follow the disparities back to institutional differences in labor law, sociocultural norms, and politics—differences that once again involve both labor institutions per se and other institutions, such as gender roles. But we also uncover and explain ample job quality variations *within* Mexican retail. Finally, Mexico's bustling ensemble of street merchants and micro retail outlets opens the question of informality in retail. In another within-sector comparison, we explore variation within and between informal retail outlets and suggest lessons for growing informal retailing in the United States.

Wal-Mart, the world's largest retailer, takes center stage in chapter 7. Here we argue that *Wal-Mart comports itself quite differently in different institutional environments*. Is it hard to imagine Wal-Mart offering higher wages than its major competitors, cooperating with unions, and being consistently underpriced by retail rivals? We show that all this and more is happening in at least some of the countries where Wal-Mart does business—providing further ammunition for the argument that Wal-Mart will adapt its practices to any changes in U.S. institutions.

Having concluded our round-the-world tour of retail jobs, we turn in the final chapter to our conclusions about retail jobs in the United States and globally, how and why these jobs vary, and what it would take to make them better in the United States. We highlight our key arguments and findings and update the U.S. picture by discussing major changes in food and consumer electronics retail and their environment since our fieldwork ended in 2007 and the impact of these changes on job quality. Fleshing out what it means to modify institutions—to the extent that they can be modified—in order to prompt job improvement, we briefly present promising policy options and grassroots strategies for improving bad jobs in retail (and other low-wage sectors). We close on an optimistic note: the global evidence tells us that inevitability is a chimera and that we *can* make retail jobs better.

WHAT CAN BE DONE TO IMPROVE U.S. RETAIL JOBS?—TWO APPROACHES

Challenging the myth of inevitability opens the door to a variety of responses. The first, which we stress throughout the book, is restructuring institutions to alter incentives. A second response that has achieved considerable traction in public discourse emphasizes enlightened employer self-interest—or, to put it crudely, getting businesses to "be like Costco."[21] The notion here is that making retail or other jobs lousy yields high employee turnover and low commitment, which undermine productivity and customer service, but that if low-wage employers flipped the script, higher-cost workers would pay for themselves in higher productivity, with Costco and Trader Joe's, among others, pointed to as potential models. Since many employers have made a myopic choice, the remedy is to teach them that they can do well by doing good.

We are skeptical about enlightened self-interest as a major lever of job improvement. We readily agree that businesses make ill-considered choices and that the linkage between job quality and productivity is real. But both our within-country evidence and, especially, our cross-country comparative evidence suggest that in the absence of policies that close off the low road (low wages, low productivity), win-win proselytizing will have little effect and the Costcos of the U.S. labor market will remain niche players. Conversely, nothing gets employers thinking harder about ways to increase productivity than blocking the easy low-wage solution—whether because comfortable but incorrect assumptions become self-reinforcing, or because businesses have calculated correctly that the benefits to them of creating better jobs will not fully offset their costs. So while we use head-to-head firm comparisons to argue that there is *some* room for enlightened self-interest, ultimately we emphasize that the widespread upgrading of jobs requires the first approach—institutional change. With its multiple analyses tracing job quality differences back to institutional divergence, this book is centered on making this case.

2 / Numerous, Young, Female, and Poorly Paid: A Profile of the U.S. Retail Workforce and Its Context

For most readers, U.S. retail companies and their workforces are old acquaintances. Consumers in the United States typically visit retail stores several times a week, and they make online purchases with increasing frequency. Many of us worked in retail as teens or young adults, or we have friends and family members who did.

Despite—or perhaps because of—the ubiquity of direct experiences of retail, it is very useful to get behind appearances and characterize U.S. retail as an employer in the aggregate. This aggregate portrait sets the stage for the within-country and across-country comparisons that make up the rest of the book. It also makes an initial case for policy interventions by detailing just how bad U.S. retail jobs are.

We start by briefly documenting retail's size as an employer. We then weave together two main themes: that retail jobs are indeed bad on average, and getting worse, and that certain people work in retail, especially in the worst jobs. We focus on the retail sector as a whole but also explore variation by breaking out findings for two contrasting retail subsectors, grocery stores and consumer electronics. We take a first look at variation in pay and other conditions within each subsector and even within individual job titles. In addition to food and electronics, we also consider the general merchandise subsector, including big-box formats such as Wal-Mart, Target, and Costco, because they are major players in food and appliance sales—and because two warehouse store chains in our U.S. study fall in this category.

RETAIL: A GIANT EMPLOYER

Retail employed 13 percent of the private workforce in the United States in 2015, accounting for considerably more than all manufacturing combined (10 percent). Retail has held its own at roughly 14 percent of employment since 1975, whereas manufacturing has declined in importance since that year, when employment stood at 27 percent.[1] Wal-Mart has become the largest private-sector employer in the country, with 1.5 million workers. Four of the ten largest employers in the country are in retail: Wal-Mart, Kroger, Home Depot, and Target (in descending order).[2]

Grocery and electronics stores are interesting in their own right. Grocery stores represent "old" retail, whereas electronics retailing is "new" retail. The two subsectors offer a series of highly informative contrasts: differences in wages and occupational distribution, in gender composition, in unionization, in industry concentration, in establishment size, and in skill requirements.

Our research focuses on stores rather than e-commerce because stores continue to represent the great bulk of retail sales and employment. Ali Hortaçsu and Chad Syverson report that e-commerce has grown rapidly in relative terms, shooting up from 0.9 percent of total retail sales in 2000 to 6.4 percent in 2014.[3] However, e-commerce's share of sales remains small compared to that of physical stores in most subsectors; music and videos are the only merchandise category in which online sales accounted for a majority of total sales (79.5 percent) in 2013. Consumer electronics retailers in our study worried mightily about online competition, but as of 2013 only one-third of computer hardware and software sales, and less than one-fifth of electronics and appliance sales, took place online—though Hortaçsu and Syverson project steady continued growth in these shares.

Figure 2.1 / U.S. Retail Average Hourly Wage (in 2014 Dollars) and Average Retail Wage as a Percentage of All Private Production and Nonsupervisory Employees, 1972–2014

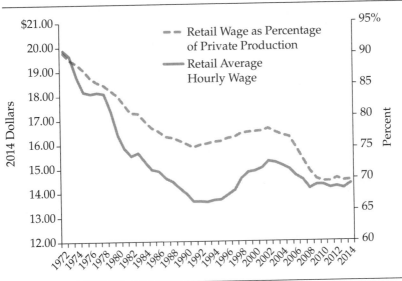

Source: U.S. Bureau of Labor Statistics 2016a.
Note: Wages in this figure and other figures adjusted for inflation with CPI-U.

RETAIL WAGES: LOW AND FALLING OVER TIME

The retail industry exemplifies the central dilemmas of low-wage work: most retail jobs offer low wages, few benefits, and little formal training. Retail trade's nonsupervisory workers have long been paid lower than the average for all private-sector workers. Of greater concern, the retail workforce has experienced overall wage loss since the 1970s, both in absolute terms and relative to other private-sector workers (figure 2.1). Retail's relative hourly wage—the wage as a percentage of the private nonfarm average—dropped from 90 percent in 1972 to 75 percent by 1991, and after stagnating for more than a decade, it dropped again in the late 2000s recession and stood at 70 percent as of 2014. This reflects the fact that the real value of the hourly wage in retail declined by 25 percent from 1975 to 1991 and has never completely recovered its early value; the 2014 wage was 72 percent of the 1972 level in real terms.[4] Indeed, retail workers make up more than one-quarter of those working at the minimum wage.[5] In 2014, the average hourly wage for nonsupervisory employees was $14.36, compared to nearly $20 in 1972 (in 2014 dollars).

In terms of total compensation, which includes employer-sponsored benefits as well as wages, retail trade workers fare even worse relative to the workforce as a whole. Average retail hourly compensation weighed in at $15.23 in 2005, only 57 percent of the economy-wide average.[6] In 2014, 43 percent of all retail workers and a scant 16 percent of part-time retail workers received employer-sponsored health insurance, as compared to 52 percent of all workers.[7] Similarly, only 30 percent of retail workers received employer-sponsored retirement benefits in 2001, compared to 48 percent of all workers.[8]

Poor compensation of store employees is not the result of lagging productivity. Retail labor productivity growth has actually outpaced economy-wide growth over the last twenty years, particularly in the last decade.[9] (The table summarizing these results and other supplementary tables and figures, along with sample sizes for estimates, can be found in the online appendix at http://www .russellsage.org/publications/where-bad-jobs-are-better.)   Some have sought to explain this pattern as the "Wal-Mart effect," driven by rapid increases in logistical efficiency in the big-box retail industry and at Wal-Mart specifically.[10] Disaggregating by retail sector reveals interesting divergences. Food and beverage stores—of which supermarkets are a part—show negative productivity growth from 1987 to 1997 (attributed by Tilly to the combination of expanding store hours and increasing use of part-time employment), relatively slow growth even from 1997 to 2007, and minimal growth over the most recent period, 2007 to 2013.[11] General merchandise, the category that includes Wal-Mart, more or less tracks the retail industry average. Electronics and appliance retailing (a somewhat broader category than consumer electronics) shows extraordinary productivity growth of 10 percent or more annually in all three periods. However, the Bureau of Labor Statistics productivity measure does not take into account the impact of productivity growth in inputs, and of course this was a period of enormous advances in productivity in electronic products. When we apply a crude correction that most likely *over*corrects for rising productivity in electronics manufacturing, progress in productivity in electronics retail gets adjusted to a more modest 2 to 3 percent since 1997 (and was negative in the earliest period).

The overall productivity growth makes sense, because retailing has come to be dominated by a few large companies that run large-format stores functioning more like a factory (with its attendant supply chain) than a mom-and-pop corner store. In 2007, 90 percent of grocery store employment and 93 percent of general merchandise employment were in establishments with twenty or more employees; electronics, a subsector with less labor intensity, had a more modest but still substantial 52 percent of employment in establishments with twenty or more employees.[12] Both the high concentration of sales in a small number of firms and the dominance of large stores mark dramatic reversals from a century ago. In 1929, 70 percent of sales were made by single-store firms, most of them small mom-and-pops.[13]

Though productivity is growing, skill requirements in retail—another pay determinant—are low. According to the *Occupational Outlook Handbook,* "Typically, retail sales workers do not need formal education. However, some employers prefer applicants who have a high school diploma or equivalent."[14] Retail workers are a bit less likely than others to have education beyond high school.[15] Over one-quarter of frontline grocery workers have less than a high school degree, and indeed many are still enrolled in high school (nearly one-tenth are age eighteen or younger).[16]

Frontline employees in retail generally train on the job with an experienced worker for a period of a few days to a month. Cashiers and stock clerks require less preparation than retail sales positions. According to the 1995 Survey of Employer-Provided Training, retail workers typically received 3.7 hours of formal training, as compared to an average of 10.7 hours across all sectors. (The survey has not been repeated since 1995.)[17]

However, we would argue that low skill requirements, rather than a *cause* of low pay in retail stores, is an *effect* of business strategies aimed at keeping wages low. For decades, retailers have avidly adopted deskilling technologies. The advent of boxed beef, which shifted most meat-cutting from the store back to the slaughterhouse, had deskilled one of the most skilled retail occupations by the early 1980s.[18] Philip Moss and Chris Tilly, in employer interviews in the early and mid-1990s, discovered a consensus that "smart" cash registers and bar codes had deskilled cashier jobs, the most numerous job category in retail.[19] Charley Richardson, in a more recent update, reported that automated "self-checkout" counters and the emerging use of "personal shopping buddies," which put a customer-activated scanner right in the shopping cart, have shrunk the cashier's role to supervision, monitoring of theft, and assistance.[20] Meanwhile, computerized ordering and a shift of stocking to outside vendors has removed most discretion from stock clerks' jobs (as well as decreased their numbers). Such deskilling reflects corporate strategies to drive down labor costs by reducing skill requirements.

If deskilling has been an outgrowth of retailers' quest to keep wages low, what kicked off that quest in the first place? One compelling explanation for falling wages despite productivity growth is the erosion of protective institutions that once sheltered retail wages—the minimum wage and unions. Whereas in the first several decades after the minimum wage was enacted in 1935 Congress routinely raised the minimum to keep pace with inflation, since the 1970s legislators have allowed the real minimum wage to slide downward, under intensive lobbying by industries that employ large numbers of low-wage workers, retail among them. The real value of the minimum wage in mid-2015 was 32 percent less than in 1968. And over the past thirty years, the retail sector shed union density even faster than the rest of the economy, reducing union coverage by 44 percent (from 7.8 percent to 4.4 percent), compared to a 41 percent decrease economy-wide.[21] Fast-growing, strongly anti-union new entrants, such as Wal-Mart, make up an important part of this story.

Another factor that is likely to have contributed to wage deterioration is the spread of discount retailing, which combines reduced prices and service levels, high volumes, and resulting economies of scale. Part of the discounting formula is lower pay, rationalized in part because expected service levels are lower. While nondiscount department stores have paid about the average retail wage, discounters paid 16 to 18 percent less, with little change in that gap, between 1990 and 2004 (more recent data are not available; see online table 2A.4).

Low Average Retail Wages and Widely Varying Pay Levels

This book emphasizes that retail workers have varying economic fortunes within as well as across countries, and that certainly holds for U.S. retail wages. In figure 2.2, we compare *relative* average wages for nonsupervisory employees in three subsectors (the two that are the focus of study and general merchandise, which encompasses warehouse stores) along with retail as a whole over the period 1991 to 2014. The only gainers are workers in consumer electronics stores. In 1990, wages for frontline workers in consumer electronics started out higher than wages for workers in grocery and in general merchandise retail, at 90 percent of the private-sector average. Their wages rose slowly for a decade before embarking in 2000 on a roller coaster ride: soaring to 109 percent, falling again, and then rising again to equal their earlier high before dropping off slightly, ending at 105 percent in 2014. Meanwhile, grocery and general merchandise, along with overall retail relative wage rates, barely budged in the 1990s and then fell after 2000. Grocery employ-

Figure 2.2 / Relative Average Wage by Retail Subsector, 1991–2014

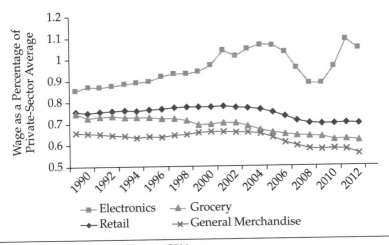

Source: U.S. Bureau of Labor Statistics 2016a.

Table 2.1 / Wages and Occupational Distribution for Grocery, Electronics, and Selected General Merchandise, 2014

	Grocery	Electronics	General Merchandise
Median hourly wage			
All occupations	$10.38	$13.65	$10.39
Cashier	9.27	9.24	9.11
Retail salesperson	11.52	11.23	9.56
Stock clerks and order fillers	10.42	11.00	10.12
Percentage of total employment			
Cashier	32%	2%	20%
Retail salesperson	2	46	30
Stock clerks and order fillers	19	2	16

Source: U.S. Bureau of Labor Statistics 2015c.
Note: Selected general merchandise includes variety and discount stores, not department stores. All data are from May 2014.

ees took the biggest hit, losing eleven percentage points relative to the economy-wide average over the period. General merchandise workers, the lowest-paid in the bunch, similarly lost ten percentage points to end at 56 percent.

Part of the wage difference between consumer electronics and the other subsectors can be accounted for by differences in job requirements. Greater technical knowledge and skill are required to sell some electronics devices, particularly complex appliances and computers.

Another factor that helps explain cross-subsector pay differences is staffing configuration, which is quite different in the three subsectors (see table 2.1). In grocery stores, the modal employee is a cashier, a job category that constitutes one-third of all jobs in the grocery sector. Cashiers mainly work in the front of grocery stores and supermarkets, either checking customers out or assisting them. Well over half of all grocery store cashiers work part-time and earn a median hourly wage of just over $9. In consumer electronics stores the modal worker is a retail salesperson—the highest-paid of the three job categories. Salespersons make up nearly half of the workforce in this subsector. Salespersons work on the floor assisting customers and answering questions. This role requires the worker to be somewhat knowledgeable about the products being sold and may include encouraging customers to buy them. The median hourly wage for salespersons in consumer electronics is over $11, about $2 more per hour than the median for a cashier. (The salesperson-cashier gaps are comparable across food and electronics retailing.) General merchandise, which includes warehouse stores, falls in between food and electronics. In this subsector, salespersons slightly out-number cashiers, but the frontline job categories are paid less than their counterparts in grocery and electronics stores.

Though it is tempting to attribute the grocery-electronics pay dif-ference primarily to skill, there is another obvious candidate: gen-der. Women's share of grocery employment is almost 50 percent higher than in electronics retailing.[22] Moreover, our fieldwork find-ings counsel skepticism about the importance of truly technical skills in consumer electronics sales. When describing what he hires for, an assistant store manager at a leading electronics chain we call Electronix told us:

> You're looking for a couple things. I think first off a general knowl-edge or at least an interest in the electronic product, so they can get excited about it. An outgoing personality. We also want to find somebody that's friendly. I will take the last two over the first two. . . . Quite frankly, I've been a very successful salesperson with a very small knowledge base around electronics. Ultimately you're selling yourself and not the product.

We know from a wide range of other research that friendliness and a "service-oriented" attitude are commonly and tacitly assumed to be inherent in women and are therefore devalued as job skills, whereas both sales ability and even limited engagement with tech-nology ("an interest in the electronic product") tend to be valued and rewarded in men.[23] Our interviews did not focus on this issue, and we did not find any "smoking guns," but it seems likely that a similar dynamic is at work in these retail subsectors.

Looking more closely at wage differences, there is vast variation in pay even within specific jobs. Tables 2.2 to 2.4 show hourly pay for four occupations at percentiles ranging from the tenth to the ninetieth. The 75/25 ratio shows the ratio of the seventy-fifth to the twenty-fifth percentile, and the 90/10 ratio compares the two most extreme percentiles shown. The disparities are greatest for op-erations managers: the ninetieth-percentile manager earns between

Table 2.2 / Hourly Pay by Percentile in Grocery Stores, Selected Occupations, May 2015

	General and Operations Managers	Cashiers	Retail Salespersons	Stock Clerks and Order Fillers
90th percentile	$65.67	$14.52	$16.98	$17.18
75th percentile	45.36	11.33	12.72	13.33
Median	32.92	9.40	10.33	10.50
25th percentile	23.37	8.77	9.13	9.14
10th percentile	17.05	8.17	8.54	8.41
75/25 ratio	1.95	1.29	1.39	1.46
90/10 ratio	3.85	1.78	1.99	2.04

Source: U.S. Bureau of Labor Statistics 2016b.

Table 2.3 / Hourly Pay by Percentile in Electronics Stores, Selected Occupations, May 2015

	General and Operations Managers	Cashiers	Retail Salespersons	Stock Clerks and Order Fillers
90th percentile	$84.12	$13.29	$24.25	$15.73
75th percentile	56.88	11.15	15.98	12.95
Median	40.86	9.53	11.33	10.89
25th percentile	27.09	8.78	9.35	9.48
10th percentile	18.60	8.16	8.55	8.61
75/25 ratio	2.10	1.27	1.71	1.37
90/10 ratio	4.52	1.63	2.84	1.83

Source: U.S. Bureau of Labor Statistics 2016b.

three and five times as much per hour as the tenth-percentile manager, and even the 75/25 ratio comes in at around two times as much. Cashiers, with the job that is arguably the most uniform, show the smallest spread, but workers at the ninetieth percentile still earn two-thirds to three-quarters more than the bottom tenth, and even the 75/25 gap is a pay difference of more than 25 percent. The pay variation for retail salespersons and stock clerks falls between operations managers and cashiers. These are not trivial disparities in pay. The extent of pay disparity varies across retail subsectors as well. For electronics retail salespersons, the 75/25 and 90/10 ratios are noticeably higher than in the other two subsectors.

Table 2.4 / Hourly Pay by Percentile in Selected General Merchandise Stores, Selected Occupations, May 2015

	General and Operations Managers	Cashiers	Retail Salespersons	Stock Clerks and Order Fillers
90th percentile	$63.84	$13.97	$14.89	$17.07
75th percentile	47.54	11.01	12.12	13.32
Median	33.70	9.24	9.95	10.63
25th percentile	26.49	8.56	8.82	9.07
10th percentile	19.72	8.01	8.17	8.30
75/25 ratio	1.79	1.29	1.37	1.47
90/10 ratio	3.24	1.74	1.82	2.06

Source: U.S. Bureau of Labor Statistics 2016b.
Note: Selected general merchandise includes all general merchandise stores except department stores. Big-box stores make up a large portion of this category.

As will be further explored in the company studies (chapters 3 and 4), the salesperson job entails a broader span of job responsibilities in electronics, even a bifurcation of jobs, across types of stores but also, increasingly, within them.

These percentile ratios surely capture differences in worker skill, store size, productivity, location, and possibly how occupations are defined; for example, the operations manager category may encompass a far broader range of jobs. Nevertheless, these pay differences also suggest that retailer wage-setting approaches differ, even within retail subsectors and for specific jobs.

Union presence also varies dramatically across retail sectors. In 2014, 14.4 percent of workers in grocery stores were union members, compared to only 2.2 percent in consumer electronics and 3.0 percent in general merchandise. Grocery stores' level of unionization is unique among retail subsectors: *the next highest unionization rate for retail is in vending machine operators* (6.6 percent). Unions' impact on retail jobs, as measured by the wage premium of union members relative to nonmembers or by union density, also diverges dramatically across regions and states in the country (see online table 2A.7). The wage premium associated with unionization for grocery workers ranges from a high of 23 percent in the Midwest to a low of 0.6 percent in the Pacific region. Narrowing the focus to large states within these regions, we see a smaller but still notable range of variation, from 9 percent in California to 3 percent in Illinois. Retail union density also differs widely, from less than 2 percent of the workforce in the South to nearly 11 percent in the West.[24]

WHO WORKS IN RETAIL?

Over the past thirty years, the retail industry's workforce has changed from female overrepresentation to a nearly fifty-fifty gender composition that is similar to that of the private sector as a whole (see online figure 2A.1).[25] In 2014, grocery job-holders included a slightly higher percentage of women than the retail industry as a whole, whose share of women workers, in turn, was slightly higher than the workforce-wide share. The percentage increases as we focus only on frontline employees (cashiers, clerks, and baggers), signaling that women are overrepresented in retail frontline jobs but underrepresented in management jobs.[26] If we split the frontline jobs into manual jobs (such as stock clerk) and customer service jobs (cashier, sales), the gender split is far more dramatic: women hold only 31 percent of the manual frontline jobs, but 63 percent of the customer service ones. Women are markedly underrepresented in consumer electronics and appliance stores, even in frontline jobs.

The employment patterns for women with children under eighteen and those with children under age six are quite remarkable. Given retail's reliance on part-time jobs, one might have expected women with young children to be concentrated in retail's front lines. However, there is virtually no difference between frontline workers and other retail workers in terms of responsibility for children. Although, as we will see, women in retail are concentrated in part-time jobs, it is *not* because of overrepresentation of women caring for children.

Young workers—those under age twenty-five and even those under eighteen—are heavily overrepresented in retail jobs; the youngest workers are particularly common in grocery stores (see online figure 2A.2). The percentage of the workforce under age twenty-five is more than twice as high in frontline retail jobs as in the overall workforce, and nearly four times as high in *grocery* frontline jobs. Young workers (notably current students) represent a reliable source of willing part-time workers, and thus a critical element in retail's labor strategy. At the same time, it is important to keep in mind that two-thirds of the frontline retail workforce is twenty-five or older—and in fact, the workforce has become older in the years since we conducted our fieldwork.

The employment of African American workers in retail mirrors the group's representation in the overall economy, whereas Latinos are moderately more concentrated in retail (see online figure 2A.3). Not surprisingly, these two groups are more highly represented among frontline employees, with Latinos particularly present in manual frontline positions. Migrants—both Latinos and others—are not particularly overrepresented in retail, even within frontline jobs (see online figure 2A.4).

Retail Hours: The Dominance of Part-Time Work

Short, variable, and often unpredictable hours set retail apart from most other sectors, marking another problem area for retail job quality. Susan Lambert and her colleagues have documented retail workers' erratic hours and the destructive work-life tensions that ensue.[27] A 2014 survey of California retail workers found that only one-third were guaranteed a set minimum number of hours, and that a slightly higher percentage got fewer hours than they would have liked. Nearly half had schedules that varied week to week, and one-quarter had to be on-call to go to work the same day.[28] And of course, variations in number of hours also translate into potentially wide swings in weekly pay.[29]

The cornerstone of this scheduling system is extensive use of part-timers. Part-time employment in retail often precludes fringe benefits and can be accompanied by lower pay scales as well. Firms rely on part-time workers as a way not just to cut costs through lower wages and benefits, but also to increase scheduling flexibility and closely match labor to customer flow. Managers use this flexibility to regularly change work schedules, improve their productivity measures, and cover evening, night, and weekend shifts.[30]

Definitions of part-time employment vary across different retail employers. Since our fieldwork found that scheduled hours are often short for full-time workers (less than forty hours weekly, sometimes less than thirty-five) as well as part-time workers, for tracking purposes we report part-time employment defined as "usually" working less than thirty-two hours per week on average.[31] Between

1992 and 2014, the frontline workforce in retail averaged about 44 percent part-time. Part-time employment has declined in frontline retail from 53 percent in 1992 to 39 percent in 2014, but part-time hours remain well over three times as prevalent in these frontline retail jobs as in the private workforce as a whole (see online figure 2A.5).

The subsectors of grocery and electronics differ markedly in their part-time shares. In 2014, 50 percent of frontline grocery workers were working part-time hours, as compared to 18 percent in electronics.[32]

Because part-time is an employment status as well as a schedule, it matters who gets part-time or full-time jobs (see online table 2A.5). It is not surprising to learn that less-educated workers (which includes youths still in high school) are more likely to work part-time than their more-educated counterparts. The gender difference is also striking. In the overall workforce, women are more than twice as likely to work part-time hours as men. This trend is partially mirrored in the retail workforce as a whole and in grocery stores. Women are still more likely than men to work part-time hours in retail, but only 1.8 times as likely.[33] The gender gap in part-time work is most muted in grocery stores, where both men and women are about equally as likely to be part-time as full-time (with part-time rates of 51 and 55 percent, respectively). Perhaps more surprising is the fact that in retail, blacks and Latinos, as well as foreign-born workers, are on the whole *less* likely to work part-time than Anglo whites.[34] It appears that young white workers and women make up the bulk of the part-time workforce in retail.

The situation of women with children merits separate commentary. Contrary to expectations, women with dependent children (under age eighteen) have a *lower* rate of part-time employment in retail than women without children.[35] Women with children under six are more likely to work part-time than women with older children, as expected. Statistically, we are seeing the impact of continuing increases in the labor force participation of women with children, combined with the large group of (childless) student-age women (plus a smaller group of older women) in retail's part-time jobs. Gap-filler jobs (jobs with fixed short-hours) for mothers are the exception rather than the rule in part-time employment in retail. We explore this issue further in chapter 3.

Importantly, retail part-timers are more likely than those in other industries to work very short hours—less than sixteen per week.[36] There is also a much higher share of workers with schedules in the sixteen- to thirty-one-hour category.[37] Cashiers (the most female of the occupational groups) are somewhat more likely to work in the shortest hours category than stock clerks (the most male occupational group), but the differences are not large.

Just a Stepping-Stone?

Poor job quality is of less concern if the jobs in question are typically just a brief stop in an upward trajectory. High employee turnover suggests that workers do move on from retail jobs more quickly than from other jobs. In 2006, retail had an annual separation rate of 46 percent, as compared to 34 percent for nonfarm employment as a whole.[38] The flip side of turnover is retention. In their report on the rate of long-term retention—eleven years in this case, that is, workers with an employer in 1992 that were still with the same employer eleven years later—the economist Harry Holzer and his coauthors note that retail's retention rate, 36 percent, lags well behind the rates for manufacturing (42 percent) and health care (56 percent).[39] However, these authors find a striking result when they calculate each company's earnings premium or deficit (the amount a firm pays above or below other firms, holding measurable firm and worker characteristics fixed) and classify companies whose payoffs fall in the top 40 percent as "good job" businesses. Retention at retail's "good job" employers was actually *higher* than in manufacturing (50 percent versus 47 percent), though it still lagged behind retention in health care. Where retail jobs are better than average for the industry, workers are more likely to stay.[40]

Exiting a poorly paid retail job does not necessarily mean exiting low-wage work. Low earners in retail are more likely than those in any other industry to be stuck at low earnings levels over time. Fredrik Andersson, Harry Holzer, and Julia Lane divide workers into quarterly earnings quartiles and focus on the lowest quartile, whom they dub low earners. Not surprisingly, retail workers are disproportionately represented in the low-earning group.[41] The authors estimate statistical models for the probability of "partial escape" from low earnings (shifting from the lowest quartile to the second or third quartile) as well as "full escape" (shifting into the fourth quartile) over the 1999–2001 period. Based on their results, low earners in retail are only 55 to 61 percent as likely to *partially or fully* escape their low earnings status, and 62 to 68 percent as likely to *fully* escape, compared to the reference group of manufacturing workers.[42] These low escape probabilities put retail workers far behind workers starting from jobs in every other major industrial group.

LOOKING BACK AND LOOKING FORWARD

The statistics we have reviewed in this chapter paint a coherent, if somewhat bleak, picture of U.S. retail employment. Retail pay is low, and despite respectable productivity growth, pay has fallen in absolute and relative terms over the long haul on average. Part-time work reigns, and schedules are variable and often unpredictable. Union representation and collective bargaining are scarce, and getting scarcer. Young people are overrepresented among employees. In contrast, women and people of color are not particularly overrepresented in retail as a whole (a change from past patterns in the case of women). However, women are, like young workers, concentrated in part-time work, and both women and minority workers are overrepresented in lower-ranking jobs. Turnover is high, but retail workers are less likely to "escape" low-wage work altogether than those in other sectors.

This portrait answers many questions about retail work in the United States but opens up others—which we strive to answer in the remainder of the book. Three sets of questions target characteristics of U.S. retail for which available statistics will not suffice. One set asks: How do retail employers make it all work (or try to)? In particular, how do they go about setting employee policies and targets? Given low pay and challenging schedules, how do retailers successfully staff stores and meet customer service needs with a low-skill, high-turnover workforce? How do managers, from the store to the corporate level, decide how many positions to cover with part-timers and how to deploy them? And how do retailers keep workers motivated?

A second set of questions ask: How do U.S. workers experience retail work? Do they view their retail jobs as careers, as stopgaps, or as something to do temporarily while undertaking other activities (education, child-rearing, phasing into retirement)? How do they gauge their responsibilities and workload? Do they feel motivated by the various strategies that employers have designed to motivate them? How do the trade-offs and the subjective experience differ for part-timers as opposed to full-timers, for women as opposed to men, for frontline workers as opposed to supervisors or managers?

Andersson and his colleagues have given us a valuable glimpse of retail workers' odds of escape from low-wage work, but standard U.S. data sources tell us relatively little about our third set of concerns: *worker mobility*. Our interviews give us both top-down and bottom-up perspectives on worker mobility. In our look from "above," managers told us how their companies tracked turnover for different job categories, estimated how many upper-level jobs were filled from within, and described career paths within and across companies. From "below," retail workers told us about their work histories and career plans and what they had observed in terms of mobility opportunities and coworker turnover. Given the high level of job churning that involves retail-to-retail job moves, the bottom-up view gave us important insights into the trajectories of employee turnover and how they result from the interaction of management and worker strategies.

This statistical overview has thus set the challenge that we seek to address in the rest of the book. Having reviewed the characteristics of retail companies, workers, and jobs, we henceforth strive to understand how retail's key actors—workers and to a limited extent unions, but especially managers—make the decisions that cumulate to these aggregate patterns, and how broader institutional structures change the terrain for that decision-making in consequential ways.

3 / Change and Variation in Retail Jobs in the United States: A View from Case Studies

Underlying the U.S. retail sector's average wages (low), hours (short), and demographics (tilting young and, in some jobs, toward women) are individual company policies and practices. The previous chapter showed that there are substantial differences in wage levels across the two subsectors of retail on which we focused the US research, food and consumer electronics. There also are substantial differences in wage levels across companies within each of these subsectors. In this chapter and the next, we use fieldwork findings in sample companies to confirm not only these wage disparities but also other differences in job quality. We use eighteen field cases to scrutinize and explain *variation* around those averages. And we pick apart the dynamics of *change* in the nature and quality of retail jobs, seeking to separate causes from effects.

Variations in job quality and dynamics are important to analyze for several reasons. First, the analysis places the retail firm itself *at the center of the web of decisions*—past, present, and anticipated ones—that most durably shape the tasks, scheduling, compensation, and mobility opportunities of retail jobs. Company- and banner-level studies allow us to account for firm decisions *within context*, be it institutional, industry-specific, or dependent on corporate history.[1] Our findings speak to enduring debates about structure versus agency: to what extent do businesses have the room to successfully pursue distinct strategies within the same market and institutional context, and what are the roles of the actors, from the CEO to rank-and-file workers, in shaping these strategic differences? Second, exploring firm dynamics through case studies helps us understand what has happened so far to retail jobs while also pointing toward likely directions of future change for retail jobs and workers. Third, case findings are valuable for identifying policy paths to improve U.S. retail jobs.

We analyze retail company cases and retailers' agency as "nested" within specific strategies for engaging the product market and for labor deployment. The strategies themselves are emblematic of the industry subsegment and broader industry structure. In turn, industry structure develops within particular institutional contexts (regulatory, customary), which differ across regions in the United States (and of course across countries). In this and the next chapter, we focus on variations in company managerial policies and practices *within* a shared institutional environment that varies little—the United States—save for some regional variations in zoning regulations and state-level minimum wage. But as we shall see in chapters 5 and 6, key features of the U.S. institutional environment regarding market, employment, and social policies make the country an outlier among high-income countries. They bear previewing here because they play an important role in retail job quality and in our field cases and frame our later extensive discussion of options for improving U.S. retail jobs (chapter 8). They include: weak zoning regulations and few or no opening hour restrictions (relative to European countries); low value of the minimum wage to which entry-level retail wages are pegged; thin and weak coverage by collective bargaining; sparse availability of affordable child care; no mandated benefits for part-time workers; and no prohibitions on short-hour schedules (fifteen weekly hours or less) and schedule fluctuation for workers in these jobs. All of these features contribute to shaping U.S. retail job quality characteristics in distinctive ways relative to other countries—but as we show in this and the next chapter, they do not entirely rule out paths to higher job quality in companies whose management aims for it.

In this chapter, we first present a general framework for understanding the determination of job quality at a particular company. We then zoom in to consider the particular roles of competitive (or product market) strategies and labor strategies and sketch out their shapes in U.S. retail. Next, we introduce our empirical study of sixteen retailers in two subsectors, food and consumer electronics, and then elaborate on the specific competitive formulas—which we term *service-driven* and *quality-driven*—adopted by each subsector in response to heightened competition. We illustrate how, within each subsector and within similar competitive orientations, there is still room for managerial maneuver and variation in labor strategies and job quality outcomes. We also note sources of tension among competitive and labor strategy goals. The chapter ends with a closer look at how work scheduling—a key strategic cost management tool for retail—meshes with patterns of labor force participation by women workers and others with constrained choices and at what the resulting "flexibility" means to these workers.

A FRAMEWORK FOR ANALYZING JOB QUALITY DETERMINATION

Markets, Institutions, and Firm Strategies

Our analysis posits a set of relationships between markets, institutions, and firm strategies that, we argue, play a determining role in job quality (figure 3.1). We lay out those relationships initially here without presuming their specific nature, then flesh out causal theories in this and later chapters, drawing on both existing literature and induction from our case studies.

In placing both the firm's market strategy and its labor deployment and human resources approach at the center, this general framework recognizes that in practice most variation in market orientation takes place *within* countries, where institutional differences are limited. This chapter and the next develop the framework for the U.S. retail sector, focusing on the left side of figure 3.1, which traces influences from markets to management strategy to job quality—though in chapter 4 we do briefly examine the impact of institutional differences within the country. Chapters 5 through 7 widen the angle to compare retail jobs in the United States to those elsewhere in the world, and here the right side of the framework takes over, since institutions differ far more dramatically across nations than within them.

Figure 3.1 / Analytical Map of Determinants of Job Quality

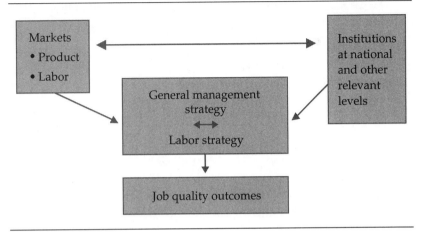

Source: Authors' conceptualization.

Competitive Strategies and Labor Strategies

The distinction between product and labor strategies is useful in an examination of the dynamics that drive job quality within the United States (and for that matter elsewhere). A *product strategy*, or competitive strategy, denotes a company's competitive formula in the market for goods and services. This strategy comprises the market segment—or combination of segments—the business targets, its mix of products, and its customer service approach or formula. A *labor strategy* governs the deployment of labor and encompasses everything from job design and recruiting to compensation and retention policies and practices.

In fieldwork in food and consumer electronics retailers, supplemented by documentary research, we asked the following:

- What strategies have retailers devised? What mixes of product and labor strategies are in force in U.S. retail chains? In particular, how do these patterns differ between food and consumer electronics retailing?

- How do these strategy mixes translate into job quality outcomes? In a cross-sectional sense, are they better or worse? In a time-series sense, are outcomes improving or deteriorating?

- What are the implications for the workforce of the choice of product strategy and the choice of labor strategy? What are the implications of the fit or lack of fit between these two approaches?

Other Findings on the Fit Between Product Strategy and Labor Strategy

Researchers have argued that some degree of alignment between the product and labor strategies is necessary for firms to sustain operations, and they expect firms to seek such alignment.[2] Still, there is room for some variation in the labor strategies that are compatible with a particular product strategy. Competitive orientations and associated labor strategies (and therefore job characteristics) differ by segment within and across businesses.[3]

But even within a market segment, multiple, distinct, labor strategy equilibria are possible (for example, Nordstrom versus Sears).[4] Indeed, Thomas Bailey and Annette Bernhardt's 1997 article on job quality in general merchandise and department stores challenged common expectations that product and labor strategies can be paired predictably.[5] In a provocative challenge to other findings in the literature on business strategy and job quality, Bailey and Bernhardt found that high-road product orientations—combining high levels of service or investments in advanced technologies—rarely involved high-road labor approaches. Bailey and Bernhardt's study indicated that retail presents both a range of product strategies and a range of labor strategies, as well as, more importantly, variation in the pairing of these.

The likelihood that a firm will adopt a particular labor approach depends not just on the firm's product strategy but also on other contextual or external influences (institutional factors and constraints, the state of the external labor market) and on internal influences (particularly managerial beliefs).[6]

Expectations for Our Study

Based on this previous research, we entered the U.S. study with several expectations. Despite Bailey and Bernhardt's cautionary finding, we expected to find that competitive success, or resilience, depends on some degree of alignment between product and labor strategies. (Wal-Mart's success story itself is an example of such a fit.) Indeed, the job quality implications of the fit between product and labor formulas matter to workers but also to the sustainability of particular strategies.

We also expected to find that certain *settings* are more hospitable to particular competitive and labor approaches. Within the United States, the timing of competitive change, the structure of regional markets, and the regional regulatory environment may all make a difference. For example, southern settings with little regulation of land use (zoning)—and therefore of retail market entry—as well as minimal labor standards regulation may make formulas reliant on higher service, higher compensation, and higher prices difficult to sustain.

Finally, we expected to find a range of variation in labor strategies within broadly comparable product strategies in a number of industries. We hypothesized that a high-road product formula, while an important correlate of high job quality, by no means *implies* good jobs. We do find in our fieldwork that there is variation in labor strategies across retailers within retail subsegments. Thus, in exploring mixes of business and labor formulas, we also explore the factors of variation within identifiable strategic mixes. In these ways, we identify in what market and regulatory environments and with what management approaches (within subsector) room for maneuver can yield higher job quality outcomes, at least for some retailers.

THE STUDY

Methodology

In all, we completed eighteen cases—ten food retailers and eight consumer electronics retailers—between mid-2005 and early 2007, before the effects of the late 2000s economic crisis began to be felt. We conducted site visit interviews in sixteen companies, not eighteen, because two companies are double cases (both food and consumer electronics). We limited the sample to substantial-sized regional and national chains, including some that have expanded beyond the United States. It is worth noting that, since the conclusion of fieldwork, three companies in our sample have filed for bankruptcy protection, two have been liquidated, and two have merged or been acquired—not uncommon fates in these retail sub-sectors. The sample was designed to reflect the range of retailers in each subsector: part of a regional or national chain, larger or smaller, unionized or not, traditional supermarket formula versus discount formula, and big-box versus traditional, full-service consumer electronics store.

The study implementation relied on securing companies' voluntary participation. The National Retail Federation provided essential help in recruiting retailers. We also contacted a number of retailers independently. We presented all of the companies with a statement outlining the benefits of participating in a study of national scope. We also offered them the opportunity to have a presentation from the researchers; none of them took us up on this offer. All companies that participated in the study received a thirty-page report of the essential findings.

In all, over an eighteen-month period starting in late 2005, forty-two companies were contacted by letter, and we followed up with successive telephone and email messages. The sixteen companies that agreed to participate (for eighteen cases) represented a response rate of 38 percent.

The Composition of the Sample

Table 3.1 provides highlights and distinctive characteristics of each of our sixteen field-study companies and illustrates the broad diversity of retailers in the two subsectors. As already noted, two case companies operate in both food and consumer electronics markets and so are counted in both categories. All of the food-only retailers except one have a regular supermarket format; the exception is a "mini-warehouse" format. One of the companies that carries both food and electronics has a warehouse format, the other uses a much smaller version of that format. Among food-only retailers, six are independent regional chains and two are what we call "cogs"—formerly independent regional chains now absorbed into national or multinational holding companies.

Among the consumer electronics–only companies, four have a big-box format and two have small stores. Two of the electronics chains sell a broad range of office supplies, including electronic equipment; we expanded the sample to include these companies

(*Text continues on p. 44.*)

Table 3.1 / Profile of Case-Study Companies and Their Business Strategies

	Geography	Format	Business Strategy
Food			
Food Chief	Cog	Regular	Under direct threat from Wal-Mart. Food Chief was revising its compensation plan and increasing the work pace and workload pressure. "Doing more with less staff."
Freshland	Regional	Regular	Freshland had implemented a two-tier wage structure and was seeking to improve levels of service, quality, and variety to compete with newcomers like Wal-Mart, but the erosion of wages and benefits was undermining these efforts.
Homestyle	Regional	Regular	Historically privately held, Homestyle had been acquired by a chain in recent years. It held its own against cost-cutting competition from other chains and from Wal-Mart supercenters thanks in part to its quality product offerings (for example, a wide range of wines) and in-person service.
Marketland	Regional	Regular	Marketland operated in a regional environment with few zoning regulations and few barriers to entry but experienced severe pressure from Wal-Mart and other regional chains that were threatened by Wal-Mart themselves.
Megamart	Regional	Warehouse	Megamart's small stores offered a narrow range of products but a large packaging of dry goods and small appliances. Some stores focused on serving small businesses such as restaurants, food carts, and clubs or associations. It had explored expanding its product range to include frozen foods.
P. A. Smith	Cog	Regular	The main competition for P. A. Smith's full-sized supermarkets, which maintained a full range of products, was other large regional and multiregional supermarkets.
The Market	Regional	Regular	Privately held, The Market held its own against cost-cutting competition from large chains. It identified "superior perishables" as the product that gave it its edge.

Table 3.1 / *(Cont.)*

	Geography	Format	Business Strategy
Food (cont.)			
Value Fresh	Regional	Regular	Sales were flat and market share had fallen over the past ten years at Value Fresh owing to stiffened competition from larger supermarket chains and overall pressure from Wal-Mart on both the supermarket and discount formats. It aimed to differentiate itself from the competition with better-quality fresh produce, meat, bakery, and deli departments. The squeeze on store monthly labor budgets limited Value Fresh's ability to grant raises and to keep sufficient labor employed in the stores. It operated in a regional market with few zoning regulations and little barrier to entry by other chains.
Jones Market			We conducted two interviews at Jones Market to collect contextual information only (not a full case).
Consumer electronics			
Electronix	Multiregional	Regular	Electronix offered a full range of equipment and services, but tiered offerings of both. It had addressed declining margins in the market for PCs and accessories (CDs, DVDs) by tiering its service options (and product packages) as high- or low-intensity. It was thus able to offer high-end home design and installation services as well as off-the-shelf products.
High Fidelity	Regional	Small	High Fidelity offered specialized audio and video equipment to a high-end customer base. The retailer moved from relying on technical knowledge for individualized product recommendation to predesigning optimal product packages that rely less on the technical knowledge of the store workforce and aim for great cost-effectiveness in sales. Under significant threat to market share from big-box stores, High Fidelity was adding services.

Office Express	Multiregional	Regular	Office Express, a diversified retailer, offered small business services, copying and printing, and electronic equipment, furniture, and traditional office supplies.
Photoworld	Multiregional	Small	In response to the market threat posed by digital equipment, Photoworld shifted from printing paper photos to offering support for self-service printing and emphasizing equipment sales.
Tech Source	Multiregional	Regular	During the study, Tech Source was designing and implementing a service "tiering" formula that would move it from an all-products offering to a tiered product offering and increased service component: off-the-shelf electronics, on the one hand, and higher-end home entertainment system design and installation, on the other. It was unclear whether the implementation would be successful.
The Office	Multiregional	Regular	The Office, a diversified retailer, offered small business services, copying and printing, and electronic equipment, furniture, and traditional office supplies.
Combined consumer electronics and food			
Bargain Warehouse	Multiregional	Warehouse	With its warehouse formula and narrow product range, Bargain Warehouse targeted middle- to high-income customers. It emphasized product selection and merchandising as well as goods "throughput" over in-person customer service, and it aimed for staff retention.
Village Voice	Multiregional	Warehouse/ small	Village Voice had a wide product range relative to its store size and operated in a relatively sheltered regional market outside of urban and peri-urban areas.

Source: Authors' compilation.

both because there is a small (and diminishing) number of large retail electronics chains and because office supply retailers are in fact important sellers of electronics. All six electronics retailers are multiregional companies. The two cases that straddle both sectors are multiregional companies.

The cases have several other key attributes:

- *Food retail sample:* Among the ten food retailers, three offer higher-end service, one offers medium service, three have low-service warehouse formats, and three are tiered-service companies. By "tiered" we mean that stores have areas that offer higher-end services (for example, made-to-order salads) while the rest of the store provides a medium level of service. The food retail sample includes two unionized and one partially unionized company. Our information on two unionized companies includes interviews with union representatives. In the other unionized company, union representatives declined to be interviewed.

- *Consumer electronics retail sample:* Of the eight retailers, two offer higher-end service, three offer medium-level service, one has a warehouse format, and two are tiered-service companies. All eight sell a mix of high- and low-technology products, and two offer office equipment and supplies.

The distinctions between high-, medium-, and low-service formats, in food retail in particular, and between high-technology and low-technology electronics offerings were not straightforward. Analytically, we would want to examine the correspondence between specific management and labor deployment practices and a retailer's choice of service level. In reality, "service level" is subject to much interpretation and fluctuation and remains a debated concept (which we examine further later in this chapter and in the next one). The contrast between a warehouse store and other types of stores is clear, however, and so is that between stores with very high service levels and others.

Fieldwork

In total, 195 interviews were conducted across the sixteen companies.[7] They include interviews with headquarters executives for human resources and operations, with regional managers, with store managers, and with a sample of frontline workers—part-time and full-time, front-end and sales-floor workers as well as those in spe-

Table 3.2 / U.S. Field Study Interviewees, by Retail Subsector and
Position

	Food	Electronics	Both Subsectors	Total
Corporate	20	23	2	45
District	11	3	3	17
Store manager	15	16	3	34
Supervisor	10	14	2	26
Full-time, frontline	12	14	6	32
Part-time	27	2	2	31
Union representative	3	0	1	4
Total	98	72	19	189

Source: Authors' tabulation.
Note: The number of interviewees (189) is less than the number of interviews (198, including 195 from the sixteen case-study companies and three serendipitous interviews) because a number of interviewees were interviewed more than once. This table includes the three serendipitous interviews (two union representatives in food and one part-time employee in electronics).

cialized departments (such as bakery, deli, photocopying, and home entertainment). Because we conducted these interviews outside of the busiest store hours, they tend to include fewer very junior, very short-hour workers and more of those who were regularly scheduled, even part-timers. In many cases, but not all, the store we visited was located near headquarters and was considered the flagship store. We attempted to factor this into our questions, often probing managers and workers with experience in more than one store (as well as in other companies) for contrasts and comparisons. We also asked for summary statistics on a variety of personnel indicators and received this information from about half of the participating companies. Three grocery chains and one consumer electronics retailer allowed us to visit two stores. All interviews were coded with qualitative software using a coding scheme prepared by the research team (see table 3.2).

DIFFERENCES IN STRATEGY AND JOB QUALITY OUTCOMES ACROSS RETAIL SUBSECTORS

With differing product markets, food retail and consumer electronics retail have adopted different product or competitive strategies. Job quality outcomes also differ across the two subsectors. Here we summarize their commonalities, then discuss their differences in both product and labor approaches on the ground—first in food retail and, second, in consumer electronics retail. We also begin to underscore factors at the individual retailer level that account for differences in job outcomes across retailers even within each subsector.

Commonality: A Cost-Cutting Priority and Its Implications

Across retail overall, and food and consumer electronics retail in particular, the standard adjustment to competitive pressures has been an ongoing focus on cost-cutting. Because a company's largest and seemingly most manageable costs are its labor costs, labor cost-cutting is the preeminent concern at all levels, from the boardroom to the store manager. Though this might at first glance seem to preclude using policy to improve these jobs, our argument—developed more fully in chapters 5 to 8—is that in fact policy that *closes off* competition based on exploitative labor cost-cutting will *open up* other avenues of competition not based on low compensation and unsustainable scheduling.

The drive to cut labor costs is reflected in compensation practices (low frontline wages and benefit rationing) as well as in attitudes toward union representation and policy stances regarding the minimum wage level. (We do not analyze the latter two dimensions because a wish to avoid or at least limit unions and opposition to a significantly higher minimum wage are virtually universal among U.S. retailers.) Importantly, cost containment or cost-cutting manifests itself in close monitoring of total labor hours used in stores (the "labor hours budget") and thus the extensive use of part-time workers and attempts to closely match labor "on the floor" to real-time customer flow and shelf stocking requirements.

We find that most retailers combine this primary, defensive cost-cutting strategy with a proactive secondary strategy that may entail changing the product mix, offering creative new service options, and improving the overall quality of goods and services. Importantly, some companies follow a third "no strategy" path— they grope for means to cut costs without having identified a proactive approach to addressing competition (at least at the time of study).

In addition to the pressures on all retailers already outlined, we find added pressures that specifically affect each of the retail subsectors on which we focus. Since we completed our fieldwork, both food retail and consumer electronics retail have faced further challenges that have exacerbated their cost-cutting and tested retailers' responsive strategies.[8] In food retail, there is growing variety in retail formats (particularly experimentation with smaller stores by large chains), and owing in part to the severe recession of the late 2000s, the "dollar store" market has expanded. In consumer electronics, big-box chains have had to contend with falling margins on computers and TVs as well as market pressure from online retailers. Moreover, retail as a whole, and grocery chains in particular, have experienced waves of buyouts by private equity firms that have exacerbated existing pressures. Private equity's demands for high returns can accentuate the squeeze on labor costs, drive staffing reductions that make it harder to keep shelves stocked, and lead to frequent changes in ownership and divestment of store buildings or other property.[9] Our fieldwork in the sixteen companies preceded some of these changes. Nevertheless, the dynamics documented in this and the next chapter portend not only retailers' patterns of adaptation to these most recent changes but also their reasons for adopting particular strategies.

Cost-cutting still leaves room for approaches aimed at improving service, quality, or the variety of offerings. Food retailers have tended to adopt *quality-driven* options, attempting to distinguish themselves through the quality and variety of goods, whereas *service-driven* electronics retailers have emphasized the provision of novel and useful services.

Quality-Driven and Service-Driven Strategies in Short

What Is Meant by Service in Retail It is critical to note that the concept of "service" is multidimensional. As used by retailers, it encompasses four dimensions. The first three form a package of consumer-oriented behaviors and knowledge that enhances the shopping experience and aims to draw and retain customers through a distinctive experience in the store:

- Attention and pleasant interaction
- Convenience (being able to get in and out of the store quickly)
- Product knowledge and problem-solving

The fourth dimension of service formulas is the *provision of additional services,* often through the bundling of services into product packages sold as "goods." These packages cover a broad range, from specialized freestanding services (appliance repair, photocopying) to installation services and service contracts, to online ordering and home delivery of groceries.

Media attention tends to focus on the first and third dimensions of service: attention and pleasant interaction, and product knowledge and problem-solving.[10] We find, however, that shopping convenience and the provision of additional services are more important to a competitive strategy—in part because, regardless of avowed goals, most companies appear to fall somewhere along a fairly narrow band in terms of interaction style and product knowledge. (Still, interviewed workers at nondiscount stores who had earlier worked in big-box retailers such as Wal-Mart, Sam's Club, and Target reported now interacting with consumers more frequently than in their former jobs.)

Quality- and Variety-Driven Food Retail   Food retailers may emphasize service in the form of better customer interactions (for example, employees greeting customers and developing other customer interaction skills as well as providing food preparation advice), but their primary competitive strategy is an emphasis on product quality and variety, a *quality-driven* strategy. Here the main differentiator is higher-quality goods, often including exotic variety. Attractive, fresh, and varied produce, meat, fish, cheese, wine, baked goods, prepared food, and deli offerings are typical. This model incorporates some service in the form of counter assistance (deli, fish) or product knowledge (wine, cheese), but the principal selling point is quality. Though standard grocery items have become commodities, fresh and attractive produce and meats are *not* universally available; by offering these, grocers seek to defend or carve out a higher-income market niche that allows higher margins.

Importantly, retailers achieve product quality and variety partly through changes in purchasing but also through greater labor input (for example, preparing food or frequently refreshing merchandise displays). At the same time, pleasant staff-customer interaction enhances the primary service dimension: shopping convenience, which is the necessary, but not sufficient, condition for retaining customers.

Strong customer segmentation within a store is impractical (but not in electronics, which we discuss later), though large food chains do use multiple banners (store names and formats) to attract distinct segments of customers: for example, Safeway's Pavilions stores target more affluent shoppers. Sometimes the quality drive extends the boundaries of retailing. To compete with restaurants, for example, some supermarkets have greatly expanded their prepared food offerings.

Service-Driven Consumer Electronics   Consumer electronics retailers follow a service-driven strategy with multiple dimensions. Its key selling points are the provision of services not offered by Wal-Mart or Amazon. Services may be packaged with high-end, specialized electronic components, but the approach stresses the services themselves. As an increasing slice of consumer electronics goods themselves become commodities, such service-based products are one area where competition is not based on cost and margins are higher.

The emphasis on new types of service *and products* has led some retailers to vertically integrate functions into the design and installation of home entertainment systems, thereby significantly altering the mix of offerings away from off-the-shelf hard goods and toward services. Other service "products" are home computer consulting service packages or the ubiquitous simple service warranty contracts.

This service-driven approach typically segments customers so as to target services to higher-end customers within a store's client population. It requires a degree of service judgment on the part of frontline workers, who must "qualify" customers' needs in order to direct them to appropriate products and services, in some cases orienting them to a specialized part of the store. Interestingly, this approach harks back to the early, more "artisanal" and technical audio stores that were largely displaced by mass retailers.

Goals in Tension and Consequences for Labor   For virtually all companies in the study, in both food and electronics retail, the goals of cost-cutting and improving quality or service are in tension, and at times in conflict.[11] These tensions have a bearing on job quality. Even when companies are making progress toward both goals, there are questions about the sustainability of such progress. The fact that cost-cutting so often undermines job quality is a key dimension of these tensions and conflicts. We find that these tensions are shared across both subsectors and are likely to illustrate endemic challenges in many parts of the retail industry.

In a pattern that transcends sectors, respondents reported having more complex jobs (due to a wider assortments of goods, stricter freshness requirements, or enhanced service expectations) but thinner staffing. Some companies have also reduced opportunities for worker earnings growth in order to meet cost-cutting goals: most notably, a number of the consumer electronics chains dropped commission sales as margins on electronic products shrank. At the same time, many of the chains in both subsectors are experimenting with new performance-based bonus systems for hourly employees. Overall, however, longer-term employees at the field study companies typically described worsening jobs.

For quite a few companies, in fact, the cost-cutting imperative has proven extremely difficult to combine with enhancing a product market approach, and they have struggled to retain standing in the market. For these companies, price-cutting competition may have occurred suddenly, making it challenging to devise ways to retain customers other than by reducing prices. Applying cost-cutting actions to an existing work organization and job structure typically results in speedups for all workers, excessive workloads (for supervisors and midlevel managers in particular), and reductions, wherever possible, of time spent on customer service. For these companies, both job quality and market survival are in a precarious state.

"ROOM FOR MANEUVER": EMPLOYER AGENCY AND CROSS-COMPANY VARIATION WITHIN A SUBSECTOR

Given the patterns identified at the subsector level, we could expect a simple correspondence between a retailer's choice of product strategy and how it deploys labor, with the resulting impact on job quality. Broadly speaking, this pattern holds true, with marked job quality differences between food and consumer electronics, as demonstrated in chapter 2.

Nevertheless, and importantly, job quality also varies significantly across retailers *within* a subsector. Even among retailers in a subsector that have ostensibly implemented the same adaptive formula (quality-driven, service-driven), there are notable differences in jobs. Furthermore, we find that there are differences—with implications for job quality—in the specific interactions between product and labor strategies, which either reinforce or undermine each other, or sometimes settle to a "draw." In this section, we first provide a picture of cross-firm variation in major, readily measurable, dimensions of job quality: starting wages, starting wages for cashiers (the primary entry-level job), incidence of part-time work, and annual turnover rates.[12] We then explore through the case studies the interrelationships of product strategy, market position, and managerial choice and how these underlie differences in job outcomes.

Differences in Company-Wide Average Job Quality: Within-Sector Contrasts

We emphasize at the outset that we present statistics from the study sample in this chapter simply to descriptively characterize the companies; we do not claim that this is a representative sample. Based on triangulation with other sources, however, we suspect that the sample is *relatively* representative—that is, our case-study companies share similar basic job characteristics with other retailers and do not display indications of being outliers.

Lower Starting Wages in Food, Greater Wage Dispersion in Electronics
In the study sample, as in aggregate statistics (chapter 2), starting pay is lower in food retail than in consumer electronics retail. Importantly, there is variation in entry-level starting wages within each retail subsector (figure 3.2). In food retail, 27 percent of grocery chains set the start pay at the minimum wage ($5.15 at the time of our fieldwork in 2005–2007). Only one company (or 9 percent) started its wages at $10 or above.

Consumer electronics companies display even greater dispersion in terms of their starting wage practices, with companies clustered into two groups: one paying at or near the minimum wage, and the other paying $10 to $11 per hour.

Cashier Wages: Factors of Variation   Within each subsector, the salary levels of entry-level, part-time cashier positions, the archetypal

Figure 3.2 / Frequency Distribution of Starting Wages in Case-Study Companies

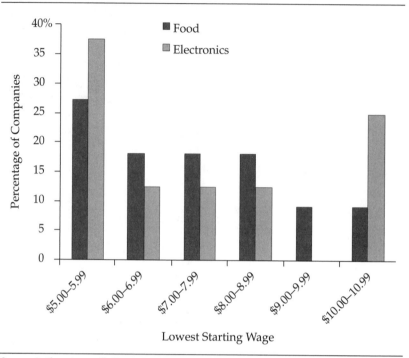

Lowest Starting Wage

Source: Authors' compilation.
Note: Both subsectors include Bargain Club and Village Voice, which sell both food and consumer electronics. The food subsector includes Jones Market (a partial case consisting of two interviews only).

position, vary across retail companies (figure 3.3), pointing toward differences in firm practices. In most food retail companies, where the cashier position entails almost exclusively cashiering, the midpoint of the hourly wage of part-time cashiers is below $9. The few companies with higher cashier wages are either unionized or partially unionized, except for one small-store retailer, Megamart, where job categories are few and broadly defined and cashiers with seniority are called upon to handle multiple kinds of tasks. In consumer electronics stores, where cashiers are more frequently called to be sales clerks on the floor, there is greater diversity of pay for part-time cashiers, though most companies pay cashiers below $9. These wage dispersion patterns within subsectors raise questions

Figure 3.3 / Frequency Distribution of Cashier Wages in Case-Study Companies

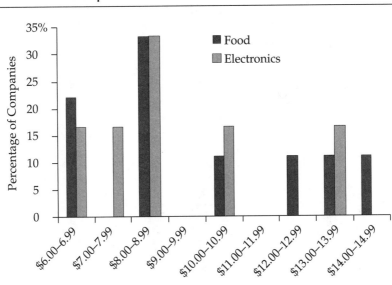

Midpoint of Part-Time Cashier Wage

Source: Authors' compilation.

about the role of company practices and are preliminary indications that sector and product strategy do not preordain all matters of job quality.

Part-time Positions Dominate but Use Intensity Varies   Part-time positions dominate in entry-level work in the sample companies in both subsectors, as they do in the industry as a whole. In both food and electronics retailers, part-time workers constitute between 40 and 80 percent of the total workforce, with one outlier at 3 percent—this electronics company relied almost exclusively on a full-time, full commission sales force (figure 3.4).

Turnover as a Correlate of Job Quality   Workforce turnover, one indicator of worker satisfaction or fit with jobs, also varies within each subsector (figure 3.5).[13] Across companies in both subsectors, three indicators—the part-time cashier wage, the percentage part-time positions, and turnover—are correlated (table 3.3). Companies with

Figure 3.4 / Frequency Distribution of Incidence of Part-Time Work in Case-Study Companies

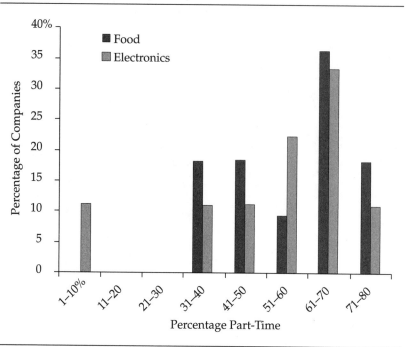

Source: Authors' compilation.

higher cashier wages are also those with a lower part-time percentage and lower rates of employee turnover. This pattern further suggests that companies adopt distinct labor deployment approaches, and that some may follow a high-road labor strategy while others follow a low-road strategy.

CORPORATE STRATEGIES ON THE GROUND: A CLOSER LOOK AT THE CASE STUDIES

What is this variation in the main indicators of job quality across retailers within each subsector telling us? We pose two questions in this section. First, is this divergence in jobs due to differences in the contexts (market, regulatory) within which particular retailers implement their strategies? We find that context does indeed matter. Second, is this variation also due to differences in retailers' choice of

Figure 3.5 / Frequency Distribution of Turnover in Case-Study Companies

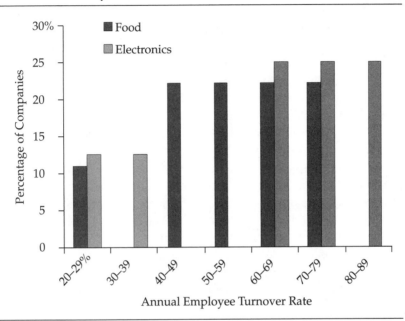

Source: Authors' compilation.

Table 3.3 / Correlation Matrix for Four Job Quality Indicators in Case-Study Companies

	Starting Wage	Part-Time Cashier Wage	Percentage Part-Time Positions
Part-time cashier wage	0.662		
Percentage part-time positions	−0.374	0.347	
Turnover	−0.311	−0.411	0.361

Source: Authors' calculation.

a labor strategy (or capacity to implement it) that they use to support their product orientation? Here again, we find this to be the case. Put another way, *there is room for maneuver* within market and regulatory contexts that enables retailers to sustain different labor approaches, at least up to a point.

Here we drill down into the case studies to elaborate and explain how differences in strategy, market position, and managerial choices underlie the range of job outcomes we observe. We use the distinction between service-driven formulas in electronics retailing and quality-driven formulas in supermarkets to guide us through indicative cases as we explore these two competitive orientations and their implications for jobs in more depth. Because warehouse stores present a special case—their store format is different from mainline stores, and they also sell both food and consumer electronics products as well as other general merchandise—we explore their product market and labor approaches separately.

For each subsector's strategy bundle, we first elaborate how chains roll out the approach, then circle back to consider the consequences for jobs. In this first pass, we explore the employment impacts at some length for food and warehouse-format chains—where strategy variations are striking—but look more briefly at their more homogeneous consumer electronics counterparts. Chapter 4 will delve into the labor-linked tensions in retailers' strategic packages and uncover subtle differences in how electronics sellers structure employment.

COMPETITIVE STRATEGIES AND LABOR STRATEGIES IN FOOD RETAIL

Food retail is part of "old retail." It displays a great variety of store formats, company sizes, labor strategies, regional patterns of consumption, and competitive settings, whereas consumer electronics is dominated by big-box formats. In recent years, mainline grocery stores—the ubiquitous format for food retail—have all adopted a quality-driven competitive strategy that relies on greater product quality and variety. Nevertheless, given the great variety of companies, their corporate histories, and their settings, this strategy plays out in varied ways that have consequences for job quality.

The Quality-Driven Competitive Strategy

Food retailers' quality-driven strategies rely primarily on extensive product differentiation rather than service provision—though a number of food retail managers commented, "Whoever figures out home delivery is going to own the market."[14] Moreover, maintaining an adequate level of customer interaction is a required component of this strategy. Because customers shop in all parts of the store, from basic dry goods to on-site prepared meals, the tension between cutting labor costs and providing higher-end services is not easily resolved in food stores. It is rarely possible to tier the levels of service provision in the store and segment the customer population, whether by spatial segregation of activities or by active customer profiling. Except for the meat, fish, and deli counters, there are few options for isolating time-intensive, knowledge-intensive, and costlier high-service options from the low-service parts of the store that require little product knowledge.[15] Therefore, food retailers avail themselves of the extensive product differentiation, in both variety and quality, afforded by retail food, which in turn requires greater labor input. The goal of this differentiation is to draw in and retain customers with higher purchasing power but also to get everyone who shops in the store to consider buying luxury or higher-labor-content products that support higher margins.

Requirements of the Quality-Driven Strategy

The quality-driven strategy entails broadening significantly the range of product offerings in the store, increasing the variety of conventional food products (for example, multiple kinds of canned vegetables) but also increasing the share of fresh produce, meats, fish, baked goods, and cheese in total offerings, as well as expanding food preparation and customization (bakery and carryout meals). These changes require more worker effort in stocking goods and also demand greater worker attention to and knowledge about freshness and quality. Quality-driven retailers also offer exotic and gourmet items, such as wine. Importantly, a quality-driven strategy includes more labor-intensive offerings, such as premade meals, meals prepared on order, and ready-to-cook meals that compete in a crowded field with the restaurant industry, gourmet stores, and food prepared at home. These bigger-ticket items, which promise greater margins, are often accompanied by counter service (though not always, as in the case of salad bars), but grocers' attempts to differentiate themselves are primarily based on food quality and presentation. This differentiation stems in part from purchasing decisions but is mostly the result of work effort in selection, preparation, presentation, and stock rotation for freshness.

Job Implications: Tensions Among Job Burden, Worker Performance, and Market Performance

We find that the quality-driven strategy has an impact on employment practices, which in turn can sustain or undermine this competitive approach. There is significant variation across food retailers in how they implement the quest for quality and variety. Job quality outcomes, in terms of both current jobs and recent trends, look better at the grocers that successfully implement a quality-driven approach. There are two possible directions of causality here. On the one hand, businesses that are struggling financially because their quality strategy is not succeeding can ill afford high-road employment practices—a significant outcome, but not a surprising one. On the other hand, and more interestingly, human resource and compensation policies that are ill suited to quality-driven competition may undermine that competitive approach, in either the short run or the long run. The quality-driven formula relies upon supervisor focus and worker effort to maintain product display and freshness and worker orientation to the customer experience. Put bluntly, quality and variety require extra work. A Food Chief store manager with twenty years at the company noted that new offerings such as "the sushi bar, the Asian bar, hot wings, salad bar, things we didn't have in the past," have required added staffing. Moreover, "the quality piece" also escalates work demands: "You're not stacking bananas six high. You've got a two-hand rule and that's it. You got to fill them five times during the day. That was a major culture shift for Food Chief. Major, major, major." Increasing variety also requires added effort, he added:

> We used to be positioned where there might be two kinds of green beans on the shelf. . . . Now maybe there's ten kinds of green beans, but all of them are three cans wide going to the back, so they're not case-packed anymore. They're hand-stacked. So we've taken some of our efficiencies out of the system.

Seemingly minor changes, such as a narrower facing display for each brand or selection, have direct implications for workload.

Additionally, to round out and capitalize on the full effect of the quality-variety strategy, food retailers recruit frontline workers for their "friendly attitude," counting on this feature to retain customers once they are drawn into the store. At the same time, the baseline cost-cutting imperative is embodied in requirements, at a minimum, that all workers be subject to scheduling flexibility (in both shift times and total hours) and that full-time workers and supervisors be "fully available."

Food retailers that face steep price-cutting competition or that choose to cut labor costs deeply run into workforce motivation walls that store managers find difficult to overcome with the few incentives at their disposal. In these cases, the two directions of causality may join in a vicious circle (and, we could argue, the company actually falls in the category of "no strategy" beyond cutting costs). As we describe job characteristics and how they are changing, we particularly search for evidence of the second causal connection—that providing better jobs is necessary if a retailer is to provide greater quality and variety—and of possible cumulative causation.

An Illustration: Successful Implementation, but with Tensions   Two food retailers, Homestyle and The Market, have been relatively successful in building up employment strategies that support a quality-driven approach. Retailers with every supermarket format in our field sample have pursued some version of a quality-driven approach, but these two companies have had greater success than others. Homestyle has bumped up initial training—a newly hired cashier reported receiving eight hours of computer-based training, whereas a cashier hired three years earlier received thirty to sixty minutes of training before starting—and invested in hiring and training managers who can more successfully motivate frontline workers. Like almost all chains in our sample, Homestyle has shifted toward hiring more managers from outside the company and even from other branches of retail, but a district manager emphasized the unique aspects of supermarket careers: "Towels are a whole lot different [easier] than bananas. . . . Perishable is such a big part of what we do at Homestyle, and do well, that people have to understand that."

At 5 to 10 percent above union scale, despite the absence of a union, pay levels at Homestyle are near the top in our sample. Only 40 percent of Homestyle's workforce is part-time—by far the lowest rate among conventional grocery stores in our sample, and among the lowest in the industry. Even so, benefits are no more generous than industry standards. The Market, on the other hand, has devised means to improve part-time jobs, the bulk of which are held by frontline workers in direct contact with customers. It pays time-and-a-half to part-time workers working more than thirty-five hours per week; throughout the industry, by contrast, retailers use part-time status to flex hours up to forty hours but not beyond, so as to avoid incurring mandatory overtime pay. Furthermore, The Market has historically provided some health benefits for part-timers. This distinctive practice is under pressure. The company moved eligibility for benefits from a tenure of six months to one year because, in the words of management, "all of our competition is moving further and further out, even our [unionized] competitors." The Market's 60 percent rate of part-time employment is closer to the grocery mainstream than Homestyle's rate, but still below that of three other chains in the study sample, Food Chief, Freshland, and Value Fresh.

These successful quality-driven food retailers have sought multiple ways to motivate the frontline workforce; most notably, they have gravitated toward incentive pay. Homestyle has implemented a workforce-wide profit-sharing bonus system. In an industry where historically only managers received incentive pay, this approach communicates equitability and feeds workforce commitment. Incentive pay is targeted to customer service. "There is probably no better catalyst to motivate your people than standing in front of them and talking about, 'You help us achieve our goals, I'm going to put money in your pocket,'" a Homestyle district manager said. "A part-time kid can understand that." Homestyle tries to reward good customer service in smaller ways as well. A store manager told us, "If an associate gets a customer compliment, for example, or something good where a customer says something or calls into corporate with something good about them, I give them two free movie passes." Similarly, The Market provides cash rewards at managers' discretion.

Homestyle has among the lowest turnover rates in the industry. It brought its turnover rate down from a range of 90 to 100 percent over the previous decade to 50 percent even amid 2006's low unemployment.[16] This rate had risen somewhat from 2003, but the increase was no great cause for concern. Management wants a degree of what it terms "healthy turnover" to renew the workforce (and keep average pay and benefit levels low) and would prefer not to see the separation rate dip below 40 percent. At The Market, department managers reported that they aimed to give their full-timers regular schedules so that they would not leave to take jobs that accommodated their preferred hours.

Despite all these indicators of success, the two companies continue to experience tensions between workforce management and business strategy. We explore these issues in the next chapter.

COMPETITIVE STRATEGIES AND LABOR STRATEGIES IN CONSUMER ELECTRONICS

Service-Driven Competitive Strategy at the Store Level

What we call service-driven retailers compete with large-scale discounters by *selling* services. Consumer electronics products are sufficiently complex that there is a market for services related to them, such as setup and repair. Broad-line mass-marketers like Wal-Mart and Target have not yet occupied this space, and online sellers cannot easily provide such services. This is especially true of more customized services, essentially quasi-luxury "goods" that can nonetheless be purveyed by mass-market chains that are willing to adopt a different tack than simply charging the lowest price. Electronics retailers' goal of expanding services is thus "an escape from low-margin hell," in the words of *Business Week*.[17] As a Technology Source store manager remarked, "We have to be more service-oriented. Margins on TVs and computers and actual boxes, product, [are] always dropping, and if we don't get that service piece nailed, then we won't survive."

One basic "service" to be sold is service agreements and extended warranties, which every electronics retailer in our sample strove to push, as do virtually all other such retailers. Commenting on the financial results of the two industry leaders at that time, one observer noted that extended warranties were estimated to account for "more than a third of Best Buy's operating profit and all of Circuit City's" in 2005.[18] Wal-Mart's 2005 entry into the extended warranty business, with policies priced at one-half to one-third the level charged by its competitors, cranked up competitive pressure in this once-comfortable corner of electronics sales (marked by 50 to 60 percent margins on service agreements, much higher than the 4 percent margins on sales of goods).[19] But nearly two years after Wal-Mart made its foray into warranties, *Warranty Week* reported that the large electronics retailers were *still* charging rates roughly three times that of Wal-Mart, indicating that this offering is still a significant revenue source.[20]

Beyond this baseline offering, we saw two distinct service-driven strategies in different segments of the market: in broad-line consumer electronics chains, and in office supply chains. Among broad-line electronics sellers, the national chain Electronix exemplifies the shift to emphasizing selling services. Electronix sells a wide range of consumer electronics products, having evolved over time from a warehouse format to a hands-on selling format. The chain offers two lines of service beyond extended warranties. On the one hand, for run-of-the-mill customers, the chain offers installation of auto sound systems and computer repair plus, increasingly, home installation. (Wal-Mart attempted to move into the installation and repair business in a pilot joint venture with Dell, but dropped the initiative.)[21] On the other end, Electronix devised a "store-within-a-store" formula in which salespeople work with high-end customers to design and install elaborate home entertainment systems that can price out at tens of thousands of dollars. Importantly, many of these services involve interaction with the customer in his or her home, which escalates the service intensity of the tasks.

Electronix seeks to expand both lines. "They wanted to get anywhere from 5 to 7 percent of the store sales from services, because the margin is available," a store service manager commented. The company emphasizes "hand-to's"—a salesperson or cashier who is helping a customer buy a small item calls attention to higher-end offerings, including the store-within-a-store, and introduces the customer to a high-end salesperson.

Electronix added key services in this portfolio by acquiring independent companies that specialize in these higher-end services. The company also in-sourced core elements of home installation, a formerly subcontracted service. Service functions are functionally and spatially segregated from routine selling, sited in distinctive locations within the store, above all in the store-within-a-store. A supervisor described that space and the shopping environment Electronix aimed to create there:

> You've got a separate divided area, a more intimate area. You know, lights are turned down low. Everything is not so bright. The music is turned down, so it's a little bit more of an atmosphere change. Then there is obviously a different level of professionalism that you get with [store-within-a-store] staff than you would get with the Electronix staff.

Another supervisor saw competitive advantage resting in the consumer loyalty generated by the quality of the company's home installation of complex systems and follow-up services:

> Home theater systems . . . can run into small snags. The wife comes home and hits the wrong button on the remote control and nothing turns on again. It's those kind of things. . . . You're gonna be the first person they're gonna call and they're gonna want it fixed instantly. Those are the times right there when you either have them come back because you've taken care of their situation right and they're gonna come back and buy things from you or they're gonna send their neighbors, their buddies, their friends to you. Or that's when the name can be dragged through the mud.

The value proposition includes product quality as well as service: the store-within-a-store also stocks specialized, high-end equipment. This supervisor continued:

> We've got a very, very vast product assortment, things that you would find rivaling your higher places like your Ultimate Electronics, and your kind of mom-and-pop shops, things that [Electronix] really never had their foot in the door before [the store-within-a-store] came along.

In pursuing this strategy, Electronix and a few other national chains aim to replicate services that were offered, until recently, only by specialized, high-end audio/video equipment stores. In short, they aim to displace these stores, and in many regions they have succeeded in doing so, either purchasing them or pushing them out.

Other soup-to-nuts consumer electronics retailers in our sample take similar approaches, though none in our sample are as successful as Electronix. The specifics vary. The strategy at Technology Source, another national chain offering a wide range of electronic goods, has the same elements as the Electronix strategy, except that Tech Source has attempted to build services within its own organization rather than acquiring specialized companies. At the time of our study, this was proving to be a less successful approach. High Fidelity, a smaller, higher-end regional chain, runs entirely like Electronix's store-within-a-store. Almost every salesperson is trained to assist customers with system design and installation. Hi Fi also sells off-the-shelf merchandise, but such sales are secondary to its core activities. The chain was struggling in the market when we studied them.

The second service-driven model we observed is more characteristic of office supply chains that include office electronic equipment as part of a range of offerings. For these retailers, margins are higher on non-electronics office supplies, but including electronic equipment helps them to draw in customers for a full range of office goods. The broad range of available products—a form of variety—is itself a sort of service offering. The Office, a nationwide chain, markets itself as a convenient seller of office supplies offering customers everything they need. The Office also has recently added copying, imaging, and printing services, which provide a high margin. A regional manager at The Office noted that photocopying now "has a real magical ability to drive sales because people are so happy with the results that we could deliver for them, that they're very pleased to pay a premium for that." In addition, salespeople throughout Office stores seek to identify small business customers in order to speedily meet their needs. A regional manager said, "We know that those users are very loyal. We know that they aren't as dependent on looking only at price to make their purchase decisions." He added that the decision to make small businesses a priority target "shifted everything, from our focus on customer service to our merchandise mix to our marketing mix." This shift turned the focus to convenience:

> If you think about what a small business user goes into [The Office] store for, they don't want to have a lot of time here. They want to get into the store. They want it to be in stock. They want

someone to help them and be friendly and helpful and help them immediately. They want to be able to find the product in the store, and they want to check out quickly.

The other office-focused chain in our sample, Office Express (OE), follows a very similar strategy. OE is a national big-box chain selling office equipment, supplies, and related services. Like The Office, the chain recently added copying and printing services. About half of its customer base consists of small businesses, and, again mirroring The Office, OE is seeking to expand that proportion because small businesses are more loyal and more oriented to convenience and service than price. The retailer hopes to differentiate itself, however, from competitors (including The Office) with a higher-service level based on helping small business find "solutions." One indication of a slightly different labor strategy was OE employees' reports of having greater independence on the job and more support from supervisors and management than they had had working for other retailers, including consumer electronics retailers. Even so, staffing is relatively thin and the use of part-time labor is high.

Requirements of Service-Driven Retailing

To what extent could niche operators, as opposed to broad-line chains, capture and hold the market for high-end services in consumer electronics retailing? Our cases do not fully answer this question, but both case evidence and observation of the market suggest that operators exclusively focused on high-end segments are losing ground. Electronix's purchase of strong competitors in entertainment systems design points to economies of scale (perhaps in marketing and purchasing) as well as scope (offering a full range of products and services). High Fidelity represents the continuation of the traditional "hi-fi shop" that caters to more sophisticated customers, with sales clerks who all are system designers, but this model's market is being usurped by larger, broader-line chains like Electronix—hence Hi Fi's market difficulties. In fact, chains have been more successful than these more specialized stores in part because all chains have moved toward a "modular" system design that combines a few base designs with a range of options, rather than designing systems "from scratch." This formula is less reliant on technical knowledge and dulls the market edge of specialized firms and their staff.

On the office side, Kinko's represented the most successful example of stand-alone duplicating services, but its acquisition by FedEx (and the conversion of Kinko's copy shops to FedEx Kinko's, now FedEx Office, copy-and-delivery outlets) and the addition of a limited range of office supplies for sale (at least in the newer and larger stores) point, again, to economies of scope.

More broadly integrated retailers are better situated than other retailers to sell services, but making service-driven strategies successful still depends on a number of factors. The requirement that employees identify high-value customers relies on sales workforce skills and the agility of the customer data management system. When sales staff is segmented, lower-end sales clerks in the main part of the store must hand off higher-end customers to the higher-end staff with efficacy. Stores must be either spatially segregated or low enough in customer density that other customers will not feel envious or entitled to high-end services. Compensation must be structured in a way that rewards big-ticket sales but does not simply absorb much of the value captured from high-value customers.

What the Service-Driven Strategy Means for Job Quality

Service-driven strategies in consumer electronics have weighty implications for the quality of jobs. Conversely, as the requirements we have recounted suggest, the success of a service-driven strategy depends heavily on staff capacity, configuration, and to some degree the form of compensation. Most fundamentally, shifting to selling more services implies changes in job content. An entertainment sales specialist at Electronix spoke about this change in words worth quoting at length:

> The biggest thing is it used to be . . . you'd have a guy walking around with a number sheet in front of him all day and [he] was gonna say you need to push X amount of boxes or X amount of dollar amount out the door, and then we'll hit revenue and we'll all be happy and we'll give a big cheer and everybody will go home. Now it's not. . . . Obviously, we're here and we're not a nonprofit organization by any means, so we're trying to make

some money, but we're trying to do it by making sure we're doing what's right for the customer. . . . If it's somebody in home theater, it's taking the two hours out of your time to make sure the customer gets the right things, leaves the store with everything they need, and making this the one-stop solution for them so that when they get home it works exactly the way it worked here in the store and it does what we told them it can do.

We heard remarkably similar narratives of change at Tech Source and Hi Fi. We explore the factors that affect job quality in greater depth in the next chapter.

NEITHER SERVICE-DRIVEN NOR QUALITY-DRIVEN: WAREHOUSE STORES

Warehouse stores sell both food and consumer electronics products and, to some extent, have different competitive strategies from either of the two subsectors. We single them out here in order to provide context for—and highlight differences with—the adaptive competitive strategies of food and consumer electronics retailers.

The low-price, self-service, and high-volume sales formula developed by warehouse stores encapsulates the competitive pressures experienced by the food and electronics subsectors. Warehouse stores sell many items in large unit quantities. They also sell a range of categories of items, typically a broad mix of general merchandise goods (home, office, personal items) along with food and consumer electronics. However, within each category, they usually sell a narrower range of brands and items than would commonly be found in food or consumer electronics chains. The store format is stripped down to essentials (hence the warehouse label), and the service formula emphasizes self-service over in-person service and reliance on consumer product knowledge over staff product knowledge.[22] The warehouse company's purchasing department plays a significant role, and the reputation of each company is based on its ability to stock products reflecting the best price-quality trade-off for the customer segment targeted by the company. Thus, product knowledge, rather than residing with the store workforce, is embedded in the product offering.

Warehouse stores are in one sense particularly able to contend with price-cutting competition from other big-box stores, particularly competition from Wal-Mart and Target, because of their store formula. Still, they are also vulnerable to this competition because they look like discounters, they advertise low prices, and their low level of in-store staff-customer interaction runs the risk of making them indistinguishable from big-box stores. Therefore, cost-cutting and close monitoring of labor-hours budgets are baseline commitments for them, as with other retailers.

Distinct Labor Strategies and Divergence in Job Quality Across Warehouse Companies

All warehouse stores operate with a standard, bare-bones store formula, but they still display differences in labor strategies. At first glance, the warehouse store value proposition appears to be rather uniform and to dictate a fairly narrow range of tasks (warehousing and stock replenishment) that require little skill differentiation among employees. Nevertheless, there are significant differences in competitive orientations and even wider ones in labor approaches across warehouse store companies. We illustrate these by comparing and contrasting the experiences of two warehouse store chains, Bargain Warehouse (BW) and Megamart (MM). Although their product market orientations differ in some ways, there are significant differences in their labor strategies. BW jobs have similar duties and training requirements as MM jobs, but they pay more, are more likely to be full-time, and provide more generous benefits.

Bargain Warehouse is a multiregional chain of warehouse stores. It sells groceries and consumer electronics items as well as a range of other merchandise. Megamart is a small, regionally concentrated chain of warehouse stores. The company sells bulk groceries, restaurant supplies, and a limited line of kitchen equipment. Both chains identify small businesses as a key customer segment; at MM, they comprise one-third of the customer base. The two chains have a similar product orientation: a similar product unit size (bulk), a warehouse format, and a narrow range of brands within each product category. For both chains, ease and convenience of shopping are key, as with all warehouse stores.

Key distinctions between the two chains include store size, product assortment, and the extent of their fresh product offerings. Megamart's stores are smaller. Its management claims a corner on the warehouse market by having a broader range of products within the food and kitchen supply categories than other warehouse stores, particularly Bargain Warehouse. One Megamart district manager noted: "We have everything [customers] need. . . . Bargain Warehouse might not have everything they need. They'd have a lot of it, but they wouldn't have it all. With us, they can get everything." In recent years, Megamart has added frozen meats and explored fresh produce displays. Within the warehouse world, where self-service is the expected norm, MM claims to emphasize customer service more than average, expecting staff to answer questions about products.

With less than half the stock keeping units (SKUs, or individual products) of Megamart, Bargain Warehouse competes on price and quality rather than assortment. Product knowledge resides with the merchandising department rather than within the store. The Bargain Warehouse human resources representative noted: "We try to provide goods to our members that give them the highest quality that we can at the lowest possible cost. We don't compromise on quality. If we can't do a good job on it, we don't carry it." Still, while it has a narrower band of products, BW stores offer a greater range of fresh products prepared on-site—baked goods, deli products, and butchery products—while Megamart has no such capacity.

Given these similarities and differences in product strategy—all within a shared store formula—we also observed quite distinct labor approaches and job quality outcomes. As noted, Bargain Warehouse offers higher compensation (particularly in frontline jobs) and more full-time jobs. Wages are higher than at Megamart and most other warehouse stores. Both part-time and full-time employees in a range of positions affirmed that Bargain Warehouse pay was higher than at other companies. The company uses the relatively higher pay as a recruitment and retention tool. One cashier reported, "The pay started out at like $10 an hour when I was eighteen. I was like, wow, ten bucks an hour, that's amazing. Everything pays like $7.50. So that's why I started here." In contrast, Megamart workers started at $7.30 per hour (in 2006 dollars) for baggers and $8.70 for cashiers. Sunday pay is also more generous at BW (doubled), while it consists of a few dollars' fixed premium at MM. Both companies have two-tiered wage scales, with higher salaries and more significant benefit coverage for full-time workers.

Importantly, both companies offer health insurance to about 85 percent of their workforce. Family benefits are provided to full-time workers (including dental and vision coverage). Health coverage for part-time workers is more extensive at Bargain Warehouse, which offers family coverage to part-time workers with hours over a predetermined threshold of workdays. Megamart offers only individual HMO-based coverage.

The two companies differ in the degree to which they rely on part-time workers and schedules. Half of the workforce at Bargain Warehouse is full-time, compared to only one-fifth at Megamart. Full-time jobs at MM are exclusively reserved for supervisory and managerial positions. At BW, full-time employees can be found in all positions. Also, minimum hours for part-timers are more generous: as a rule, they work a minimum of twenty-five weekly hours, whereas there is no such minimum policy at MM. Importantly, many part-time workers at both companies "flex up" to forty weekly hours, though they are considered part-time for pay and benefit purposes. They may remain in this status for extended periods of time, sometimes for years.

This difference in reliance on part-time labor (50 percent at Bargain Warehouse versus 80 percent at Megamart) relates to their benefit policies. According to the BW human resources chief: "In our world, we give everybody benefits. You're actually putting fewer people through the benefit pipeline [with fewer part-timers]. . . . There are some efficiencies in having fewer people." But as with the higher compensation, BW's lesser reliance on part-time workers also aims at keeping turnover in check and enlisting worker involvement in the running of the enterprise. In contrast, part-time jobs at MM are considered low-commitment positions; a store manager noted: "Part-time is just temporary work."

Despite these differences, jobs in both companies are strikingly similar in the range of duties and the training required (little—except for a few specialty departments). Each worker has main areas of work, but all perform a wide range of tasks because they fill in as needed. There are two main task configurations: working primarily in checkout and helping out with stocking as needed, or being primarily responsible for stocking in one area but filling in at checkout or stocking in other areas.

In the next chapter, as we examine the factors that undermine job quality, we include examples from warehouse stores based on comparability of jobs: examples from warehouse food preparation and display departments and from food stores are discussed together, as are examples from warehouse electronics departments and from consumer electronics stores.

THE MEANING OF FLEXIBILITY IN U.S. RETAIL: SCHEDULING PRACTICES, GENDER ROLES, AND ACCOMMODATION

Thus far in this chapter, we have relentlessly viewed strategy through the imperatives of competitiveness. Here we flip the viewpoint and focus instead on significant qualitative dimensions of retail jobs and how they manifest themselves in what we term *lived job quality,* that is, aspects of jobs that workers gauge differently depending on their needs and expectations. To a great extent, the role match between worker and job arrangement determines lived job quality and, in turn, affects retailers' success in implementing a specific labor approach. In retail, aspects of lived job quality reveal the interactions between *managerial strategies and agency,* as manifested in scheduling practices, and *accommodation by workers* to the structure of jobs and compensation and to social norms and institutional practices related to gender roles and care responsibilities.

Gender roles and dynamics play a significant part in the story of retail, and in how women workers in particular fare. In fact, the study subsectors of food and consumer electronics were initially chosen in part because of their differing gender composition. We expected the contrast between male-dominated consumer electronics and the (relatively) female-dominated food retail environment to provide some insight into whether structuring jobs to take advantage of traditional gender roles (women as secondary earners and "relationally" oriented, men as primary earners and "technology" oriented) would result in far lower job quality in retail food. We also expected that contrast between the subsectors to illuminate the job features in each that make jobs more or less hospitable to women workers in terms of work-family balance. However, we found the picture to be more complex and nuanced in terms of the forces that shape workers' lived job quality. Lived job experience in retail revolves around the key dimensions of compensation and scheduling and the use of part-time work. Part-time work draws parents (read: mothers) in retail, but also is the primary scheduling and work arrangement for *all* entry-level workers, both male and female, in both subsectors.

Retailing is a mix of product selection and in-person service. The industry relies on standardized modes of customer interaction but also on multiple less rationalized and more intangible social interactions.[23] For some jobs, hiring policy explicitly selects for such social skills. Furthermore, many jobs are created by labor strategies that rely and capitalize upon secondary earners and sometimes—some would say often—assume all women to be secondary earners. Hence, "role match" affects how individual workers perceive job quality.

Part-Time Gap Fillers and Time Adjusters

The notion of lived job quality is most useful for assessing the quality of part-time jobs, which are ubiquitous in both subsectors. From a firm's standpoint, part-time jobs allow significant savings in compensation and operate as "shock absorbers" for variations in customer flow and financial fluctuations in the business. Retailers have four main motivations for making use—sometimes extensive use—of part-time work. First, part-time work allows them to match staffing to peak days and hours, reducing "excess" labor. They can extensively vary staffing levels over the day or week and reduce labor hours with minimal notice. This matching ability is particularly valuable in the context of recent just-in-time inventory management systems. Second, the classical argument that, in repetitive work, workers with short hours are more productive holds sway with retailers. Third, part-time employment is an exit option, because in much of retail part-timers are paid lower wages and receive fewer or no benefits. A fourth, less obvious advantage is that managers can use hours allotted to part-timers to mete out rewards or punishments (even inducing quits rather than having to fire problem employees), with no added cost to the labor budget. A produce manager at P. A. Smith explained how this can work:

> Usually [workers who are not working out] come to me and ask me why they're not getting more hours. . . . You know, "My hours are getting cut back and why is that?" I'll say, well, I explain it to them. "You know, I'm given X amount of hours to use, and if I see someone is more productive than someone else, if you were doing my job, who would you schedule?" I throw it back on their

lap and let them see what impact their being unproductive has on the department. Then they make the decision to either step it up and be productive. If I notice that they have reacted to it and are getting more productive, I compensate them with giving them more hours. But if they're not, you know, they don't get more hours and . . . they have to pick up another part-time job at that point or move on or something.

A Tech Source store manager recounted a similar experience:

One [person who quit recently] was a gentleman who was here when I got here who did not fit into that team atmosphere. Basically what happened was one of my seniors, summertime came and his availability opened up, so I started giving him more of the hours because he was a better associate for that, and the other gentleman, his hours dropped. . . . He ended up probably catching on and he just quit, just stopped showing up.

Part-time hours can also be used to reward, as a customer service lead at Tech Source noted: "Say merchandising doesn't have enough hours and Joe Schmoe is really good at computers. Well, we can bring him over to computers where there are extra hours to give him a better schedule and paycheck." From workers' standpoint, however, part-time work ranges from a mixed blessing to a curse. Workers assess part-time jobs in terms of the extent to which the job suits their job expectations, which take into account the constraints of the work environment and schedules.

Along with other researchers, we find that a picture of part-time job quality cannot be painted with a single brush; there is significant variation in how workers experience part-time schedules. Stores use two kinds of part-timers: gap fillers and time adjusters.[24] *Gap fillers* are employees working short-hour "arrangements": they are deployed on regular schedules and work predictable time slots. *Time adjusters,* by contrast, are deployed at variable times and have variable total work hours.

Gap fillers include many in-school youths who work short hours, most often in evenings and on weekends, and have declared their availability to be clear and limited. An electronics manager reported that, because his store was not open evenings, he did not make use of college students. Gap fillers also include parents and those with other care responsibilities (such as elder care); they often are adults but can also be young workers with responsibilities at home. A large group consists of mothers who work during school hours. Gap fillers may also hold multiple jobs, using their retail earnings to supplement their main job. Supervisors and managers tend to schedule these two groups according to their availability.

Time adjusters are in a different situation altogether. They have been hired part-time, to work a low level of hours, typically fifteen to twenty hours weekly, because all entry-level hiring is part-time. They are in a way station to full-time work and usually are expected to flex up to forty weekly hours—sometimes staying at that higher level for weeks or even months.[25] A P. A. Smith produce manager observed, "I'm sure there's people that work here that work forty, forty-eight hours part-time every week . . . for a long, long time. [P. A. Smith policy says] they're considered for full-time, but there's only so many full-time positions available." Incentives are strong for time adjusters to be available to be scheduled to work "whenever."[26] They experience variability and unpredictability in when they work as well as in the total number of hours they work. Though the situation of part-time workers employed as time adjusters is particularly difficult, an increasingly prevailing trend is for full-timers to also become time adjusters. A number of big-box retailers ration work hours for full-timers as well: they set the standard workweek at thirty to thirty-five hours, demand full scheduling flexibility in exchange for full-time status, and expect these workers to flex up to forty weekly hours.

Regardless of whether they are gap fillers or time adjusters, part-time workers in nearly all our case study companies and retail as a whole often have a lower hourly wage and benefit package than similar workers in full-time positions.[27] Thus, the major pay progression path offered by retailers requires the ability and the opportunity to move to a full-time position as a first step.

The Lived Part-Time Experience and the Meaning of Flexibility in Retail

The appeal of retail work, particularly frontline retail work, is the option to work short hours, but the drawback of retail work is the difficulty of reconciling these short hours with responsibilities outside of work. For time adjusters, working extra hours entails schedule unpredictability, with consequences for life outside of work. For gap fillers, schedule predictability is achieved at the cost of low earnings due to low hours and few options for mobility. Both groups must contend with lower hourly pay and limited fringe benefits.

How are these trade-offs perceived by workers and managers? We would expect gap fillers to report few scheduling conflicts. Indeed, in many of the interviews, gap fillers reported that they worked solely the hours they could. A clerk in a warehouse store who was also enrolled in college worked twenty to twenty-five hours per week, most of those hours on Saturday, Sunday, and one weekday. He sometimes worked up to thirty hours weekly, but "never more." An electronics salesperson reported working only up to thirty hours and was not looking for more hours because he also was enrolled in college. One sales associate noted that the only way to move up would have been to take on full-time work, but doing that was impossible with his school schedule.

Parents—usually women—who work a schedule that fits with their children's school schedules are particularly appreciative of the access to short hours, as the following comments from a grocery store customer service associate illustrate:

> Most of all, I like working here because the hours are flexible for my needs, and I do have a thirteen-year-old boy at home. My priority is being a parent . . . and my child, taking care of them, first priority for me. So I send him to school and I come here . . . in the morning. . . . Then before he gets home, then I [can] be home before him. For me, it's worked out great here.[28]

A supermarket cashier noted: "When I got hired, I said, 'No nights, no weekends.'" Another grocery cashier reported similar accommodation to her constraints: "I can't work past 1:00. That's the latest I work because then I go home with my daughter and my husband goes to work."[29]

Indeed, both groups of part-timers also reported a fair amount of trading of shifts as well as manager tolerance and willingness to accommodate adjustments in schedules. The cashier who could not work past 1:00 PM also noted: "There's a board where you can write down days where you're unavailable and try to get people to cover your shifts." Another interviewee said: "My manager is very willing to work with my schedule . . . and, if I need a day or something, that's when we switch or whatever."

Short notice adjustments to the schedule are the responsibility of department supervisors and store managers to handle and "make it work." As an electronics salesperson remarked, "There is always a chance they can make that [adjustment]. It all depends on your manager." And certainly supervisors themselves frequently mentioned the need to juggle schedules and the complications that entailed, including having to pressure regularly scheduled full-timers to pick up the extra workload.[30]

In unionized food stores, unions have striven to establish somewhat depersonalized rules for scheduling and have tended to rely on a seniority system for scheduling preference. Therefore, some experienced the rule as fair and some did not. A deli worker at a union grocer noted that if she ran into a scheduling problem, "I'd probably, like, talk to my manager. A lot of times, like, you don't get what you want. It's difficult."

We are mindful of the fact that because the companies selected the interviewees, the workers we met were probably relatively satisfied employees on the whole. Nevertheless, even in this group of relatively satisfied workers, flexibility was constructed and understood within the given constraints of the labor market, the job structures in retail, and the socioeconomic context (for example, child care affordability). Gap fillers took short hours because they found few other ways to work. They also found part-time jobs to be far more "flexible" than steady full-time jobs because they could ask for reduced work hours occasionally, or even for significant stretches of time.

The first grocery store associate with a child quoted earlier looked into other job options, but "every place you go, they're demanding hours 9:00 to 5:00. But for me, I still want to be a priority for my son." A single parent reported that she quit another retail job and took her current one because it allowed her to get home two to three hours before her child went to bed. She would have loved to work more hours, but on a schedule that would allow her time with her children.[31]

Here lies the dilemma for adult gap fillers, most of whom are women with caretaking responsibilities for children or elderly people. They have resolved the immediate difficulties of caregiving caused by the lack of affordable child care and sparse paid family leave by gravitating toward retail because of the opportunity to work part-time.[32] But part-time work comes with limited compensation and scheduling constraints. Working short hours is possible—daytime grocery cashier jobs have steady and predictable short hours—but short hours also hem women in and leave few pathways for progression. Any option to move up requires full availability (being able to work anytime) and a willingness to adjust to fluctuating total hours.[33]

We also note that gap fillers who request a change in regular hours usually request a reduction in their steady hours. A reduction in hours is always easier to get than an increase. In effect, the fact that most workers in stores are part-time workers (with low guaranteed hours) enables managers to reduce a worker's hours if the worker requests it without changing their job arrangement. This is the context that workers and managers describe as "flexible."

Time Adjusters' Perspective on Part-Time and Full-Time Differentials

Time adjusters—both women and men—had a far different view of scheduling "flexibility" than gap fillers; they experienced it as variability in when they worked and, importantly, how many hours they worked each week. They may have gravitated to retail because they could not keep up with a consistent full-time schedule, but they also wanted more work hours and knew that the first step to advancement was conversion to a full-time job. They reported wanting, and getting used to, higher levels of hours than the minimum guaranteed.

One cashier noted: "I was kind of upset with this week thing. They gave me [an] eighteen-hour week, and I was kind of hoping for thirty, like I normally get. Sometimes they'll give you less hours because they're training other cashiers and they need to balance the hours." In a company that had implemented severe labor budget reductions in recent years, another cashier observed: "Some people, they work over thirty-two hours, but they're just not considered full-time. And that makes them so mad." A human resources officer concurred: "There's probably plenty of thirty-plus-hours part-time employees that just are not full-time because the stores are not able to make anybody wholesale full-time if they want to, because of the expense of the benefit packages." An electronics manager reported that he had lots of part-timers who experienced great fluctuation— such as five hours one week but twenty the next, when a coworker was out. However, he "cannot schedule them steadily for as many hours as they'd like."[34]

The Implications of Short Hours for Workers and Managers

Within the confines of an exacting scheduling environment and minimal worker bargaining options, some workers settle for short hours. As noted earlier, the limited availability and relatively high cost of child care also play a part. Short-hour schedules have an impact not only on workers but also on management's labor deployment options.

Gap fillers in particular do not take on additional hours and, importantly, do not wish to move up to full-time status because of the expectation that they will be available to work over a much broader span of the day and week. For the same reasons, some time adjusters want—and work—more hours than they are regularly scheduled to work, but do not necessarily wish to make a commitment to working full-time or to move to higher (management) levels. A cake decorator who worked nearly full-time hours highlighted the dilemma of turning down promotion options that would have made greater demands on her time in order to handle child care scheduling constraints: "I wouldn't want to move up, and definitely working in a twenty-four-hour department, I wouldn't want to . . . have to be called in the middle of the night to fry doughnuts." Even in unionized food retail, full-timers are consistently required to be flexible as to when they are scheduled to work. A union company worker noted that she could get a full-time schedule of thirty-seven and a half hours guaranteed only "with lots of flexibility." In this demanding environment, even time adjusters retain some level of control over total work hours and scheduling relative to full-timers.

A recent trend will complicate the trade-offs faced by workers, time adjusters, and full-timers alike: a number of retailers have issued explicit requirements that full-timers have "full availability"—in other words, that they be willing to work any schedule and adapt to schedule changes week to week. For example, one electronics retailer issued written notifications to full-timers of such a requirement. According to one manager, "Some did not want to do it" (and the full-time to part-time ratio declined rapidly). The interviewed workers seemed to have settled for low earnings as a trade-off for having some degree of predictability in their work schedule—that is, in their time away from home. This accommodation creates complications especially for single parents, mostly single mothers, who need predictability but also seek a higher number of hours on which to count every week. Moreover, the long-term consequences are likely to be especially problematic for single parents because they are the least well positioned to access even first-line supervisor positions given the requirements of these jobs and the institutional and social norm constraints within which caregiving is organized.

Since the end of our fieldwork, militancy in retail, fast food, and other sectors that rely heavily on part-time workers has called attention to the exacting trade-offs faced by part-time workers in these sectors. Many rebel, particularly as these sectors have recruited greater numbers of older workers with families since the Great Recession and the resulting slack labor market. Movements for higher pay and more hours have highlighted differential pay, insufficient hours (thus insufficient earnings), and unpredictable schedules and the disruption they cause to family life and to opportunities to line up other jobs.[35] These movements have also highlighted the consequences of the use of more advanced scheduling software—the ever-finer "slicing" of customer flow into stores—for workers who face shorter shifts with irregular scheduling. We return to these issues in chapter 8.

CONCLUSION

We have laid out the competitive strategies devised by retailers in the two subsectors and the demands these strategies generate in terms of management, skill mix, and worker behavior at the entry and middle levels of the job ladder. We have also explored how the "labor budget," a key management tool, drives staffing decisions and also meshes with the labor supply decisions of some categories of workers to yield the ubiquitous retail schedule patterns of heavy use of part-time and increasingly variable hours. Women workers, for example, exemplify the experience of working with constrained options, such as care responsibilities, while also bringing—or being perceived as having the ability to bring—an orientation to in-person service, a legacy of ingrained perceptions of gender roles. We also have pointed out likely tensions between competitive goals and labor strategies. Using company case studies, we illustrated the range of the job quality outcomes (compensation, hours, turnover) present in companies with seemingly comparable competitive strategies.

This variation prompts us to perform a deeper comparison of companies' approaches to similar competitive or labor issues and to examine more closely the sources and implications of tensions among retailers' goals. We do so in the next chapter, where we sift the qualitative case study material to explore conflicts between the requirements of product strategies and labor strategies. That chapter analyzes the features and consequences of these tensions not only for job quality but also for the sustainability of the approaches taken by several case-study companies.

Finally, this chapter has raised important issues regarding the role of the broader institutional context in the United States—for employment as a whole and for the retail industry in particular—in how it affects both employer strategies and worker choices and their implications. These issues surface repeatedly as we examine the environment of U.S. stores.

4 / Competitive and Labor Strategies: Addressing Sustainability

We found that retailers' strategic responses to competitive pressures have job quality consequences, but that companies vary sufficiently in strategy implementation to yield differentiated job outcomes. The confluence of these strategies with the ever-present drive to control labor costs creates tensions in workplaces. In this chapter, we revisit sources of cross-company variations in strategy and resulting job quality. We inquire more deeply into clashes between product and labor strategies as well as conflicting goals within product strategies. Fleshing out this picture requires in-depth exploration and documentation of company case studies. In analyzing the cases, we ask to what extent current company strategies are *sustainable*.

We have centered our case-study analysis on three primary inquiries:

1. *Why is job quality different across companies?* How do institutional factors, market factors, and especially managerial practices (including both company-level strategy and local manager preferences) come into play?

2. *How much of an impact does cost-cutting have on strategy implementation?* Here we find that, where labor cost-cutting is primary, conflicts among goals are particularly difficult for managers to address.

3. *How do clashing strategies affect corporate sustainability?* We find that these frictions threaten corporate sustainability in three ways: they

worsen job quality, they directly undermine company survival, or they do both.

The chapter discusses job quality variation and analyzes the underlying interstrategy tensions for each subsector in turn: food retail, consumer electronics, and warehouse store formulas. Because food retail is the largest and most differentiated sector, we give it greater attention in this initial discussion. The chapter then analyzes strains between product and labor strategies that are common to all three sectors. The chapter closes with a brief overview of recent market changes that are likely to further impact retailer practices and ultimately job quality, particularly for frontline workers.

JOB QUALITY AND THE QUALITY-DRIVEN STRATEGY IN FOOD RETAIL

In addition to the quantitative differences in job quality across food retail companies summarized in chapter 3, there are clear *qualitative* differences in strategy implementation and job characteristics across companies. We first explore one obvious difference—unionization. We then consider variation in how companies implement a quality-driven strategy given their market position and also, importantly, their commitment to a particular labor strategy. We flag inconsistencies within their strategies and describe the resulting implications for workers as well as for the retail companies. Finally, we identify the market factors that increase the odds of the quality-driven strategy yielding better job quality outcomes and fewer tensions.

Unionization: A Differentiating Factor

What explains differences in the quantitative and qualitative features of jobs across companies? In food retail, one powerful factor is the presence of unions and collective bargaining agreements.[1] Unionized retailers do not necessarily offer significantly higher pay, but union wage scales, by including a greater spread of wage levels *within* job categories, represent the likelihood of greater reward for seniority and work experience in these retailers. Furthermore, unionized retailers provide more generous benefits to full-timers (paid time off, insurance) and tend to provide health insurance to part-timers. In our study sample, the three unionized chains (one only partly unionized) provide health insurance for part-timers that seems comparable to that offered to full-timers.

Nevertheless, unionized food retailers adopt scheduling practices similar to those of non-union competitors. They make significant use of part-time schedules (65 to 71 percent of the workforces in the fully unionized companies Food Chief and Freshland) and also require weekend work. One difference with non-union food retailers is that managers consider seniority in giving workers a choice over scheduling. Another distinction is that unions negotiate limits to wide schedule swings for part-timers; at one company, one-quarter of part-timers are guaranteed twenty-five weekly hours, while others have wider fluctuations. This contrasts with non-union settings, where guaranteed hours are usually lower or nonexistent.

Unionized food retailers in our study also do not differ markedly from the non-union retailers in turnover and patterns of mobility. Still, the two fully unionized retailers have turnover rates at the low end of the range of our study sample. Their rate of promotion from within is similar to that of other food retailers in the study.

Union impacts on retail jobs are compounded by regional differences in regulatory environment, regarding both product markets and employment; the South, for example, is both a low-unionization and low-regulation environment. We return to these regionally varying factors later in the chapter.

Different Implementations of the Quality-Driven Strategy

Beyond collective bargaining impacts, there are other significant differences across companies in how the quality-driven strategy plays out. As we saw in chapter 3, job quality contrasts also arise from differing labor strategies and managerial practices. These strategy differences may stem from a decision to target different market niches, or to adopt a distinctive labor strategy within a broadly similar market.

Perhaps the best-known contrast among companies is that between the giant retailer Wal-Mart and the warehouse club Costco. Where Wal-Mart operates a labor model with low wages, thin benefit coverage, low and variable part-time hours, and high turnover,

Costco is on record as aiming for higher-than-average wages, more predictable hours for part-timers, and some benefit coverage for part-timers—with results like labor turnover less than one-third of Wal-Mart's.[2] Costco's strategy stands out to such a degree that President Barack Obama featured it in his January 2014 State of the Union speech. Costco has adopted a labor strategy intended to foster worker productivity; higher-than-average compensation is designed to limit undesirable turnover and promote worker effort. This labor strategy aims to support a business strategy consisting of a targeted higher-income warehouse shopper (shopping for good prices on quality products), a limited range of goods, and high volume.[3] Our study cases display a number of important additional variations on this theme.

Successful Implementation of the Quality-Driven Strategy: Homestyle and The Market   To illustrate differing applications of the quality-driven strategy, we revisit in greater detail two resilient examples of this strategy—Homestyle and The Market—whose strategic approaches were presented in the previous chapter. These two regional chains have managed to continue growing in the face of stiff competition while others have lost significant market share, sacrificed job quality, or foundered. Homestyle defines its competitive advantage as "quality and service." Its market niche is college-educated customers with higher income and a taste for fine food and wine. It is thus able to offer higher-quality products and indeed is "number one with variety and merchandising" in its market and "the largest purveyor of wine" in its home state, according to an executive. A Homestyle produce manager commented that in the early 1980s, when he first started at Homestyle, "all the stores were just pretty . . . standard grocery stores. Since then, Homestyle has gone to a lot bigger, nicer look." The two stores we visited presented their food (particularly produce and prepared foods) very attractively. Homestyle defines restaurants as direct competition. In the words of the company's vice president for human resources:

> We don't want our folks to eat out! Our clients are the ones that like to go to the nice restaurants as well. So when the economy gets tight, people will tend not to eat out as much, and therefore we need to be able to offer that different solution. . . . So we have chef-prepared meals that are restaurant quality. A lot of folks in-

stead of eating out will have that at home. Pick up a bottle of wine
on your way out.

Homestyle competes head to head with Wal-Mart, but where
Wal-Mart has entered a Homestyle market area, Homestyle stores
have only seen limited sales losses of about 20 percent. A store manager commented that, with the opening of a nearby Wal-Mart, he
had seen an impact on sales of cleaning and paper products, but
"they put their groceries in the store, a few aisles of it, and I really
didn't see an impact there." Despite losses to Wal-Mart, Homestyle
has been able to continue growing total sales through expansion.
Consistent with defining a niche distinct from that of Wal-Mart,
Homestyle continues to practice "hi-lo pricing" (based on weekly
sales on selected items) rather than the "everyday low prices" approach championed by Wal-Mart and other discounters.

The Market, another regional chain using hi-lo pricing, also now
aims at higher-end customers. According to a regional manager, a
thirty-six-year veteran, the result of The Market's "quest to be
leading-edge" has been that "goods and services has grown and become more complex, [and] much more specialized work [is] being
done: . . . custom-cut meats, fresh seafood, scratch bakeries. . . . People want something that's new and different and unique that their
neighbor . . . doesn't have." A store manager repeatedly referred to
The Market's perishables departments as one key to retaining customers, adding that although he had not had to face Wal-Mart, he
had heard that other The Market stores had prevailed despite Wal-
Mart's arrival because of superior perishables and service. The Market has experienced steady, moderate growth while other chains in
the region have contracted.

Though we have emphasized quality and variety, service is definitely part of the formula. In fact, interviewees at both Homestyle
and The Market would disagree with our characterization of their
strategy as quality-driven: Homestyle's vice president for human
resources and the store manager we interviewed at The Market both
pointed to service as their main competitive advantage. Among the
dimensions of service, these and other interviewees focused on attention to customers and keeping wait times short. Nevertheless,
we stand by our "quality-driven" label: based on their descriptions
and our direct observations of service levels, their service does not
distinguish them from most other nonwarehouse supermarkets in

the sample (though it does distinguish them from Wal-Mart). A district manager at the regional grocer P. A. Smith, another chain that emphasizes service as well as product quality and variety, also noted that standards of service quality are often aspirational and, if anything, are getting harder to meet:

> Companies will say we're really customer-driven, we're customer-oriented, customer is number one, all of that, but I think what they deliver to the consumer is far less than that, and I think they tolerate far less than that, and I don't think P. A. Smith is an exception with that. . . . To go back [fifteen or twenty years ago], we had customer-driven programs, mystery shoppers, and all those type of things, that said, "Okay, how good are you with the consumer?" I don't think that's a whole lot different now. The ability to execute might be different, because anytime you go from managing 75 to 100 people to managing 250 people, you know, that's gonna be very different.

Still Homestyle and The Market respondents were correct in the sense that without an adequate service level, retailers' delivery of quality cannot win and hold on to customers. The two companies have taken a number of steps toward ensuring this; Homestyle, for example, has initiated bonuses for frontline workers and strengthened training.

Service in the more substantive sense of providing information and advice based on product knowledge could complement a quality strategy more directly by helping to develop customer tastes. The human resources vice president at The Market illustrated how worker knowledge translates into service quality, which, in turn, fosters sales of higher-quality and more varied products:

> We have to really teach people about the products because I believe that if people understand the products, they will naturally talk to the customers, because people want to share their knowledge. We did a knowledge-based training in our meat department, and it was the most successful customer service training we did. We taught every single meat associate how to prepare the meat. . . . What we were teaching them is, get excited about the products.

However, this approach to service is the exception rather than the rule. In fact, the context of this vice president's anecdote was a complaint that this remained an isolated experiment and that most service training consists of "just telling people to smile."

Built-In Tensions Among Successful Quality-Driven Grocers   Delivering the quality-driven strategy at the store level builds in significant tensions despite changes in labor deployment. Strains appear to stem from the combined effects of increasing demands on employees and trimming staffing levels, with the resulting coordination demands and workload increases. At Homestyle, there has been pressure on staff schedules and total job demands for managers, supervisors, and frontline workers because staffing gets "a little tighter every year," according to a front-end manager. A full-time customer service associate has to be available to be scheduled to work anytime. Worker assessments of the workload impacts varied somewhat. A customer service manager remarked, "I think we just do a lot—one person can do a lot in one day." A produce clerk at the same store had a less positive view: "If they weren't gonna give any more hours, and they're not going to, they'd have to come up with a better system of being able to get it all done without killing people."

At The Market, as at Homestyle, pressure is significant. In the words of interviewees, including regional managers, there are "incredible" demands on managers; they are expected to be "hands-on" and to work long hours. To implement quality goals, the product displays and the overall look of the store have become quite important. Everyone at headquarters and in the store says that they want the store to look attractive—indeed, the store we visited looked quite appealing. This emphasis generates significant workload: one manager lamented that customers "do not realize what it takes to make the store look like this."

Tensions and Conflicts Among Competing Goals: When Cost-Cutting Rules

In other food retailers, tensions between management goals and workforce capacity at the store level have escalated to the point of threatening the quality-driven strategy. We find that, with these retailers, cost-cutting has taken primacy, often with divisive impacts on the workforce.

Value Fresh avows a commitment to high quality and service, but at the store level cost-cutting translates into a squeeze on monthly labor budgets, which regulate labor hours in the stores. These cost-cutting pressures also have an adverse impact on training resources and the ability to grant pay raises. The resulting workforce difficulties threaten, in turn, to thwart store managers' ability to maintain quality and service. The company, which has experienced competition in recruiting entry-level workers, offers wages pegged at the same level as Target and Wal-Mart—close to the minimum wage—making retention difficult.[4] Changes affecting midlevel management and supervisors have played a part. With more manager recruitment from outside (college graduates), those in place see fewer promotion options and, we surmise, fewer reasons to strive for quality and service goals.

Freshland and Food Chief, the two fully unionized companies in the study, have also cut staff, thus increasing workloads and "doing more with less," in the words of a Freshland manager. A Freshland produce clerk glumly spelled out the implications:

> The amount of work [has] gone up quite dramatically. But it's just basically they cut labor in order to either make more money or obviously there's competition so they have to trim the fat somewhere in terms of labor. If there's the same amount of work that needs to be done, then obviously we have to take up the slack. . . . There's just less of us, so it's kind of suck [it] up and do more work.

At these unionized chains, the change with the most dramatic consequences has been the implementation of two-tier pay scales, with a lower wage cap for newly hired clerks. At Freshland, management described the two-tier structure as inevitable. "With competition like Wal-Mart," said a district human resources manager, "it's difficult to pay our employees a higher wage while maintaining competitiveness." But in limiting upward mobility, this change clashes with a company strategy based on high commitment and "fierce loyalty." Employee turnover has climbed, and service levels have slumped. When we visited, Freshland had just launched a new "engagement" initiative, but the initiative consisted mainly of cheerleading plus coaching based on mystery shoppers. A store manager directly linked two-tier pay with higher turnover: "I think that they didn't know to what extent this last [union] contract would just make for a deluge [of turnover], because that was never part of our culture. . . . They're hoping this engagement piece, having people more aware and conscious or feeling 'part of,' will help that."

At Food Chief, likewise, a newly adopted lower wage cap for new workers was seen as a departure from tradition, and it raised concerns about worker commitment. "Only the people at the top of the scale got . . . progressive increases. People in the lower ranks were frozen. That's a huge, huge, huge change from what they're used to. They're used to seeing a 3 [or] 4 percent increase every year of the contract." Partly to address workforce motivation shortfalls, Food Chief recently launched employee rewards programs (small cash bonuses at manager discretion) tied to customer service. However, implementing a radical culture shift while having fewer incentives to offer workers presents a daunting managerial challenge. Meanwhile, Food Chief's implementation of the quality-driven strategy coupled with its cost-cutting has resulted in the reallocation of resources toward fresh products and "enhanced" stores (with more offerings) and away from standard stores—"to try to get to the bottom line," in the words of a regional manager. The impact on overall product quality and customer service is unclear at best.

In addition to commitment difficulties, a second potentially problematic consequence of higher turnover, scantier staffing, and increased pressures on managers is the *thinning of the internal pipeline for supervisors and managers* (also an issue in consumer electronics, as we will see). First, fewer employees aspire to move up within the company, as a Freshland cashier explained:

> There's not a whole lot of people that want those [head cashier jobs]. The big downside for that is they only make a quarter more an hour, but now you have a lot more responsibility. You're now responsible for running that front end. You're responsible for closing the store and making sure things are being taken care of and customers are taken care of.

That slim twenty-five-cent raise is a direct consequence of the pay cap for new hires. Meanwhile, managers who are lucky enough to have effective full-timers amid lean staffing are reluctant to let go of them, impeding the flow to higher-level jobs. At non-union Value Fresh, a human resources official observed:

> Something that I noticed over the last five years that has changed significantly is the ability to career-path individuals into a department manager training program from within the company. My theory as to why that has happened has to do with the relationship of the hours adjustments over the last X period of years and because the hours get down so tight where you have so few key people, the go-to gal or the go-to guy that I know I can ask them to do anything and it will be done, the managers don't want to give them up.

This official summed up Value Fresh's challenges and how they impeded store success by wryly commenting, "Everybody is vying for that food dollar, and you have to find a way to make it work. Wages are the easiest thing to control. It gets to a point where you can control yourself right out of business."

The Impact of Market and Regulatory Factors on Food Retailer Labor Strategies and Sustainability

Another set of elements *outside* the labor dimension structure the viability of competing on product quality and sustaining key features of job quality. Three such elements appear to help companies succeed in this quest: a historical emphasis on quality, being privately held, and operating in a relatively sheltered market. To some extent, these three factors are interdependent. For example, having been privately held may have given a company the autonomy necessary to adopt and maintain a higher-end strategy. Likewise, operating in a relatively sheltered market segment facilitates adherence to a consistent strategy. We elaborate how each of these components plays out in our case-study companies.

First, it is an advantage to have started at the higher end of product offerings and customer service when competitive pressure ratchets up. In the face of price-cutting competition, it appears to be easier to maintain an upmarket position—retaining an image as well as customers—than it is to transform from a midlevel retailer to a higher-end one.[5] Both Homestyle and The Market, for example, had built a reputation for quality long before the most recent wave of competition, though, to be sure, each has taken added steps to cultivate that reputation in the current environment. A Homestyle store manager emphasized company history: "We've always stood for cleanliness and trying to have a niche out there in the market to try and be a little bit better and also [to offer] better products than anybody else. That's always been what we stood on."

Still, it is possible to make the transition upmarket. Food Chief, a unionized regional grocery chain within a multiregional holding company, has responded to low-price competition from Wal-Mart and others by seeking to move upmarket to middle- and upper-income customers and now emphasizes meat and produce quality, a variety of new fresh and prepared food offerings, cleanliness, and service, as well as its identity as the "hometown market." According to a regional human resources director, "Fifteen, twenty years ago, [our appeal] was price. . . . For many years, our tag line was 'low-price leader.' To be perfectly honest, we had to take that back now that we're dealing with more Wal-Marts." But now, she added, "we're known in [Food Chief's home region] for our fresh produce. People come . . . for our produce. We just launched a big meat campaign where we have a certain line of beef that you can only get at Food Chief and it's very high-quality. You know, freshness, cleanliness, and price." A Food Chief store manager emphasized variety: "If I were to say there's a Wal-Mart across the street and why would they come to Food Chief versus a Wal-Mart or a Target super center, I would probably say, the variety, the assortment."

Second, being privately held appears to buy food retailers some leeway to implement a quality-driven strategy. It has enabled some retailers to make investments with longer-term horizons and to use reserves to address recent competitive pressures. At the time of our study, Homestyle was privately held (with strong though decreasing family presence in management); it has since been acquired by a national retail corporation. The Market is privately held and to a significant degree is employee-owned. Management at The Market credits being privately held and majority-employee-owned for the company's ability to make investments with longer-term returns.

Conversely, others have noted that firms that carry more debt (often as a result of private equity ownership) experience greater pressure to yield higher short-term returns and thus to cut costs.[6]

Being privately held and historically a higher-end chain facilitates a firm's implementation of a quality-driven strategy, but these factors do not suffice by themselves. Freshland also is a privately held, unionized, regional grocery chain with banners ranging from warehouse to upscale and a strong family presence in management. But, as noted, its cost-cutting to narrow the gap with Wal-Mart has undermined a labor strategy built around loyalty, longevity, and commitment.

The third factor in successfully competing on product quality, operating in a relatively sheltered regional market, allows some companies to take a more deliberate approach to implementing a quality-driven strategy. Operating with enough stores in areas experiencing little or no direct competition enables companies to anticipate competitive changes and learn from the experiences of some of their urban stores that confront stronger competitive pressure.

Another market-sheltering issue arises in regions with more laissez-faire land use policy, especially in the Southeast and in south-central regions: new retailers can easily enter the market, generating more price- and convenience-based competition, which results in shrinking market shares for those in place. This dynamic makes it harder for the quality-driven model to succeed because the competitive terrain shifts quickly, eliminating the lead time for adjustment. These regions typically also have low rates of unionization, further undermining labor strategies anchored in job quality. Some interviewees noted the significant regional variations in land use policies and their market consequences. At the southern food retailer Marketland, the human resources vice president emphasized the region's institutional peculiarities:

> If you look at the U.S., if you compare . . . the density of supermarket stores in the Northeast versus the Southeast, there's a huge difference. Your average volume of a supermarket in the Northeast is probably four times what it is here. You just have a whole different dynamic. So that means it's that competitive, and it means it keeps the prices down. Here you're constantly fighting

for more customers, so it's a very challenging environment to operate in.

Similar issues challenge Value Fresh, a regional grocer struggling with price-cutting competition. Value Fresh uses two main store formats: its stores are mainly midrange supermarkets offering fresh produce, deli, bakery, and meat products, but they also target middle- and low-income shoppers with "every day low price" discount stores with a narrower range of offerings.[7] In the midrange supermarkets, the company aims to differentiate itself from the competition (both Kroger and Wal-Mart) with higher levels of service and better-quality fresh food departments. However, land use regulation in Value Fresh's area is relaxed, making it easy to locate a new supermarket. All twenty independent grocery stores in its headquarters urban area closed over the past two decades owing to a mix of direct competition from discounters like Wal-Mart and the expansion of multiregional chains seeking new markets to remedy *their* losses to discounters in other regions. The consequence for Value Fresh: flat sales and a falling market share in both principal formats over the preceding two years.

A final type of market sheltering is stiffer state or local labor standards. For example, a higher state minimum wage raises the floor, closing off low-wage competition to some degree. Higher labor standards tend to correlate with tighter land use regulations—state and local minimum wages, for instance, are set higher in the Northeast, upper Midwest, and Pacific Coast regions.

ELECTRONICS AND THE SERVICE-DRIVEN STRATEGY: DIFFERENCES ACROSS COMPANIES IN AVERAGE JOB QUALITY AND DEGREE OF JOB INEQUALITY

The service-driven strategy has somewhat different implications for jobs in broad-line electronics than for those in office equipment and supply stores. But across the board the imperative of cost-cutting—while simultaneously expanding service strategies—generates tensions for most retailers, undermining the workforce capacity and engagement needed for successful implementation of a service-driven strategy.

Broad-Line Consumer Electronics Companies: Degrees of Job Segmentation

For broad-line consumer electronics purveyors like Electronix and Technology Source, one powerful impact of the service-driven strategy is workforce segmentation—the separation of a store's staff into distinct tiers. The criterion for entry into the upper tier is advanced technical skills (computer repair, auto installation) or advanced sales skills plus in some cases managerial skills. Although the sales jobs involving systems design require some technical skill as well, managers at several chains told us that they were shifting away from recruiting and training for advanced technical skills and instead emphasizing "sales ability." In home installations, an important added overlay is the "general contractor" skills involved in coordinating installers' work. These management skills are a mix of ability to coordinate services and communication-oriented "people" skills. The combination is required to carry out the scheduling of component deliveries, the cost estimates for alterations (wall modification for wiring and installation), the meshing of physical alterations with the electronic work, and the appropriate ongoing communication with the customer.

Segmentation implies large differences in job quality, somewhat tempered by variable pay as an important motivational tool for *all* workers, even low-level ones. At Electronix, for example, pay differences illustrate a job quality gap across positions. Part-time sales staff in the main part of the store earn from the minimum wage up to $10 an hour, whereas in the high-end section—the store-within-a-store with specialized high-end products and services—part-timers can earn up to $16 an hour, computer repair techs can earn $19 an hour or more, and supervisors earn up to $26 an hour (in 2007 dollars). We will return to Electronix's wage disparities, but for now, the broader context for these wage figures is important: nonsupervisory workers in electronics retailing averaged $18.31 in 2007 (when we completed our fieldwork), 43 percent more than the average retail worker and 62 percent more than the average grocery employee.[8]

To further motivate lower-level employees to deliver "hand-to's" to the store-within-a-store, Electronix and Tech Source mobilize peppy frontline management, including "fun" games and activities, all built around team-building and internalization of sales goals and techniques. Both companies also implement a small variable bonus—taking account of department and storewide performance—and "instant bonuses" in the form of gift certificates distributed by managers to recognize outstanding service. Variable pay partly serves to mitigate the significant pressure on even lower-level employees to "qualify" (profile) customers and hand over appropriate ones to the store-within-a-store. One elite sales manager described the process of teaching employees how to qualify customers:

> The [store-within-a-store] pros' other job is to . . . go out fishing. What that means is they're gonna go out looking for the customers that would have any interest to shop in that area of the store and hopefully catch those customers and bring them back to that room. Also, when they're out fishing, what they're gonna spend their time doing is coaching and training employees on how do we qualify customers to get them into that room.

Despite their similarities in approach, the two broad-line consumer electronics companies display some striking differences in job outcomes. The two retailers differ greatly in the degree of within-company job inequality (table 4.1). Within-company gaps across jobs are noticeably greater at Electronix than at Tech Source, most strikingly when contrasting part-time and full-time workers. At Electronix, full-timers have a higher base number of hours and can reach higher wage levels, whereas part-timers start at a lower wage and suffer a greater wage penalty relative to full-timers than part-timers at Tech Source. Electronix store managers also earn more than their Tech Source counterparts relative to hourly workers.

How can we explain the divergences between these two otherwise similar chains? Electronix appears to be more tightly focused on the importance of selling higher-end services, especially the design and installation of costly home entertainment systems. Achieving this goal depends on differentiating the store-within-a-store with "an atmosphere change" and "a different level of professionalism" than with the rest of the staff, in one supervisor's words, based on acquiring a boutique seller and importing that company's staff and techniques.

Tech Source also seeks to sell more high-value-added services,

Table 4.1 / Selected Indices of Inequality at Electronix and
Technology Source, 2006

Characteristic	Electronix	Technology Source
Starting hourly wage for part-time workers[a]	$5.15	$6.00
Top of wage range for full-time sales[b]	Over $19 an hour	$18 an hour
Health plan for part-timers?	No	Yes (individual)
Base hours for full-timers	36	30
Full-time/part-time hourly wage ratio, cashiers	1.24	1.00
Full-time/part-time hourly wage ratio, regular sales	1.71	1.18
Store manager/part-time cashier hourly wage ratio[c]	4.83	3.41

Source: Authors' calculations from the field study.
Note: Wage ratios are calculated at the midpoint of the respective ranges.
[a]Varies by region; the lower end is shown (same region for both firms).
[b]For a specific metro area.
[c]Calculated omitting bonuses and assuming store manager works forty hours weekly (an unrealistic assumption, but comparably so across the two cases). The Tech Source manager salary figure comes from a single store; the Electronix figure is the ratio of chainwide midpoints.

but has approached this market by building capacity in-house rather than by acquiring a specialist retail chain. And whereas top human resources executives in Electronix emphasize "service as one of the big differentiators going forward"—in the words of the director of field human resources—Tech Source's top human resources executive responded to the same question about competitive advantage by first talking about price and product assortment. He went on to bemoan falling margins on computers, adding, "That's where the service business hopefully will kick in." Moreover, he highlighted the recent extension of limited health benefits to part-timers as a "retention vehicle" to reduce turnover. One of his deputies argued that "this shows we do value you" and described part-timers' health coverage as part of a broader shift, under the leadership of a new CEO, from a "dog-eat-dog . . . very competitive . . . results at any cost" culture to one where "there's value on people." The tone is different from that of Electronix's vice president of field human resources, who prioritized giving employees "skills and knowledge and tools . . . to do great things . . . be creative . . . bring their full selves to work and think while they're there."

In short, despite very similar selling strategies, on the terrain of labor strategy Electronix emphasizes rewarding individuals for doing more and seeks to differentiate higher-end sales, whereas Tech Source is using its compensation to communicate that *all* employees, even lowly part-timers, are valued. In relative terms, one HR strategy promotes differentiation, the other inclusion.[9]

Office Equipment Stores: Contained Job Segmentation

In the alternative service-driven model of office equipment stores, where options for within-store spatial segmentation and customer-base segmentation are limited, segmentation in pay is significant, but not as pronounced. Reviewing senior employee wages at The Office stores at the time of our fieldwork, we find that a part-time cashier was paid $9.60 an hour, an office equipment salesperson was paid $13.63, and a copy center supervisor was paid $15.75. The Office uses other carrots and sticks to motivate employees: significant opportunities for salary growth with longevity (the three employees just described started at $7 to $8 an hour); a small bonus based on department and company performance; and intense reliance on customer surveys and "mystery shoppers" to monitor employee behavior. These incentives are linked, since, as one manager explained, "the weighting of the customer service index [in the bonus] is growing."

Shared Sources of Tension in Labor Management in Consumer Electronics

Consumer electronics retailers share several practices that they deem necessary to successfully implement the service-driven strategy. As in the grocery sector, these practices in turn generate tensions in managing labor. Their service-driven competitive strategies depend on both cost control and the appropriate mix of soft skills (customer assessment and service) and hard skills (product knowledge). But the cost containment goal can clash with other requirements of the model, notably the need to keep the workforce motivated and engaged in the project of enhanced customer service.

Cost Control and Worker Motivation: Commission Pay   The abandonment of commissions tied to sales appears to be an important correlate of success in the service-driven strategy. As margins on consumer electronics goods fell, commissions made less and less economic sense, adding to unit labor costs while contributing little in terms of margin on added sales. Among broad-line electronics retailers, Electronix dropped commissions early, Tech Source eliminated them later, and Hi Fi was still using them when we spoke to them (though it had cut the commission rate as margins shrank). The three companies' handling of commissions maps exactly onto the degree of their market success. Apparently, timely redesign of the compensation system—cutting effective pay for some while spreading incentives to all workers—may have enabled some companies to better address the tension between cost-cutting and worker focus on service provision.

Commissions were never present at the two office supply sellers in our sample, but both at one time used "spiffs"—special cash incentives for selling high-margin items such as extended warranties. Office Express still uses spiffs to induce employees to sell extended warranties, whereas The Office has shifted to a bonus system and dropped spiffs because they motivate what a store manager called "bad behavior"—for instance, inducing an employee to discount the sales price of an item in order to sell the service plan. Again, The Office's no-spiff policy correlates with better performance.

Staffing, Training, and Turnover   In addition to seeking new forms of workforce motivation, the other ubiquitous challenge threatening the service-driven strategy is that all of these companies are trying to cut costs, as they seek to narrow price differences with Wal-Mart and online sellers and even increase the service component of their offerings. Thinner staffing, for instance, jeopardizes the service-driven model. An Office Express middle manager complained that:

> we're real shorthanded, especially during those peak times. It makes it real hard to help out every single customer that we get in the store, juggling between all of them. Obviously you want to

give the customer a great shopping experience. It's a little hard when you're running back and forth between customers.

Reduced resources for training can likewise undermine service. At The Office, an office equipment salesman noted that "a lot of the cross-training is what hit the floor when they cut the payroll," and he blamed the precipitous decline in training for reducing workers' ability to help out across jobs. In turn, frontline workers' lack of polyvalence may erode key elements of the service-driven strategy, such as identifying potential higher-end customers and building a coordinated sales workforce with both technical knowledge and people skills.

Importantly, increased job requirements and broader job content seem to have caused turnover, which was already high in settings with many part-time and disproportionately young workers, to rise in some companies. "There's a lot more requirements in the jobs these days," said a sales supervisor at Technology Source. "So, therefore, there is a lot more things to mess up on. Therefore, there's a lot more ways to have turnover." Turnover makes it even more difficult to instill a customer service orientation and train employees in the skills needed to qualify higher-end customers.

Furthermore, as in food retail, turnover in the electronics sector seems to deplete the number of those in the pipeline who are ready to move up to management roles. Also contributing to a shortage of managerial candidates is another consequence of lean staffing— with inadequate staff coverage, managers must work dauntingly long hours to problem-solve and perform necessary tasks.

JOB QUALITY CHALLENGES WITH THE WAREHOUSE STORE FORMULA: WORKLOAD AND MOBILITY OPPORTUNITIES

Warehouse stores (which sell both food and consumer electronics products) also experience workforce challenges in fully implementing their retail model, even as they generate price-cutting pressure on companies with conventional store formats. Though warehouse stores are, by design, light users of labor resources, their cost control drives still leaner staffing, generating labor motivation challenges similar to those in the other subsectors.[10]

As warehouse store companies, both Bargain Warehouse and Megamart expend few resources on training frontline workers beyond initial orientation and cashier instruction. Training resources are earmarked for workers who are positioned to move up; these employees receive extensive training that is either area-specific (for example, food preparation at Bargain Warehouse) or focused on product features. Frontline workers not on that track complain of insufficient training. At Bargain Warehouse, an appliance department clerk grumbled, "That's a challenge for me, to try to learn as much as you can while you have your other duties."

Since both companies have cut their total labor hours budgets, some workers expressed feeling overwhelmed. One Bargain Warehouse employee described, for example, the intensity of checkout lines on Saturdays: "It just seems like it snowballs and gets later and later and people get angry that their breaks are an hour late." Megamart deals with an additional challenge: its smaller stores are laid out in such a way that clerks have to load large, heavy items onto store shelves themselves (rather than with heavy equipment such as forklifts, as in other warehouse stores). This requirement is a source of burnout and turnover among middle-aged employees.

Both companies share with other retailers the challenges with the pipeline for promotion beyond frontline positions. Full-time employees in both companies expressed their doubts about moving up into management positions, owing to the increase and variability in hours. "The time constraints for this place are pretty severe on a manager," a Bargain Warehouse cashier observed. "You typically have to start out on the floor working 2:00 in the morning to 10:30, and that's just rough. It's salaried, so they can work you whatever they want." BW managers are expected to work weekends, whereas some full-time hourly workers can get a weekday schedule. The same concern about hours factors into decisions to bid for a supervisory position at Megamart as well. As one full-time worker noted: "The forty hours are okay for me. I know that if I were to put in [for manager], I think it would be fifty to sixty hours." Another reason workers hesitate to move up is that managers often are transferred across several locations.

Both companies experience challenges with providing upward mobility opportunities, but for different reasons. At Megamart, the lack of full-time job opportunities makes for long waiting periods and tends to feed turnover. In contrast, the greater number of full-time opportunities at Bargain Warehouse and the company's general better treatment of part-time workers make for low turnover. Ironically, the low turnover generates long waits for promotion, particularly in regions where warehouses are few and far apart geographically. This limitation is mitigated by the fact that Bargain Warehouse is growing and opportunities arise with each new store—which is not the case for Megamart.

The Impact of Warehouse Stores' Market Positioning on Job Quality and Labor Strategy Tension

Bargain Warehouse and Megamart illustrate that, even within warehouse retailing's relatively narrow band of store format and product offerings, there is notable leeway in how a warehouse store deploys labor, manages work hours, controls compensation costs, and ultimately addresses clashing goals. BW shows that a strategy that relies on relatively higher job quality can *in some cases* enable a warehouse store company to take full advantage of its product market approach. BW pushes the envelope in part through changes to the warehouse formula, including distinctive "add-ons," such as fresh bakery and deli items, that could be labeled "quality-variety" strategies adopted within a part of each warehouse. In turn, these additions attract a higher-income customer segment willing to pay extra for these items, despite having initially been drawn to the warehouse by the good price-quality ratio and the generally low prices on a variety of goods.

Bargain Warehouse's larger store size and the fact that the company itself is larger and growing may also enhance the benefits of retaining workers, permitting a labor strategy of relatively high compensation that lowers turnover. Relatedly, BW's hours of operation are shorter than Megamart's, reducing the demands for holiday and weekend work and for "full scheduling availability." At 20 percent for all employees, including summer hires, staff turnover at BW is remarkably low for retail. Though still low by industry standards, Megamart's turnover rate, 40 percent, is much higher. Over the ten years preceding our fieldwork, MM's full-time turnover rates ranged from 8 to 18 percent annually, but part-time turnover varied between 56 and 82 percent.

With its labor strategy yielding jobs of lower quality in terms of compensation and schedules, Megamart has developed and re-tained market share by differentiating its *product* strategy. It has combined the convenience aspects of a warehouse store with broader product choices that reflect the expertise of the headquar-ters purchasing department, and it has added a modicum of knowledge-based within-store service for appliances, especially ap-pliances tailored to small businesses (such as restaurants). Me-gamart has been able to maintain operations with comparatively low-paying jobs and undesirable schedules because its sales ap-proach does not require its frontline workforce to acquire significant knowledge.

Taking a pared-down warehouse approach to food and consumer electronics and delivering a narrow version of retail service and a limited variety of goods, these two companies illustrate the range of autonomy that is possible. Embedding quality assurance in head-quarters purchasing departments reduces significantly what is needed on the store floor from workers in terms of knowledge and display maintenance. Nevertheless, a company that does not per-ceive a need for greater workforce engagement shows a different degree of commitment to job quality than one that uses higher com-pensation and more generous benefits to attract a more engaged workforce, thus limiting the costs of turnover and improving shop-pers' in-store experience.

A SUSTAINABILITY CRISIS? SHARED CHALLENGES AND TENSIONS ACROSS SECTORS

For most retailers, even those with market success, ongoing dilem-mas in workforce management affect the chances of their continued market success and ability to improve job quality. Here we revisit these dilemmas more comprehensively. Overlaying product and la-bor strategies in both sectors are ever-present cost-cutting pressures and the resulting lean staffing policies. Where cutting labor costs dominates other goals, contradictions between product and labor strategies erupt in conflict and affect the enterprise. These pressures play out in similar ways across food retail, consumer electronics, and warehouse stores. In brief, the resulting deterioration of job quality in some retailers triggers difficulties with worker motivation at a time when strategic choices require *greater* frontline worker effort to deliver quality, to qualify customers for targeted services and products, and to sell product packages effectively. Here we paint a composite picture of these shared retail challenges, then extrapolate on the points raised for each subsector.

Lean Staffing, Job Quality, and Worker Engagement

The lean staffing imperative shapes the jobs of both retail managers and frontline workers. In grocery stores in particular, managers find it difficult to make short-term adjustments in the labor budget, which has no "cushion." Also, the manager has little room to accommodate temporary (but recurrent) staff shortages when workers call in sick; a Value Fresh store manager noted: "You can't really hire somebody to work one day a week" in order to make up for temporary shortfalls. In electronics as well, the schedules of salaried managers absorb the consequences of lean staffing combined with extended store hours. At Photoworld, "When . . . someone doesn't show up for work, you know, they [the managers] cover the hours."

Lean staffing also has ramped up short-hour part-time schedules (under fifteen hours), and the greater variability in scheduling that results shapes the "lived work experience," as we discussed in chapter 3. Short hours draw in workers who, finding one near-minimum-wage retail job equivalent to another in a nearby mall ("for a dime difference in hourly wage," to paraphrase supervisors), can more readily "job-hop." Managers also note an increase in the number of teenage employees who subordinate their part-time retail job to other commitments (sports, schoolwork) and increasingly write off reliability as a job requirement.

Long-standing issues for women workers in retail are exacerbated by recent trends. Part-time work compelled by family responsibilities combined with scarcity in affordable child care confines many women to "gap filling," that is, working regularly scheduled part-time jobs. The sustained shift to part-time positions with the requirement to adjust upward to forty hours—often a precondition to any kind of regular full-time work, in first-line supervision and above—further strengthens the obstacles to promotion that women already encounter. We noted in interviews that though a few women had risen to managerial rank—and accommodated to variable hours—no regional or district manager was a woman.

Crucially, the spillovers from tight labor budgets undermine worker engagement, fueling widespread high turnover in the sector. Retail has long had high turnover, but the change we observe in our sample is that *even companies with historically low turnover,* relative to industry averages, reported increased rates.

To induce desired frontline worker behaviors, retailers have experimented with a variety of new variable-compensation incentives. In the short run, the highest payoff may accrue to bonuses linked to the sale of "attachments," such as extended warranties or supplementary equipment, but as consumer sophistication grows, this tactic is likely to lose effectiveness. More intriguing future prospects are suggested by an office equipment seller's experiment with tying bonuses to departmental and storewide customer service ratings, and grocery store chains' consideration of ways to create financial rewards for customer service even at the level of part-time employees (both discussed earlier).

Reduced worker engagement also creates pipeline problems for managers, who need a "bench" of potential, tested candidates for promotion. As a Megamart human resources official observed, the "key carrier" job is "like a first-line supervisory position. That's why getting keys is a big deal. And some people don't want to step into that role. They don't want the responsibility. So that's why some people just remain part-time associates and never go up to that key level."

A Further Complexity: Changes in Recruitment and Promotion Practices

Contributing to turnover but also raising other workforce management concerns are complex changes in recruitment and hiring for junior and senior management positions in stores. Managers at headquarter or district levels are constantly formulating plans for staffing managerial positions. New provisions go beyond the traditional building up of the bench of internal candidates for managerial positions to include a mix of recruiting from outside the company, and even from other sectors, and escalating educational requirements (for example, requiring a college degree for store managers). Such efforts, especially attempts to formulate and recruit for the generic elements of retail management abilities, are bound to have some payoff. However, they are also likely to further limit the movement into retail's management ranks of less-educated workers, who historically have been able to scale this in-house ladder. These trends will probably have particular repercussions for women workers, who have recently won opportunities to move up to assistant store manager and store manager positions.

Lean Staffing and Manager Overload

The Manager's Complaint High turnover and other workforce management challenges have resulted in supervisory and managerial work overload. Managers juggle sometimes irreconcilable imperatives, with consequences for the entry-level workers who implement their decisions—including heightened pressure or contradictory directives. Workers aspiring to move up witness firsthand the downside of promotions, which, in spite of pay raises, also come with the shift from hourly to salaried compensation and therefore take the "lid" off maximum work hours. As a result, some workers resist promotions or seek them in other parts of retail or other service industries.

Managers' testimonies illustrate how the challenge of matching competitive strategies with lean staffing has made their jobs difficult to sustain over time. At food retailer P. A. Smith, a store manager painted a grim, detailed picture that linked a variety of sustainability issues: leaner labor budgets, worker speedup and frustration, added demands on managers, and concerns about meeting rising service goals:

> P. A. SMITH STORE MANAGER: [Tighter labor budgets are] a major challenge. You know, we have great expectations out there. We have to have the store right 24/7, seven days a week. We want a clean store. We want to give great service. We want to make sure the shelves are full. When the labor budget gets pulled tighter and tighter like it has been, how do you make all that happen, and it's become quite tough.
>
> INTERVIEWER: How have [the workers] adjusted?
>
> P. A. SMITH STORE MANAGER: There's frustration. We try to do some things. We try to have luncheons here and there. . . . We're out walking the stores constantly. . . . trying to recognize

the positives, trying to give them a pat on the back. . . . But there's definitely frustration. . . . When you get in those stores that's really cranking out high volume, like here on Friday, Saturday, and Sunday, if you're that coworker short that you know you really need, you can really see the frustration in the faces. [Frustration at not being able to get their] job done . . . the way they want to get their job done. I mean, we can . . . get the product out, but we're kind of killing ourselves to do it. Before, ready to stock and talk to the customer. Now it might just be stock and having your head down. We're not getting that good customer contact that we probably should have.

INTERVIEWER: What do you see are some of the big changes coming down?

P. A. SMITH STORE MANAGER: Changes we see here are, I think the expectations are gonna rise with the new competitor coming in, whether it's a [*names high-end chain*] or a private independent coming in. Our expectation level is gonna grow, and the people who come in and walk our store from our corporate office, their expectation is [too]. Our concern is with the tight labor budget and how it's really put a strain on things. . . . We don't want our people to get frustrated because someone [from corporate] comes in and maybe this one is turned like this when it should have been turned like that.

At consumer electronics retailer Tech Source, one department manager similarly spelled out the multiple expectations that contribute to stretching responsibilities and work hours when matching customer demands and organizational needs with tight staffing—and described how his own job had been degraded:

[When I was away] . . . things got a little out of control with certain products, you know, open box and returns that we have to resell. We don't want them out there, you know what I mean. There was more than I had ever seen before. . . . Staffing is always a problem too. That seems to be a common thing . . . finding time to get these things done sometimes. You know, I'm on a fifty-hour workweek, if not more. Sometimes it's six days a week, whatever the boss says. They want me to go out and recruit . . . on my day off, which I told them no. . . . It's something that I should be able to do on my time that I'm here, especially if it's fifty hours [but I don't have time]. . . . Just having the time to get everything done because when you don't have enough associates, you have to prioritize on what's gonna get done. Generally speaking, it's the customers.

Dissecting Manager Overload   Across the three subsectors, these two managers' experiences appear typical. Managing with tight staff hours is difficult: "You can't run the store any tighter than we run the store," noted one store manager at Value Fresh, which had squeezed labor costs. Another Value Fresh store manager lamented, "You shouldn't have to do it, work twenty-four hours." Importantly, labor budgets, though tightly controlled, exclude manager hours, so managers are not "penalized" for their own long work hours.

We heard across sectors that managers often work fifty-, sixty-, even seventy-hour workweeks. "We average ten-hour days. When you work Sunday, you work six to eight, so that's sixty. I never go home on time. I work at least sixty hours a week," a Marketland store manager said. "We're not asked to work six days, but that's just the reality of the business," remarked the P. A. Smith manager we earlier quoted at length. He added: "A soft week is fifty. There's been weeks in the seventies." A Homestyle store manager told us he comes in at 6:30 or 7:00 in the morning and walks the aisles to check stock until 2:00 PM. "My goal is, I don't use the bathroom till I get these done," he said. "At two, my help comes in so I pee and eat." At Photoworld, whose consumer electronics stores are small, full-time schedules run a minimum of forty-five hours, but managers work longer.

The heavy workload is made harder by competing priorities. Managers suffer from what a Freshland grocery store manager called "the funnel effect": "We have a group of people down in our corporate headquarters . . . whose whole job survival is to create. All those people there are doing that, and it all comes down the funnel and drops right on me. My job is to implement it." At electronics retailer High Fidelity, where store managers are expected to sell as well as manage, a manager ruefully commented, "This morning, to give you an idea, I had sixty-seven emails that I haven't even dived into yet. My Daytimer is now full from now until 6:00, and it's 11:00. So there's a lot of tasks that are on the table, and the difficult part is saying, 'Okay, how do I prioritize these?'" In addition, managers are ringing registers and stocking shelves when staffing is short. On one visit we even saw the manager of a store with roughly 200 employees mopping a spill because he couldn't find anyone else to do it, and during another we saw the manager straightening up shopping carts.

From Managers to Frontline Supervisors   The staff who are next in the line of command bear the consequences of this overload as well. Particularly in consumer electronics, the heavy workload spills over from managers to supervisors and even full-timers. At Tech Source, responsibility for drawing up schedules may devolve for stretches of time from the overburdened store manager to department heads, even though it is not the preferred managerial choice. A full-time entertainment sales lead at Electronix who had become "the de facto supervisor" complained, "I spend a lot of my free time either thinking about work or dealing with work." Because Electronix had scaled back on sending entertainment salespeople to training programs, he had to provide the missing instruction. At The Office, cutbacks in part-timer training mean that a full-time office equipment salesperson was constantly compensating for "basic errors that they're making that they shouldn't . . . things that they should have learned probably in the first week or two, but a lot of times they've been here for four months and nobody just went over those little basic things." Thus, frontline supervisors and full-timers witness firsthand the workload impacts but also the service quality consequences of corporate lean staffing imperatives and the adjustment strategies of their managers.

As we have pointed out, observing managerial overload also reduces these workers' interest in being promoted to manager. This is particularly the case in food retail: managers noted that the pipeline for potential assistant managers has atrophied, and regional managers expressed concern about their pool of store manager candidates schooled in the ways of the company. The lack of promotion-ready candidates makes it challenging to develop consistent performance across stores.

Addressing Overload   Interestingly, at several chains—Food Chief, Office Express, and The Office—executives and managers claimed success in recent efforts to reduce managers' hours. Although we do not doubt the good intentions of such initiatives, we are skeptical of the stated results. At Office Express, the vice president of store operations declared, "We've said . . . we don't want you to work [long hours]." But an Office Express district manager told us that he worked seventy hours a week, adding, "I know there are some [other district managers] that do what I do," and that most store managers worked forty-five to fifty hours per week.

JOB QUALITY LOOKING FORWARD: RECENT DEVELOPMENTS AND LONG-TERM PROSPECTS

Over the course of the study, and in the few years since we completed fieldwork, consumer electronics retailers have undergone rapid change and accelerated competitive pressures. Food retailers have experienced heightened competition from small-store formats, including dollar stores, and a more gradual rise in online sales. Our fieldwork did not capture the adjustment of retailers to these very recent changes. However, our assessment is that, while details differ, these most recent changes simply intensify the trend we found toward escalating pressure to both cut costs and distinguish offerings based on quality, variety, and service. In the last chapter, we draw on secondary sources as well as our own research to address the future of U.S. and global retail, and we put together what is known about current pressures with what we have learned about retailers' adaptive strategies to earlier waves of competition. In closing this chapter, we offer a brief preview pointing from our fieldwork forward.

Two chains in our sample exemplify diametrically opposite strategic directions. The food retailer Freshland, with a two-tier compensation system, has experienced a surge in discontent and turnover: managers accustomed to a well-compensated and highly motivated workforce now struggle to keep workers engaged. The company seeks to improve service, quality, and variety to compete with newcomers like Wal-Mart, but wage and benefit erosion undermines such efforts. In contrast, Bargain Warehouse, despite some recent trimming, continues to offer high wages and benefits, even to part-timers. Attracting motivated workers, this company is able to run a highly efficient operation and win the loyalty of customers of above-average income. Few if any of the other companies in our sample are going through as painful and difficult a transition as Freshland. Conversely, few are likely to successfully implement a strategy like Bargain Warehouse's and capture a higher-end market. Most retailers will probably "muddle through" somewhere between these two extremes.

Given the pressing cost-cutting imperative—ratcheted up by dollar stores on one side and online retail on the other—average job quality in retail will most likely continue to slide, through further reductions in compensation, speedup, and heightened demands for employee flexibility to facilitate just-in-time staffing. Perhaps equally importantly, customer segmentation and an increased role for variable compensation at all levels of retail organizations are likely to intensify job stratification, with small numbers of workers garnering higher earnings and greater autonomy (though perhaps longer schedules more driven by customer needs) while others experience job degradation. This pattern would enable retailers to retain and reward workers with desired skills and management potential, yet such stratification coupled with stricter promotion criteria would sharpen inequality in an already very unequal work setting. Ultimately, as we explore in chapter 8, departing from these likely outcomes in a more worker-friendly direction may depend more on public policy or grassroots organizing than on shifts in underlying competitive trends.

5 / Comparing Retail Jobs in the United States and Western Europe

Chapters 2 through 4 plumbed commonalities and divergences in U.S. retail jobs. We demonstrated that despite the predominance of bad jobs in retail, there is still (limited) room for retailers to chart different job quality courses. In this chapter and the two that follow, we place those same U.S. retail jobs—captured by aggregate statistics (as in chapter 2) by our eighteen in-depth cases (as in chapters 3 and 4) and by other sources—on a larger global canvas. We start, in this chapter, by comparing U.S. jobs with those in five Western European countries, tracing differences in jobs to disparate national institutions.

Though we opened the book by contrasting French, German, and American shopping experiences and retail jobs, there is a baseline of similarities. Across five European countries—Denmark, France, Germany, the Netherlands, and the United Kingdom—and the United States, retailers face similar competitive trends. Retail jobs share similar tasks and workforces as well as low wages relative to other sectors. In all these countries, retail leads in initiating "exit options" from the legal and institutional environment for labor.[1]

But even with the proliferation of exit options, national institutions do generate important differences. To highlight how institutions interact to yield such results, we focus here on those differences, both between the United States and its European counterparts taken as a whole and among the European countries. To sharpen this focus, we largely abstract from the variations in retailer strategy and job quality *within* a country that occupied much of chapters 3 and 4. We highlight outcomes in two frontline occupations: cashiers and stock clerks/salespeople. By tracking institutionally driven divergences in jobs while recognizing the ways in which the retail industry evades institutions and diffuses practices across borders, we look at both sides of what we call a national-sectoral model of job quality determination. Crucially, if institutions shape job quality, then altering institutions through public policy can make jobs better.

In each of the six countries, both the contours of retail employment and the policy environment are constantly shifting in ways large and small. In our analysis, we freeze that process, presenting a snapshot pegged to the mid-2000s timing of the six-country fieldwork so that quantitative data and the qualitative, fieldwork-based data refer to the same moment, allowing an in-depth comparison.

The next section gives a quick first look at key differences in retail jobs and in employment-related institutions across the six countries. We then take a step back to conceptualize cross-national job differences and institutional impacts on that variation. We explore those institutional effects in practice in an overview and four subsections analyzing key dimensions of job quality: schedules; work organization, tasks, and skill composition; turnover and mobility; and compensation. In each case, the institutions that yield cross-national job quality differences point to policy options for the United States. The chapter closes by summarizing lessons from this U.S.-European comparison of retail jobs.

CROSS-NATIONAL VARIATION IN RETAIL JOBS AND IN LABOR INSTITUTIONS: A FIRST LOOK

Retail workers toil at varied levels of pay, and with varying employment status and conditions. Table 5.1 charts three of these variations. Retail's low-wage share—the percentage of retail workers falling below a low-wage threshold of two-thirds of the national median—ranges widely, from less than one in five in France to nearly one-half in the United Kingdom. The share of part-time workers differs considerably, from less than one-third in France to more than two-thirds in the Netherlands. U.S. retail workers fall in the middle of the pack in low-wage share and at the bottom in the

Table 5.1 / Cross-National Variation in Selected Retail Job Characteristics in the Six Countries, 2002 and 2006

	Retail Workers Earning Low Hourly Wages, 2006	Annual Labor Turnover, 2002	Part-timers Among Retail Workers, 2006
Denmark	23%	36%	50%
France	18	20	28
Germany	42	20	47
Netherlands	46	27	70
United Kingdom	49	26	51
United States	42	50	28

Sources: (1) *Retail workers earning low hourly wages:* Authors' compilation, based on the percentage falling below two-thirds of the national median, from: Westergaard-Nielsen (2008, 72) for Denmark; Askenazy, Berry, and Prunier-Poulmaire (2008, 220) for France; Voss-Dahm (2008, 258) for Germany; van Klaveren (2009) for the Netherlands; U.K. Office of National Statistics (2005) for the United Kingdom; authors' calculations from U.S. Bureau of Labor Statistics (2005) for the United States. (2) *Turnover:* Eurostat (Statistical Office of the European Commission) calculations from EU Labour Force Survey (various years) on behalf of IAQ, for European Union (EU) countries except Germany; Bundesagentur für Arbeit (2005) for Germany; "Job Openings and Labor Turnover Survey" from U.S. Bureau of Labor Statistics (2015b) for the United States. (3) *Percentage of part-timers:* EU Labour Force Survey (Eurostat, various years) for EU countries; U.S. Bureau of Labor Statistics (2007) for the United States.

Note: "Part-time" is defined as less than thirty-five hours a week in the Netherlands and less than thirty-two hours in the United States; in other countries, the definition of "part-time" is based on the worker's self-classification. "Low" wages denote hourly wages below two-thirds of the national median. The percentage falling below two-thirds of the threshold is calculated in 2002 for Denmark and Netherlands and in 2005 for the United Kingdom and the United States. The percentage of part-timers among U.S. retail workers is calculated for 2007.

rate of part-time employment, but stand out with much higher turnover—U.S. retail turnover is more than double that in France and Germany.

A variety of factors might explain cross-national differences in job characteristics and quality. They could result from compositional differences—for example, the mix of small, large, and supersized stores. Differences in market structure (degree of monopoly power, exposed versus sheltered markets, and so on) could also be important. However, we argue that a particularly compelling explanation for divergent job patterns in the six countries is found in several institutions—those regulating labor markets, those governing product markets, and those shaping social reproduction.

Despite their increasingly neoliberal tendencies, the five European countries jointly still diverge substantially from the United States in their portfolio of institutions.[2] In particular, they generally have more inclusive institutions that protect those at the low end of the workforce. Except for the United Kingdom, all these countries have multi-employer bargaining in place covering most or all workers in retail, regionally or nationally. In France and the Netherlands, and to a more limited extent Germany, this centralized bargaining is supported by state-mandated extension throughout the sector of the agreements' basic compensation provisions. Germany, Denmark, and the Netherlands have extensive vocational training programs, with strong roots even in retail, for Germany in particular.

But as this summary indicates, there are also differences *among* the five European countries. One notable distinction groups the United States with France, the Netherlands, and the United Kingdom: a statutory minimum wage (Germany adopted a minimum later, in 2014). Moreover, we will see that though superficially similar, centralized bargaining plays out quite differently in Denmark than in the other countries, where exit options have eroded its solidaristic effects.

Table 5.2 summarizes in advance our findings about which institutions matter in shaping job outcomes. The table's very telegraphic summary underlines the numerous ways in which national institutions intervene in job quality.

EXPLAINING CROSS-NATIONAL DIFFERENCES IN JOB CHARACTERISTICS

How do we begin to explain cross-national job differences? Two bodies of sociological literature about the determinants of job quality are particularly relevant. One literature studies the practices of *individual multinationals* outside their home country in order to assess the impact and interplay of multinational home-country "dominance" effects (the effects of dominant firm practices and their dissemination of home-country norms regarding employment) and the societal or national effects generated by host-country institutions and social norms on management practices and employment systems.[3] This literature takes as its primary point of entry multination-

Table 5.2 / Summary of Cross-National Job Quality Differences and
Their Institutional Drivers

Job Feature	Notable Country Differences	Institutional Explanations
Sustainable schedules	Advance notice (Denmark and Germany), minimum number of hours (France), collective say by workers, part-time parity in compensation (European Union versus United States)	Collective bargaining, national regulations, required works councils at all workplaces, EU directive on part-time parity
Work organization and skills	Broad jobs in Germany and to some extent in Denmark and the Netherlands	Vocational education
Worker mobility	U.S. elevated turnover	Distinctive U.S. corporate strategy, shaped indirectly by varied institutional differences
Compensation	Smaller low-wage share in Denmark and France	Collective bargaining, high national minimum wage

Source: Authors' compilation.

als' managerial practices, which reflect such influences and, in turn, help determine job characteristics.

A second group of analyses starts from observed differences in average job quality and analyzes the contribution of societal institutions to these differences using *sectorwide* cross-national comparisons. Authors use selected job characteristics as the point of entry for comparing systems of employment. Starting from a microlevel analysis, they move up to locate jobs within systems of employment embedded within a constellation of interacting social and economic spheres. Previous comparative research on retail jobs along these lines has scrutinized both market and institutional differences. Jean Gadrey and Florence Jany-Catrice compared U.S. and French retail. They found that U.S. retailers offer "higher quality and more services for the same average basket of goods sold," and that they "finance" the additional value added by providing lower compensation to workers.[4] Going even further than Bailey and Bernhardt to challenge the oft-predicted correlation between high performance and job quality, Gadrey and Jany-Catrice concluded that in fact the U.S. high-road service advantage *depends* on low compensation.[5] More recently, Jany-Catrice and Steffen Lehndorff offered an ambitious six-country (Denmark, Finland, France, Germany, Portugal, and Sweden) comparison focusing on how institutions shape nationally specific patterns of fragmentation of work and working time in retail, suggesting some institutional effects that we explore further in this chapter.[6]

Other research in this second group has sought to theorize the different subsystems affecting jobs. For example, Christophe Baret, Steffen Lehndorff, and Leigh Sparks examine working time in retail in three European countries and Japan, and Bosch and Lehndorff analyze multiple service industries (including retail) in ten European countries.[7] This scholarship draws on concepts initially developed by Marc Maurice, François Sellier, and Jean-Jacques Silvestre to provide analytically meaningful categories for cross-national comparison of work and employment systems and capture societal effects constituted by norms and institutions.[8] Bosch and Lehndorff summarize four main spheres of influence on work:[9]

• Product markets and consumers, including the parameters of competition and product market regulation

• Management strategies, including corporate governance and technology

• The labor market and associated institutions and norms, public policy, customers, and industrial relations

• The welfare state and gender relations, including family structures and taxes and benefits.[10]

Both literatures approach these issues through sector-specific studies, thus setting sectoral characteristics regarding market, production technology, and the organization of work as mediating processes for economic forces and societal effects. Trevor Coiling and Ian Clark argue that sector effects, growing out of shared practices in a company's particular sector, interact in important ways with the dominance effects of a multinational's home country, either enhancing or weakening host-country effects.[11] Within Gadrey, Lehndorff, and Thierry Ribault's framework, market and organizational structures differ systematically by sector.[12]

The analysis we present resonates with both literatures in recognizing the role of sector characteristics in mediating the effects of broader market and societal forces. We posit that national business systems (which form home-country effects abroad) will be expressed differently by sector, and that sector patterns will take different shapes in different nations.[13] Thus, we develop the notion of a *national-sectoral model* that combines societal and sectoral effects.

A U.S.-EUROPEAN COMPARISON OF AVERAGE JOB OUTCOMES IN RETAIL

Industry Overview

Before digging into cross-national differences, we start with commonalities. Indeed, the core tasks performed by clerks and cashiers in retailing are quite similar in all wealthy countries: workers must take goods from the stockroom to the shop floor, replenish shelves, answer customer questions (and sometimes solicit customer purchases), ring up sales, and receive payment. Likewise, retail hours invariably extend beyond standard daytime shifts to include evening hours, weekends, and in some retailers nights. The intensity of retail sales also varies by season. Retailers in the United States and Western Europe alike have responded to nonstandard operating hours and seasonal swings by making substantial use of part-time labor.[14]

Retail sectors in the United States and Western Europe are similar in other ways as well. All have recently been rocked by three new forces: the diffusion of intricate information technology for supply-chain management and optimal staff scheduling; the spread of aggressive discount chains; and a set of institutional changes in the labor market that can be characterized as neoliberal. These neoliberal institutional changes have weakened workers' representation and increased labor regulations' flexibility—often to the point of relaxing labor regulations for particular subsets of workers.[15] Indeed, in all six countries, retail is a laboratory for changes in labor market

Table 5.3 / Sample Structure of Retail Case Studies in the Six Countries

	Food Companies	Consumer Electronics Companies	Comments
Denmark	5	3	Three food retail companies also sell electronics.
France	6	2	Two food retail companies also sell electronics.
Germany	4	4	
Netherlands	4	4	
United Kingdom	4	4	
United States	10	6	Two food retail companies also sell electronics.

Sources: Compilation by Carré et al. (2010) based on: Esbjerg et al. (2008) for Denmark; Askenazy, Berry, and Prunier-Poulmaire (2008) for France; Voss-Dahm (2008) for Germany; van Klaveren (2008a) for the Netherlands; Mason and Osborne (2008) for the United Kingdom; and Carré and Tilly with Holgate (2007) for the United States.

institutions; the sector often leads with experimentation in this regard.

As in the United States, in each of the five European countries, a research team conducted interview-based case studies of large retail companies in food and consumer electronics retail. Worker interviews and focus groups zeroed in on our two target jobs of cashiers and stock clerks/salespeople.

The number and composition of cases is detailed in table 5.3. The U.S. sample (already described in detail in chapter 3) was designed to be twice as large as the others because it represents in some sense the "baseline" for international comparisons, and the retail industry there is larger. In countries where researchers came up short on electronics retailers—as we did—they adopted the same solution: they examined both food and electronics in big-box retailers that sell both, building two cases within a single company. There was some unplanned heterogeneity across country samples. For example, the German researchers were not able to gain access to discounters, whereas the other country teams were able to include them; the U.S. sample, unlike the European ones, included two chains in the electronics category that principally sell office equipment and supplies. Nonetheless, the samples are quite strongly comparable across countries.

Relying on national patterns and on these case-study findings, we review four dimensions of job quality: schedules; work organization, tasks, and skill composition; turnover and vertical mobility; and compensation.

Schedules

Work schedules are a primary dimension of retail job quality in Europe as in the United States. In the Dutch case studies, for instance, many workers complain of unilateral employer decisions concerning working times and days off. British employees lament having insufficient work hours and little schedule flexibility to meet their needs as well as being required to work evenings and weekends. In this section, we first summarize common features of work schedules across the six countries. We then explore the U.S.-European differences—above all in how much control workers have over scheduling—before briefly discussing differences among the five European countries.

Common Features of Retail Work Schedules   As in the United States, the retail workforce in Europe is disproportionately (and increasingly) part-time. Table 5.4 presents aggregate rates of part-time work. The proportions of part-time workers are even higher in the case-study stores, which are generally larger than the typical retail establishment. For example, in the U.S. cases, part-timers make up 50 to 80 percent of the store workforce (with a couple of exceptions), which is well above the 28 percent industry average.

Table 5.5 demonstrates that high concentrations of women and younger workers come along with high proportions of part-time jobs. In each of the six countries, the retail workforce is disproportionately female (though in the United States the overrepresentation is minimal). Workers under age twenty-five are likewise universally overrepresented in retail. When we compare the representation of women and young workers in food retail, with its higher rate of part-time employment (and lower-paid jobs), with their position in consumer electronics, where the opposite is true, we generally find larger female and young worker percentages in the former (not shown).

Table 5.4 / Part-Time Employment in Retail by Country, 2006 and 2007

	Denmark, 2006	France, 2007	Germany, 2007	Netherlands, 2006	United Kingdom, 2006	United States, 2007
Part-time in retail employment	49.7%	27.7%	52.0%	69.8%	50.2%	27.9%
Part-time in total employment	23.6	17.2	25.8	46.2	25.5	18.6
Ratio: retail part-time percentage to total part-time percentage	2.1	1.6	1.8	1.5	2.0	1.5
Ratio: food part-time percentage to retail part-time percentage	NA	1.8	1.3	1.1	1.3	1.4
Ratio: electronics part-time percentage to retail part-time percentage	NA	0.6	0.4	0.5	0.6	0.8

Sources: Compilation by Carré et al. (2010) based on: European Commission (2007) for part-time in total EU employment; EU Labour Force Survey (Eurostat, various years) for EU retail; and Askenazy, Berry, and Poulmaire (2008, 221), U.K. Office for National Statistics (2006); and van Klaveren (2008b) for retail subsectors; and Bundesagentur für Arbeit (2007) for all German statistics. For U.S. statistics: U.S. Bureau of Labor Statistics (2007) for part-time in retail; subsector part-time imputed by combining March 2007 Current Population Survey data with 2007 Current Employment Statistics (CES) (U.S. Bureau of Labor Statistics 2016a); U.S. Bureau of Labor Statistics (2015c; table A-18) for part-time in total employment.
Note: Ratios of food and consumer electronics retail part-time percentages are calculated from 2004 data, except France (2003) and the Netherlands and the United Kingdom (2005). Definitions of part-time status differ by country; see table 5.1 note.

Table 5.5 / Women and Young Workers Employed in Retail, by Country, 2006

	Denmark	France	Germany	Netherlands	United Kingdom	United States
Share of women in retail	57.0%	63.3%	70.6%	60.9%	61.5%	49.4%
Share of women in total	46.4	46.3	45.4	44.9	46.7	48.1
Ratio: retail percentage women to total percentage women	1.2	1.4	1.6	1.4	1.3	1.0
Share under age twenty-five in retail	48.5	19.3	15.6	44.7	34.0	28.6
Share under age twenty-five in total	13.6	8.9	10.7	15.3	14.0	13.6
Ratio: retail percentage under age twenty-five to total percentage under age twenty-five	3.6	2.2	1.5	2.9	2.4	2.1

Sources: Compilation by Carré et al. (2010) based on: for EU statistics: authors' compilations of EU Labour Force Survey (Eurostat, various years) for share in retail; European Commission (2007) for shares in total employment. For U.S. statistics: U.S. Bureau of Labor Statistics (2015a) for female shares; U.S. Bureau of Labor Statistics, CPS (March 2006), for young workers.

The heavy reliance on part-time work offers the same advantages for European retailers as outlined earlier for U.S. retailers (see chapter 3). Employers can match staff head-count to customer flows using fixed-schedule "gap filler" part-timers and flexible "time adjusters." Retailers can also reap the advantages of higher productivity in the first few hours of a worker's shift. As a manager in German food retailing noted: "The productivity of people with short working hours is simply higher. After five or six hours, an individual worker starts to run out of energy and to slow down, while two workers can complete a lot of work in four hours each."

The third advantage to retailers of widespread part-time employment is that it opens up exit options that allow them to evade normative, legal, or collective bargaining standards for compensation, fringe benefits, and social insurance. The specifics vary. In the United States, as we saw in chapter 3, the inferior wage and benefit packages given to part-timers themselves represent an exit option. In Germany, a key exit option is the "mini-job"—a short-hour part-time job often paid below the collectively bargained scale, in violation of the law (see the section on compensation).[16] In Denmark, the Netherlands, and the United Kingdom, a lower statutory or collectively bargained wage scale for younger workers has opened up an important exit option. In France's highly inclusive employment relations system, there are few formally specified exit options, though as a practical matter legal and collectively bargained requirements are less rigorously enforced in small retail establishments.

Although we discuss the impact of these varied exit options further later in the chapter, it is important to point out here that the high concentration of women and young people has helped to make exit options viable for firms in all six countries. Because these groups tend to be weakly organized and poorly represented in unions and works councils—the representative bodies of the workforce mandated regardless of union status—employers can execute exit options with little public fuss. We note that, unlike in some other low-wage industries, immigrant labor is not commonly used to facilitate exit options in retail. Immigrant labor (by which we mean foreign-born or noncitizen workers) is not widespread, ranging from 4 to 13 percent of the retail workforce in the six countries. There is some immigrant overrepresentation in U.K. retail compared to the workforce at large, but immigrants are underrepresented in Denmark, Germany, and the United States.[17]

U.S.-European Differences in Work Schedules   Despite these common features of retail jobs in the United States and the five European countries, the United States stands apart in a number of ways. Given the importance of schedules as a job quality parameter, these U.S.-European contrasts are noteworthy. Recall that in the U.S. company cases, full-time workers increasingly are not guaranteed full-time hours; in a number of the food and electronics chains, full-timers are guaranteed only thirty-two or thirty-five weekly hours, out of forty that traditionally and legally have constituted a full-time schedule (see chapter 3). This system turns full-time workers into another group of time adjusters while minimizing the risk of incurring the overtime pay premium. This practice was not encountered in the European cases. Some European retail full-timers do flex their hours *upward* from a full-time base, particularly consumer electronics employees motivated by commissions and, more generally, German full-timers socialized by that country's strong vocational education system. Even in the relatively liberalized British labor market, seven out of eight case-study firms use overtime rather than temporary workers to handle demand variations.

U.S. workers have less individual and collective choice, control, and advance notice of work schedules than their European counterparts. U.S. retailers typically inform workers of their work schedules three days to two weeks in advance, with shorter notice and more schedule variation in food retail than in consumer electronics. The combination of lean staffing with the high turnover and unreliability of short-hour part-timers frequently compels managers to change staffing and adjust schedules on short notice; the low rate of union representation and lack of mandates on schedule notification enable them to do so.

In contrast, the most extreme European cases are Germany and Denmark, where retail collective bargaining contracts require retailers to post schedules twenty-six and sixteen weeks in advance, respectively (though breaches of these mandates are rather common, especially in smaller retailers). German, Danish, and Dutch codetermination laws also require retail employers to negotiate scheduling with their works councils.[18] In response to worker preferences, German and Dutch works councils in grocery stores have used their legal right to negotiate scheduling to achieve compromises on flexibility for management and workers. German and Dutch retailers use sophisticated software to work out schedules that conform to worker preferences, whereas U.S. retailers press new employees to list the maximum possible hours of "availability" and penalize employees who do not offer the desired flexibility, giving them fewer hours and promotion opportunities.[19] Workers' main recourse is to swap shifts with coworkers, subject to management approval (also a common strategy in European stores).

In the United States, store managers (and to a lesser extent supervisors and full-time workers) are acutely aware of the difficulty of scheduling and often must solve scheduling problems by working extremely long hours themselves, sometimes up to sixty or seventy hours. (In the European countries, store managers also reported working long hours, but not to the same degree; in Denmark, by contrast, even in food retail with its longer hours, managers reported working "only" forty-five to fifty hours.) Above the store level, however, U.S. higher-level managers and executives expressed little concern about scheduling. In contrast, in many European companies, especially in Germany and the Netherlands, the difficulty of organizing satisfactory employee work schedules is a topic of discussion up to the executive level, and even on corporate boards.

In Denmark, Germany, and the Netherlands, the countries with more corporatist labor relations and robust unions in the workplace, work hours are further shaped by both store hour regulations and collectively bargained shift premia. Danish, Dutch, and German stores are barred from opening most Sundays (France permits only a few Sunday openings a year, except in tourist areas), and super-discounters and consumer electronics stores operate even fewer hours. Danish, German, and Dutch retail collective bargaining agreements stipulate premium payments for overtime hours, night work, and work on Saturdays, Sundays, and public holidays. Moreover, such premium payments are also prevalent in France and the United Kingdom, in both union and non-union settings. In contrast, U.S. restrictions on store hours were imposed only at the state and local levels, and most such restrictions were already gone by the late 1980s. The U.S. cases show companies (including unionized ones) decreasing or eliminating pay differentials for off-shifts and Sundays.

However, even in the countries with strong unions, the bite of working-time regulation seems to be weakening. Some regulations, like shift differentials, already exempt some vulnerable groups and are coming under further attack. With the liberalization of opening hours in the Netherlands in 1996 and Germany in 2006, employers have begun to press for reduced premia for nonstandard work times. In the Netherlands, as early as 1998, retailers negotiated the elimination of premia for Saturdays and work between 6:00 and 8:00 PM. In Germany, unions successfully resisted employer efforts to reduce shift differentials in 1999, but with opening hours now less regulated, employers have made the abolition of premia their main demand, triggering a series of hard-fought strikes. Even in strict France, 2015 legislation allowed stores in a dozen Paris "tourist zones" to stay open until midnight and on Sundays.[20]

Despite these recent shifts, European retail workers continue to have more tools for exerting control over their schedules than do their U.S. counterparts. The long reach of union agreements and the presence and legally sanctioned role of works councils, as well as differing norms, are the main factors explaining these U.S.-European differences. Ongoing opening-hours restrictions in some European countries also limit schedule variability. Even in the United Kingdom, which is farthest toward the U.S. side of the spectrum in scheduling, unions and growing public sentiment are pushing to limit "zero-hour contracts" that offer no minimum hours guarantee, and in 2015 unions won a ban on "exclusivity clauses" that require 24/7 worker availability without any assurance of getting hours.[21]

Differences in Work Schedules Within Europe   The five European countries themselves differ in work schedule patterns, as our discussion has already revealed. These differences result from a combination of labor supply differences (themselves provoked in part by differing family and welfare state policies; see chapter 6) with divergences in employment-related institutions. Danish and Dutch retailers—motivated in part by lower bargained or legislated rates of pay for young workers—have extraordinarily high levels of youth employment (table 5.5). French and German retailers, in contrast, rely more on women workers, whereas U.K. retailers lean heavily on both workforces.

In each country, a specific history underlies the demographic pattern. For example, in Denmark, working women have shifted from part-time to full-time work since the 1970s, supported by government-sponsored child care and a tax system that assesses each spouse separately. In response, retailers have turned to youths for part-time staffing. In the Netherlands, on the other hand, the influx of women that took off in the 1980s reversed in 2003 when a price war put pressure on wage costs. Retailers responded by availing themselves of the statutory youth subminimum wage. Adult women complained that they were "bullied away" and replaced by cheaper young workers, many of whom (50 percent) were students whose low income was made viable by a generous state student grant system. In France, for decades, large majorities of women have preferred full-time work, bolstered by a universal child care system. Retailers rely on women to cover part-time schedules, but these schedules are unpopular.

In fact, France is something of a special case, with the state playing a particularly prominent role in typical French fashion. On the one hand, French law has set the full-time workweek at thirty-five hours. On the other hand, pressed by unhappy women workers, French retail food unions have won a minimum part-time-hour threshold of twenty-six hours.[22] In combination, these provisions reduce the part-time/full-time hours gap to its lowest level across the six countries. With this minimum hour requirement and a mostly adult workforce, only 16 percent of French part-timers work fewer than twenty hours per week; in the other European countries those working fewer than twenty hours per week range from 53 percent (Germany) to a staggering 77 percent (Denmark). The United States falls between France and the rest of Europe, with 34 percent of part-timers clocking fewer than twenty hours.[23]

In summary, work schedules are a critically important element of job quality in retail. In most of the European countries, unlike the United States, collective bargaining and legislation reinforce workers' influence over their schedules. However, retailers in Europe too are leading in experimenting with institutional loopholes. Combined with their pervasive use of part-time labor, experimentation pushes them to recruit particularly vulnerable populations (women with care responsibilities, youths), facilitating their use of exit options from regulating institutions. These options range from German mini-jobs to British, Danish, and Dutch youth subminimum wages. In some cases, these options dovetail with workforce preferences. In particular, students and some women take gap filler jobs precisely because they want short, fixed work hours. The overrepresentation of women and younger workers, in turn, implies that other institutions—notably government support for child care, the tax treatment of married couples' earnings, and student grants—are modulating the industry's labor supply.

Work Organization, Tasks, and Skill Composition

Though sales activities as a whole have much in common, the task and skill profiles of workers vary depending on the business strategy adopted. With retailers that adopt a self-service strategy, customer advice and service are reduced to a minimum. A high-service strategy places much greater demands on staff availability and skills. Thus, the market segment in which companies position themselves is a crucial factor in determining job content.[24]

This background might suggest that institutional factors have little or no direct influence on tasks and skills in sales retail, and that business strategy is the major determinant. But the case studies do show institutional influences on these jobs, through product market regulations and training institutions. We start this exploration by providing snapshots of retail jobs in the six countries.

As we have seen, virtually across the board in U.S. food retailing, quick checkout is part of the service pledge, affecting how often employees are shifted from other departments to the registers. Likewise, in most U.S. food stores simple service tasks like bagging are a central element of customer service, boosting the share of workers with narrow task profiles. However, variety-oriented U.S. food retailers require special and often craftlike skills in preparing and presenting fresh food. Looking at the consumer electronics subsector, we see an even greater diversity of job requirement profiles. Some stores concentrate on selling mass-market products off-the-shelf. Others focus on selling specialized items, such as technically sophisticated home entertainment systems, and services, such as installation, that require significant sales and technical skills.

Adding Europe to the picture reveals other within- and cross-country differences in grocery retailing. Service-oriented British supermarkets tend to focus on labor-intensive features like the availability of sales staff to answer customer questions or short wait times at checkout. Employee bagging was found in the United Kingdom but not in any of the other European countries. *Within-*country differences loom large in France. There, as in other countries, small-scale discounters follow a pure self-service concept that sharply contrasts with that of French hypermarkets, which traditionally offer specialty cheeses and fresh fish at full-service counters, leading to a more heterogeneous and sometimes even sophisticated set of tasks.

Comparing French and German product market regulations, such as zoning and pricing rules, reveals how a country's job structure is influenced—at least indirectly—by institutional factors. In France, the barriers to entry for large stores—which include zoning regulations (1973 and later), periodic freezes on the authorization of large stores (for example, 1993 to 1996), and store size limits (1996)—set hurdles to the expansion of sales space. As a result, established French hypermarkets, with high service levels and plentiful product variety, face limited competition and dominate the food retail market. In contrast, Germany, where such regulations are absent, has one of the highest selling-space-per-inhabitant ratios in Europe.[25] Winners in the expansion of Germany's selling space are low-price, no-frills discounters like Aldi and Lidl, which have gained at the expense of other formats with more varied merchandise and more differentiated jobs.

What can be observed with regard to frontline retail activities? In particular, is technology an equalizer of task and skill demands in sales jobs across countries? As in the United States, and sometimes in advance of U.S. technologies, European retailers have long found ways to speed up and automate goods handling by using information and communication technologies.[26] The use of advanced technology in goods handling and customer self-service, described as "lean retailing," offers retailers ways to achieve high productivity with low labor costs.[27] In such a system, knowledge demands on employees are low. In extreme cases, the only tasks left for sales staff are simple, routine activities such as shelf stocking. This scenario can clearly be linked with a high-performing business–low-wage system.

We found substantial *within*-country differences, rather than clear differences between countries, in the presence of highly automated high-performing business systems.[28] In Germany, for example, one company stands out as a world leader in the use of labor-saving radio-frequency identification (RFID) technology, whereas in another, automatic goods ordering has been rejected for strategic reasons, leaving the reordering of products as a standard task for sales staff.

Task- Versus Function-Centered Work Organization   It is insufficient to state a connection between business strategy, customer segmentation, and workforce segmentation to explain the varied pattern of tasks and skills in retailing. Such a statement understates management's leeway in bundling single tasks into actual jobs.[29] These management decisions are influenced by labor market institutions, and in particular by training institutions.

In general, there are two polar ways to bundle tasks. On the one hand, retail jobs can be organized based on a strict division of labor. Then workers perform individual, easily delimited, *tasks* usually assigned to them by supervisors. On the other hand, jobs can be organized so that personnel perform many distinct tasks with a high degree of self-direction. Their job is to fulfill a *function* within the work process. According to David Marsden, function-oriented organizations of work are based on "the employee's output or contribution to the collective effort of production or service provision."[30]

We found nationally specific patterns of work organization (figure 5.1). In the United States and the United Kingdom, particularly in the big-box formats in food retailing, the dominant form of work organization is based on a strict division of labor with most workers performing rather narrowly defined tasks and only a few (full-time) workers or supervisors having broader process and product knowledge. High employee turnover is a fundamental reason for this choice of work organization. Individual tasks are isolated from each other and can therefore be quickly learned and easily monitored.

However, the easy substitutability of workers is not the only important argument in favor of a task-centered work organization system, with a correspondingly low level of individual freedom of action. Employees' skill levels also play a crucial role (see the discussion of training institutions in a later section). Entry skill requirements in U.S. supermarkets are minimal. A U.S. grocery manager stated laughingly that the qualification for getting hired was "having a pulse," while others spoke of "paying attention." Never-

Figure 5.1 / Patterns of Work Organization in the Six Countries

Type of work organization	Task-centered work organization	← →		Function-centered work organization
Position of country	**United States, United Kingdom**	**France Netherlands, Denmark**		**Germany**
Type of training system	No retail-specific training institutions	← →		Retail-specific training institutions

Source: Authors' analysis based on Marsden 1999.

theless, U.S. and British case studies show that task-centered work organization can be accompanied by some degree of horizontal task variability. In British supermarkets, when checkout lines grow longer, stockers are sent to the registers. A sales assistant in a U.K. discount retailer commented: "We go where we are needed; it could be on provisions (for example, dairy or produce), or it could be queue-busting on the checkout, or we could be doing replenishment." Similarly, U.S. sales workers are deployed to different departments as need arises, particularly in consumer electronics, where such shifting is the norm. Such ad-hoc adjustments are made necessary both by the cost-cutting strategies adopted by retail companies, which have cut staffing levels to a minimum, and by temporary short-handedness due to high labor turnover.

The counterexample to the U.S. and U.K. task-based system is Germany, where most retail employees have completed vocational training. Ordinary sales assistants take responsibility for the whole distributive process, including ordering goods, taking goods out to the shop floor, stocking shelves, merchandising products, and giving customers advice. Hence, tasks are *vertically* integrated, from beginning to end of the selling process, and salespeople have significant discretion; they do not receive daily instructions from supervisors. At the same time, tasks are narrower from a horizontal perspective. Sales assistants handle only one merchandise line; they do not move between departments, and they never work at checkouts. They are expected to optimize the product assortment in order to improve sales. If this requires a change of assortments, the addition of new products, or revised merchandising, they must coordinate these changes with team leaders. Though the potential of vertically integrated tasks for job quality is obvious, there are special demands too, such as the delegation of responsibilities for tight cost control downward from managers. A German supermarket manager's comment illustrates the reliance on trained workers: "I can put pressure on the permanent workers. They have the basic knowledge for me to be able to discuss particular developments, objectives, and plans with them. They have a background in retailing and know what it's all about." Thus, vertical integration of tasks within a cost-cutting environment constitutes an attempt to "exploit awareness," that is, to make use of, but not necessarily reward, worker attention and skill.[31] Owing to their specialized skills, German retail workers are more likely than workers in other countries to have internalized the belief that what they do at work contributes to firm performance.

In U.S. consumer electronics in particular, we found other means of stimulating worker engagement, such as games and team-building exercises that are linked to achieving sales and coordinated by managers. In some big-box stores, the duty manager holds regular, sometimes daily, motivational meetings around team coordination and store performance results.

Comparison with Dutch and Danish supermarkets shows that store size also influences the strictness of the division of labor in day-to-day operations. Dutch and Danish supermarkets typically have small sales spaces, and most position themselves as discount stores offering mass-consumption goods at permanently low prices with minimal service. Most supermarkets employ many young people in marginal part-time jobs; measured in full-time equivalents, however, the number of employees per store is rather small. Although formally these young people perform narrow tasks, in practice, "everyone is trained to do everything" to maintain the efficiency of the work processes. In some stores managers assign tasks, and in others peer groups of workers organize flexibility themselves. A Dutch supermarket manager explained: "We maintain clear policies to keep lines short through the flexible opening of new checkouts. If necessary, we ask staff from counters and from the ranks of experienced stockers to join. Yet we don't feel the need to formalize or reward these practices." In practice, this deployment pattern is very similar to that of U.S. retailers.

The influence of store size on the degree of division of labor is also evident in consumer electronics. In smaller stores, sales assistants usually handle the whole sales process, giving advice to the customer, ringing up the sale, and then "taking ownership" of the after-sale service arrangement. Larger stores show more specialization, with cashiers running cash registers without engaging in the sales process.

The task profile at checkouts in large grocery stores is a special case. In the United States and France, cashiers' tasks are monitored for speed, pushing the worker to perform. U.S. managers periodically post individual scanning results on a public wall in the work area for all staff to see and, in at least one case, on public display within the store. This places lateral pressure on workers, who often prefer to quit the job if their scan rate falls below standards rather than be fired or passed over for raises. Similarly, supervisors in France provide weekly individual scanning results to cashiers. In contrast with both the United States and France, German and Dutch laws *ban* individual reporting of scan rates, owing to privacy considerations. In the Netherlands, before individual scan rate reporting was prohibited, it was attempted as part of a drive for faster performance. Food retailers had no problem accepting the legal limitations because they had found that, with the checkout speed already quite high, it led to increased error rates.

Training Institutions and Their Impact on the Skill Level We have argued that skill formation affects how tasks emerging from company business strategies are bundled into jobs. Therefore, sector-specific training institutions should matter. The basic principles of skill formation differ widely in the six countries. Low-skilled and semiskilled employees dominate U.K. and U.S. retail employment, and there is no notable vocational training system for retail frontline jobs. France also has no countrywide vocational training system in retailing that develops skills tailored for the retail trade, but in the country as a whole a consistently strong emphasis is put on general education. Almost half of retail employees have a French Baccalauréat degree.[32]

Absent a vocational training system tailored to retail firms' needs in these three countries, more emphasis is placed on job-specific training. For example, French food retailers provide extra training to specialized employees working in fresh fish, meat and cheese, and baked products. Induction training takes longer for these employees than for ordinary sales workers, and they are likely to undergo continuing training as new products are released and new hygiene regulations (covering fresh food) are enacted. Consumer electronics retailers also tend to invest in in-house training, given that they sell more complex and expensive products. Ongoing training is typically organized using a "snowball" model: internal trainers are trained in new products through seminars or training modules delivered via the Internet, and then these trainers pass this information on to colleagues at training and work meetings. In addition, training by suppliers plays a much more prominent role in consumer electronics than in food retailing.

German vocational training institutions provide apprentice training and continuing training programs specialized for the retail trade. The role of vocational training institutions, which are governed by unions, employers' representatives, and federal authorities, is to provide training curricula that fit the needs of retail companies as well as to issue standardized certificates. In general, training includes theoretical study in school and practical learning in firms. Despite a decline in total retail employment, the number of newly concluded training contracts in retail has not declined in the last fifteen years. A remarkable *81 percent* of all retail employees have completed a two- or three-year vocational training program.

Denmark and the Netherlands also have traditional vocational training institutions, but make far less extensive use of them in retail. About one-third of Danish retail workers have vocational training certificates. In the Netherlands, where an industry-based vocational training system matured later, only about 15 percent have such a certificate. The Netherlands and, even more so, Denmark show that changes in the workforce composition alter both the qualification structure of a sector and the role of training institutions. In both countries, the growing number of young people working as sales assistants for a limited period of time has shifted training patterns. In food retailing in particular, young workers are trained through on-the-job training, using e-learning modules and quick training by experienced workers. Even though firms could make use of the sector-specific vocational training systems, they do not use these "higher-level institutions" for the bulk of new recruits.[33] The consequences of this shift in pattern are twofold: the core of trained workers in food retailing will decrease over time, and the competition between a short-term pattern of skill formation and traditional policies that are oriented toward the long term and associated with vocational training will lead to an "exhaustion" of training institutions. Wolfgang Streeck and Kathleen Thelen define this exhaustion as a gradual breakdown of institutions over time through depletion.[34]

Norms and Their Implications for Worker Experience Beyond the task structure, workers' experience with workload and pressure is also susceptible to social norms regarding customer service. For example, European cashiers in food retailing sit, whereas they are mandated to stand by companies in the United States. In Denmark, France, Germany, and the Netherlands, this practice is reinforced by national ergonomic standards and the Labor Inspectorate.

Work organization also responds to customer service expectations, but these expectations turn out to be malleable both upward and downward. With the partial exception of the United Kingdom, European grocery customers expect to weigh produce and bag their groceries. In the United States, bagging is provided and is considered an integral component of customer service except in self-checkout counters. Also, produce displays are expected to be very attractive even in midrange U.S. food stores, an expectation that generates a workload not present in other countries.

Turnover and Vertical Mobility

Mobility in retail jobs has two key dimensions: vertical mobility and labor turnover—"moving up or moving on," in the felicitous phrase of Andersson, Holzer, and Lane.[35] Given a retail job pyramid with many entry-level jobs and few higher positions, opportunities for upward mobility are more limited than in many other industries. This presents retailers with three options: (1) tolerating high turnover in some jobs, (2) recruiting significant numbers of workers who do not aspire to mobility, or (3) creating some opportunities for growth even *within* an entry-level job (through enriched content and opportunities for compensation growth). As we will see, retailers in the six countries use all three solutions, but to varying degrees. We start by examining turnover—because retail is distinctive in its high level of employee turnover—and then turn to upward mobility.

Turnover   Labor turnover has several important effects on various dimensions of job quality, making it an important job characteristic in its own right. First, high turnover can depress productivity by creating a workforce dominated by those lacking experience and firm-specific knowledge. Second, elevated turnover in low-end jobs results in very few workers actually exercising the option to move up. Conversely, high turnover in mid- and upper-level jobs opens up space for upward mobility for those who remain. Finally, when turnover is high, it is relatively easy to achieve a norm shift about what constitutes an acceptable job or schedule. Expectations of newer cohorts of workers can be ratcheted down. Managers at a U.S. electronics chain that eliminated commission payments several years ago acknowledged that the action had been very demoralizing for employees at the time, but current salespeople were content. One commented, "I like not working on commission"; another, newer hire exulted over a 3 percent raise in his hourly rate after ninety days on the job, oblivious to the absence of commission pay.

We found considerable differences in retail labor turnover across countries. U.S. retail has by far the highest churning rates (50 percent per year, thirteen percentage points higher than the U.S. economy-wide average), with Germany and France (both 20 percent) at the bottom (see table 5.1). Quantitative data and the case studies themselves suggest three reasons for these variations in churn. The first two stem from the observation that separation rates are typically higher where unemployment is lower (hence other jobs are more available) and the workforce is younger. As shown in figures 5.2 and 5.3, with the exception of the United States, the correlation between the turnover rate and both unemployment and the percentage of the workforce under age twenty-five is quite strong.[36]

Age and unemployment are mediated by a third factor (actually a set of factors) that we call "context," comprising institutions, labor market conditions (including the *interaction* of age structure and un-

Figure 5.2 / Scatter Plot of Labor Turnover and Unemployment Rate with Fitted Line from the Five European Countries, 2002

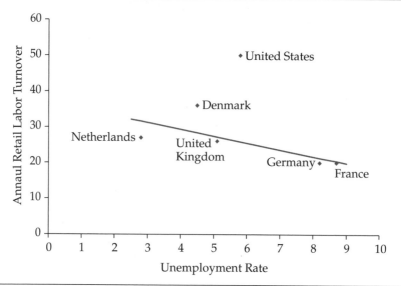

Sources: Authors' compilation from OECD (2003) for comparable unemployment rates; for turnover rates, see table 5.1.

employment), and firm strategy. As can be seen in figure 5.3, retail turnover in Denmark is slightly above the five-country fitted line based on age structure, whereas Dutch turnover falls somewhat below it. This corresponds well with what managers and workers said about young people's behavior as retail workers: Danish interviewees described young workers as "transitional," whereas their Dutch counterparts commented that many young workers, particularly immigrants, were "stuck." This difference, in turn, can be linked to the disparities in labor market opportunities between the two countries, but also to Denmark's famed system of "flexicurity," which enhances labor market mobility.

The largest discrepancy from the dominant turnover pattern, however, arises in the United States, which has a far greater separation rate than would be expected based on either the age mix or the unemployment rate. Interviews with U.S. retail managers and executives revealed a corporate strategy so pervasive that it has become institutionalized: these managers literally "tuned" turnover

Figure 5.3 / Scatter Plot of Labor Turnover and Percentage of
Young Workers with Fitted Line from the Five European
Countries

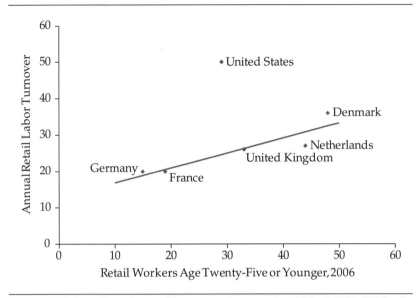

Sources: EU Labour Force Survey (Eurostat, various years) and March 2006 CPS for the
percentage age twenty-five or younger. For turnover rates, see table 5.1.

levels. On the one hand, because pay raises, particularly in retail
food, are closely linked to seniority, managers seek to keep labor
churning high enough to maintain low average wages. "Your [aver-
age pay] rate constantly goes up," a supermarket manager explained. "You have to cycle in the lower end to balance the rate out."
On the other hand, they seek to ensure that enough of the desirable
workers are retained and groomed for internal promotion. This
two-sided strategy can be recognized in the European countries as
well, but European retailers tend to emphasize the retention side
quite a bit more, tilting toward having better jobs overall rather than
a large "turnover pool." As we explored in the work organization
section, longer job tenure may be a side effect of higher commitment
to developing employee skills, whether because of an apprenticeship system that offers a strong platform for doing so (Denmark,
Germany, Netherlands) or a high wage floor that obliges retail managers to keep productivity high (France).

Also, consideration of institutional factors and corporate strategies counsels us to look beyond the age profile of the retail workforce as proximate cause to consider underlying influences on this profile. France and Germany, the two countries in our sample with the lowest retail turnover rates and the lowest percentages of young workers in retail, are also the two countries with the *highest* proportions of women workers in retail. These high concentrations of women, in turn, are closely tied to France's family policies supporting female labor force participation and German policies promoting mini-jobs with tax advantages that are particularly beneficial to married women. Alternatively, the possibility that an older workforce is the *result* rather than the cause of a lower propensity to quit directs our attention to nondemographic influences on turnover. We have already cited the vocational training system and a high minimum wage as incentives for retailers to strive to hold on to workers; it is equally reasonable to argue that German workers' strong vocational training and French workers' high relative wages (see next section) induce workers to stay in retail jobs. Indeed, as a rule, churning can be brought down with higher wages and benefits, and even in the United States, selected retail companies reduce turnover this way. Segmentation offers compensation opportunities to one slice of the workforce, with the part-time/full-time distinction serving as a key divider in the United States: in one U.S. grocery chain that provided detailed statistics, the turnover rate for part-timers is twelve times as high as for full-timers.

Vertical Mobility   Despite the varying national contexts for upward mobility, we mainly found commonalities. In all six countries, retail management posts are predominantly filled by promotion from within. However, the odds of promotion for shop-floor workers, especially in food retail, are low given the high ratios of workers to managers, as we have pointed out. Given the flat employment structure of stores, management is virtually the only path for advancement. Promotion opportunities for those in place are further limited by the growing practice of recruiting managers externally. Moreover, in most countries a gender gap can be seen: women are broadly underrepresented in management ranks. Gender norms as well as expectations of what managers will sacrifice for the job shape these outcomes. Country experiences vary somewhat, owing to different degrees of accommodation of parental responsibilities, but a shared pattern nevertheless rules.

Across countries, vertical mobility appears very much shaped by work design and market structure. In German food retail, promotion opportunities are limited, and in particular, gendered segmentation patterns and processes are evident. Segmentation in career opportunities starts as early as the selection process for vocational training positions. Managerial positions at the store level are predominantly occupied by men, and the more companies use potential consideration for management positions as a criterion for allocating initial training slots, the more disadvantaged female applicants are. This mechanism works in step with the widely held view among male managers that investing in women's advancement is a waste of resources. Moreover, a willingness to work long hours (over forty-five per week) and to be geographically mobile are essential preconditions for promotion from within. These two constraints, which are not directly linked to the business processes at stake, are also reported in the Netherlands and the United Kingdom.

Denmark's retailers offer some contrast. In food retail, unlike in the other five countries, channels of upward mobility seem relatively open. Those starting as apprentices or trainees can access comprehensive training programs that have been set up by the industry to address competition for workers. Denmark is a country that has fashioned its labor market institutions to foster labor mobility and limit underemployment and unemployment.

Compensation

Retail trade is consistently a low-wage sector in all these countries. We start this section by exploring the role of national institutions in two countries with comparatively low shares of low-wage workers in retailing, France and Denmark. In contrast, the three other European countries give insight into the dynamics that drive an increase of low-wage work—specifically, the use of exit options. Strikingly, the ultraliberal United States, with the lowest rate of collective bargaining coverage, has the same incidence of low-wage work in retailing as Germany, which despite its tradition of strong representative structures, has allowed the creation of numerous low-paid jobs via the mini-job option. Following our look at overall wage differences, we examine the gender pay gap, the related wage gap between food and electronics retailing, and the role of commission sales in the latter.

National State and Labor Relations Institutions with a "Bite" Some national institutions set effective barriers against firms' drive to lower wages and depress working conditions. U.S. law does not mandate hourly wage parity for part-time and full-time workers, while under a European Union directive (which has the force of Europe-wide law), European part-timers are entitled to the same hourly wages as full-timers if they perform the same jobs, and all those working over a minimum threshold (usually twelve hours per week) must be covered by national social security systems. The lack of quasi-mandated universal health insurance (prior to the implementation of the 2010 Affordable Care Act in 2014) and pension coverage (except for very limited Social Security) also makes the U.S. situation exceptional.[37] Compared to their European counterparts, U.S. retailers have greater incentives to use part-time as a "status" in order to ration access to employer-sponsored benefits. "The fringe costs associated with part-time associate versus full-time associate are dramatically different," a U.S. grocery chain executive remarked.

The differential bite of national institutions becomes particularly clear when we contrast the United States to the two countries with the lowest incidence of low-wage work in retail, France and Denmark. In France, the high value of the national minimum wage (SMIC) relative to the national average pulls up the retail wage distribution and contributes to the lowest incidence of low wages in retail of all the countries in the study. The national minimum wage is well above contractual wage levels in retail and provides a floor that lifts most workers above the low-wage threshold, despite reports of frequent minimum wage violations. In contrast, the real value of the U.S. minimum wage has been set relatively low. Retail entry-level wages are pegged close to it, and often barely above it, so the U.S. minimum wage does influence retail wages but does little to raise them.

France's SMIC is a far more potent tool than collective bargaining in that country's retail sector. In fact, despite the significant *indirect* impact of national union federations on wages via the setting of the national minimum wage level, the direct impact of collective bargaining on retail wages is limited because French retail unions are weak in the workplace. France's mandatory contractual extension of pay provisions is thus ineffective in the sector. French product market regulations complement the SMIC in limiting low wages. Regulations, by limiting store size and expansion and thus constraining big-box competition, make comparatively high wage levels (and a smaller share of low-wage employment) possible.[38]

Strong union representation in Denmark, expressed in collective bargaining agreements that enforce significant wage compression, contributes to the other case of minimal low-wage retail employment. Collective bargaining coverage is significant—it was 69 percent from 2004 to 2006—and even those retailers that do not sign on to the collective labor agreement (CLA) adhere to its conditions.[39] Furthermore, the Danish social partners (which include the Danish Employers' Federation) have agreed that no member firm will pay gross wages of less than 12 euros ($16.20) per hour.[40]

In contrast, U.S. retail collective bargaining coverage is the lowest among the six countries: less than 6 percent in 2007.[41] Unionization clearly affects compensation for workers in U.S. retailers, but unlike Denmark, there is little spillover to non-union workers. Furthermore, U.S. workers lack access to other worker representation structures, such as works councils, that could affect wages. Though in decades past U.S. retail unions won significant gains for their workforce, in their current weakened state unions at many companies have been compelled to accept slower wage increases, lower wage ceilings, and benefit cutbacks, sometimes in more dramatic increments than their non-union counterparts. Such concessions often take the form of "two-tier" contracts specifying inferior terms for new hires.

The cases of Germany and the Netherlands—with a share of low-wage work that is about the level of that in the United States (Germany) or even slightly higher (the Netherlands)—show that the existence of collective bargaining institutions does not necessarily raise relative wages. In Germany, the high level of low-wage work in retailing partly results from a continuously decreasing coverage rate of collective agreements in recent years: only about half of all retail employees were still covered by collective agreements in 2006 (a twelve-point drop from 2003 in western Germany). Even the administrative extension of collective bargaining agreements in the

Netherlands, which compels similar or identical agreements across the industry, is not by itself sufficient to yield a low incidence of low-wage work given the high percentage (44 percent) of workers under age twenty-five who receive youth subminimum wages. In both countries, retail firms dispose of viable exit options, to which we now turn.

The Dampening Effect of Exit Options and Weak Enforcement   Exit options open the door to excluding certain groups of workers from the industry's prevailing wage level. Consequently, they widen wage dispersion within the sector. Exit options' impact on the pay structure can be "self-energizing" and grow over time when firms follow cost-cutting strategies: if certain groups receive lower wages than others, they may be substituted for those who are better paid. Just as there are country-specific options for employers to achieve schedule flexibility, there are nationally specific "Achilles' heels" for worsening compensation. In addition to exit options, which are primarily aboveboard means to bypass national (and sometimes sectoral) institutions, the six countries also display some degree of weak enforcement of regulations, with further implications for compensation.

Youth subminimum wages are the most salient manifestation of a wage exit option in retail. Such subminimum wages are more broadly used in food than in consumer electronics retail. Denmark, the Netherlands, and the United Kingdom offer youth subminimum wages. In the latter two countries, such wages have a legal basis, though they differ widely in size and impact. (The youth subminimum wage for a sixteen-year-old is 62 percent of the adult minimum wage in the United Kingdom and 35 percent in the Netherlands.) In Denmark, the subminimum wage is set in collective labor agreements. The youth subminimum wage is consistent with the United Kingdom's low-regulation model, whereas in the other two countries this wage offers an exit from institutional arrangements (relatively high collectively bargained wages).

Youth minimum wages in Denmark and the Netherlands have played a significant role in staffing decisions, cost control, and ultimately the share of low-wage work in retail. They have created strong incentives to use very young workers and students in both countries. In the Netherlands, the statutory youth subminimum

Table 5.6 / Retail Workers with Wages Below Each National Low-Wage Threshold, by Subsector, 2003

	Denmark, 2002	France	Germany	Netherlands, 2002	United Kingdom, 2005	United States, 2005
All retail workers	23%	18%	42%[a]	46%	49%	42%
Food retail	29	26	29	57	64[b]	35
Consumer electronics retail	15	3	27	19	—	18

Sources: Compilation by Carré et al. (2010) based on: Esbjerg et al. (2008, 141) for Denmark; Askenazy, Berry, and Prunier-Poulmaire (2008, 220) for France; Voss-Dahm (2008, 258) for Germany; Structure of Earnings Survey (Centraal Bureau voor de Statistiek [CBS] 2003) for the Netherlands; U.K. Office of National Statistics (2005) for the United Kingdom; and U.S. Bureau of Labor Statistics (2005) for the United States.
Note: The low-wage threshold is two-thirds of the national median gross hourly wage.
[a]The retail-wide percentage includes both full-time and part-time workers, whereas the subsector figures include only full-timers.
[b]For 2001.

wage introduced by the government in the 1970s led to the replacement of adult women with very young workers in food retail when price wars flared between 2003 and 2006. More Dutch retail workers fell below the low-wage threshold than in any country but the United Kingdom (table 5.6). Prodded by the protests of young members and the downward pressure on adult wages, union leaders recently requested that adult wages be paid from the age of eighteen onward. In Denmark, the impact of the youth subminimum wage is mitigated by other institutional features regulating compensation, even in the presence of a high share of young workers. The retail subminimum wage, though about 30 percent lower than the (bargained) adult wage, is still high. As noted earlier, the national agreed-upon wage floor is high, and wage compression prevails in bargaining; retail labor agreements have high coverage and are often adhered to by nonsignatory employers.

Though a national minimum wage, if high enough—as in France—can lift the retail wage distribution and limit the incidence of low-wage work, its effectiveness is limited in cases where it is set relatively low and in an environment with weak workplace-level unions. For example, in the United Kingdom the national minimum wage (NMW) is still low relative to the median wage. Furthermore, British retailers reacted to increases in the NMW by reducing bonuses and shift pay differentials—leaving retail workers at low relative earnings levels. An executive of a food chain commented: "We pay just a tad over the minimum wage. . . . We used to [go] higher than that, but you know how it's hiked up. . . . We would probably have been around fifteen to twenty pence above it." Furthermore, as noted earlier, the United Kingdom also has a youth subminimum and a high share of young workers (33 percent under age twenty-five in 2006)—a higher share than in France, though not quite as high as in the Netherlands and Denmark. The result, in combination with the very limited grip of collective bargaining, is an even higher incidence of low-wage work than in the United States.

In Germany, the increasing use of mini-jobs—short-hour part-time jobs with a maximum monthly income of 400 euros ($637 in 2008)—accounts for the relatively high incidence of low-wage jobs in retail.[42] In 2004, nearly nine of ten mini-jobbers received hourly wages below the low-wage threshold, whereas only one-third of full-time employees in German retail were low-paid. The pay difference is connected to the special national regulation of mini-jobs. By law, mini-jobs should provide a subsidy to job holders by exempting them from tax and mandatory social security contributions. But in practice, and contrary to the law, most mini-jobbers never receive this subsidy because retail firms appropriate the benefit by offering lower wages—without being penalized by the state. Married women, socially protected by their husbands' entitlements, and young workers in mini-jobs may not object to unequal wages because, in the absence of mandatory social protection contributions, their wage level seems sufficient. However, in companies where works councils strongly represent employees' interests, it has proven possible either to prevent the use of mini-jobs altogether or at least to monitor developments closely in order to forestall a differentiated pay policy. Germany also adopted a national minimum wage in 2014, but it is too early to tell to what extent that will close this wage exit option.

The case of German mini-jobs illustrates how the self-reinforcing effects of exit options can result in a wider deterioration of income opportunities. Mini-jobs fit retailers' needs for gap fillers to cover peak times and do not cut off access to trained personnel, thanks to the presence of a high percentage of skilled women among mini-jobbers. Women often agree to work a marginal part-time mini-job because they see it as a means to combine work and family responsibilities (in the absence of other viable options) and social norms still accommodate a secondary earner role for trained women. When combined with easy access to the mini-job option and declining coverage of collective agreements on pay, an institution such as the apprenticeship system that is geared to developing skills, upholding wage levels, and equalizing male and female earnings potential does not forestall the growth of low-wage jobs as effectively as in the past. Thus, the case of Germany shows that occupational skills do not necessarily protect workers—in particular female workers—from low wages. Furthermore, not only is the extension of mini-jobs a gateway for low-wage work within retail, but it also has become a driving force for the degradation of female employment in Germany as a whole. Ironically, mini-jobs were established by one institution and accepted by another that in other contexts have done the most to bolster earnings. The German state imposed the mini-job option, and works councils agreed to the establishment of mini-jobs in some big retail companies partly with the intention of protecting core worker employment conditions by sacrificing the "peripheral" newer hires.

In retail, exit options—aboveboard means to debase pay—coexist with opportunities for outright violation of employment standards. Multiple and scattered workplaces make the monitoring and enforcement of labor standards difficult, particularly if there are weak or no institutions of worker representation at the work site. To varying degrees, the case studies reveal instances of minimum wage or overtime pay violations.

The Gender Wage Gap in Retail   Behind average wage differences are within-country pay disparities. The mean gender pay gap in wholesale and retail is especially large in Germany and the Netherlands: according to WageIndicator data, 22 and 21 percent, respectively—while in the United Kingdom and France it is 16 percent.[43] In comparison, the U.S. wage gender gap is relatively moderate, though still significant: women in frontline retail jobs in 2004 earned 12 percent less than their male counterparts.[44] Danish women's disadvantage in hourly compensation is even smaller, at 10 percent.[45] Gender sorting across retail subsectors and the wage penalty due to interruptions in paid employment play a role, as do the constraints on the vertical mobility of female retail workers. Within countries, the gender gap is likely to be smaller where wage-leveling institutions such as unions are stronger. At a unionized U.S. grocery chain, a woman cashier approvingly noted, "You get your pay raises per hour, hours worked. So that's fair. I know in some businesses you hear how men make 20 percent more than a woman in the same job." We later discuss the gender wage gap as it arises in analyzing various aspects of compensation.

Pay in Food Versus Electronics Retail   In all countries, the share of low-wage work is much higher in food retailing than in consumer electronics (table 5.6), and the company case studies conform with this pattern of disparity. One possible explanation points to the significant differences between food and consumer electronics retail productivity, but the data, limited as they are, do not appear to bear this out. Indeed, food retailing has 6 percent higher productivity than electronics in the United States, 22 percent higher in Denmark, and 19 percent higher in the Netherlands.[46]

As we pointed out in chapter 2, the obvious alternative to explain pay differentials would be a historical gender bias in pay structure, given that men make up the majority of the workforce in consumer electronics and women constitute the majority in retail food. In 2004, the share of women in Europe's retail food sales occupations ranged from 68 percent in Denmark to 85 percent in the Netherlands, while it was 53 percent in the United States; in consumer electronics, the share of women workers varied between 17 percent in Denmark and 40 percent in France and stood at 30 percent in the United States. Gender patterns may play out indirectly as well; consumer electronics retailers may have to compete with information technology—another male-dominated sector—to attract knowledgeable salespeople and technicians. We further scrutinize the food-electronics pay gap in the following analysis of the practice of commission pay.

The Role of Commission Pay and the Gender Composition of Consumer Electronics   Consumer electronics retail has historically relied on commission pay, a practice that highlights gender-patterned behavioral expectations and appears congruent with the relatively high proportion of men in the sector (as compared to food). We expect that commission pay plays a role in the higher pay in consumer electronics than in food retail. Given that male workers concentrate in parts of retail where commission pay is in effect, they stand to benefit from higher compensation. Commission pay is not always associated with higher pay, however, as we will see in the Netherlands.

Electronics retailers in all five European countries very much rely on commissions as an incentive. (As we have seen, U.S. electronics retailers rely much less on commissions.) Pay based on individual sales levels motivates a sales process that entails greeting customers, offering detailed product information and advice, and securing after-sales service contracts. Collectively bargained pay can coexist with commission pay, but has divergent outcomes across countries. In two German retailers, the collective agreement sets a bonus level on top of base pay, but there also is the expectation that individuals will negotiate additional bonuses. These can be substantial, reaching as much as 25 percent of collectively agreed basic pay, according to one store manager. In the German cases, collective voice appears to increase the relative share of fixed (guaranteed) pay in total compensation. In one case that involves neither a collective agreement nor a works council, the fixed pay is one-third lower than in settings with bargaining. Commission pay can also undermine collectively bargained base pay, although its record is mixed enough that we would not consider it an exit option. The Dutch retail study found that commission pay is accompanied by lower collectively bargained wages because social actors have the perception that individuals can improve their compensation with commission.[47]

Nevertheless, commission pay, while still prevalent in European countries, is under pressure, owing to falling margins on major video and audio consumer items as well as personal computers; these pressures are felt most acutely in the United States and, to some degree, Denmark. Some Danish case studies include reports by management that a slowdown of sales growth raised questions about continuing with commission pay. Major U.S. big-box consumer electronics retailers have already moved away from commission pay in recent years in order to cut costs. It was possible to implement this change quickly—basically overnight—because there was no consultation with any representative bodies, since unions and works councils are absent in U.S. consumer electronics retailing.

The U.S. cases reveal that ending commission pay is associated with declining pay levels for sales staff and a growing use of part-time workers. Shifts away from commission pay generate motivational issues for the sales workforce that management must address. It remains to be seen whether the removal of commission pay will result in a decline in male representation in consumer electronics retailing.

In sum, national institutions that set basic conditions for pay directly affect the incidence of low-wage work in retail. National institutions such as collective bargaining and a national minimum wage raise the wage floor when they are geared to do so, as in Denmark or France. However, we find that exit options from the institutional framework, such as a youth subminimum wage or mini-jobs, allow a significant number of low-wage jobs to be created even in settings with collective bargaining, an apprenticeship system, and other institutions geared to maintain job quality and relatively higher compensation.

LESSONS FROM THE SIX-COUNTRY COMPARISON
Shared Pressures, Different Trade-Offs

What aspects of the national institutional settings in which retail jobs are embedded make these jobs better or worse? To answer this question we have explored how job quality outcomes in the United States (with its thinner web of formal regulatory and bargained mechanisms) diverge from those in European countries as well as how these outcomes differ among the latter.

Concerns about the role of the institutional setting are particularly salient because, as noted at the outset, retail leads other industries in experimenting with changes that affect the labor market and job quality. Pressures on job quality have been high in all six countries as retailers have adopted supply-chain management strategies based on advanced technologies, along with employment strategies aimed at cutting costs. Across countries, pressures to fend off competition from low-cost retail models have translated into market strategies that go in the two opposite directions of increasing service and customization or pushing for self-service. Attempts to cut labor costs have been consistent. Across countries, retailers have availed themselves of existing exit options from particular features of their institutional environment and also have led the push for introducing *new* exit options. These efforts have resulted in varied patterns of exclusion and disparate work conditions across countries as each national web of institutions offers specific options for exit and closes off others. Thus, while retailers' uses of exit options dilute the impact of societal effects—the institutional and normative factors that traditionally ensured a high degree of shared employment conditions in many European countries—they have done so in ways that are unique to each nation, producing a national-sectoral outcome.

Trends and Variations in Job Quality

In general, retail jobs have gotten worse across all six countries over the past two decades. First, there has been a general liberalization trend in labor and product market regulations within all these countries. *Which* policies are implemented and *how* they are implemented vary greatly across countries. There are also nationally specific exit options, such as the youth subminimum wage in the Netherlands and mini-jobs in Germany.

A second effect is that retailers have adjusted by shifting to heavier use of part-time workforces with weaker bargaining power (for example, mothers with young children and low-skilled young workers), who bear the brunt of adjustment and the sharp edge of cost-cutting. For European retailers, part-time employment has been closely related to several key exit options (notably mini-jobs and a youth subminimum wage). The heavy use of part-time workers is emblematic of employment segmentation and has also been associated with thwarting union organizing.[48] Furthermore, social norms for what constitutes an acceptable job or schedule have changed: high turnover and young hires have made the ratcheting down of the expectations of newer cohorts of workers an easy transition to achieve.

Why are some countries' retail job outcomes better than those of other countries along certain dimensions, even given this broad negative trend? We observe that some historical institutions—those with a "bite"—continue to demonstrate a strong societal effect on job quality. Our key findings on schedules, work organization, mobility, and compensation illustrate their impact.

In terms of the institutions and norms affecting work schedules, the primary contrasts between the United States and the European countries are the thorough lack of government regulations of hours of operation in the United States and the nearly complete absence of worker schedule regulation. The country has led the way in 24/7 store operation. The only significant remaining regulation on work schedules is the weekly overtime premium. In contrast, unions, works councils, and store hours regulations all play a role in store and worker schedules in the European countries. German and Danish regulations require that work schedules be set far in advance (four to six months), a mandate that would be considered unmanageable by U.S. retailers. In France, the combination of a thirty-five-hour full-time workweek with a (nationally extended) labor agreement specifying a minimum of twenty-six hours for part-timers has narrowed the hours gap between part- and full-time workers. We examine scheduling issues in France in the next chapter.

In the absence of hours regulation, and with little union presence, social norms regarding reasonable workloads and hours can erode. Witness U.S. grocers that are progressively eliminating the wage premium for Sundays and other nonstandard work times. In contrast, hourly wage premia, typically mandated by collective labor agreements, are common in all the European countries, though employers are seeking to chip away at them.

The way tasks are organized is clearly affected by the interactions of national institutions, social norms, policies affecting the reproductive sphere, and labor market context. The education and training system, primarily the vocational education system, plays a role in Germany and, to some degree, in Denmark and the Netherlands, facilitating a broader job profile than in other countries. However, rather than ensuring that graduates of the vocational system all have good-quality jobs, the combination of vocational education and exit options results in retailers having access to skilled secondary part-time workers—in Germany, women with family responsibilities who end up in mini-jobs, and in Denmark and the Netherlands, (trained) young people subject to youth wages.

Workforce turnover and upward mobility affect the managerial choice of work organization and, conversely, are affected by job quality and workforce expectations. As we noted at the outset, separation rates are far higher in the United States than in the other countries, especially given the middling concentration of young workers in the retail sector. U.S. retailers' labor strategies rely much more than those of their European counterparts on workforce churning to keep average wages low. Vertical mobility patterns do not show readily explicable cross-national differences; instead, the strongest finding across all countries is that significant barriers impede women's movement into management.

The institutions with the most influence over compensation vary across countries. In some nations, state regulation, rather than collective bargaining, has the most significant impact. In France, the state-set minimum wage has more impact on retail wages than contractually bargained wage levels; the high minimum wage floor essentially reaches the "ceiling" for many frontline retail jobs, significantly boosting their wages. In the United States, in contrast, the minimum wage has historically set a low floor for the industry. On the other hand, state policy may enable retailers' use of low-wage exit options, as with Germany's state-imposed mini-jobs.

Worker representation institutions also continue to impact compensation. In Denmark, high union density and unions' commitment to wage compression lift most jobs above the low-wage threshold. In contrast, in the United States, because unionization and collective bargaining are by now limited to a few companies (where wages are higher), ripples from the "union threat effect" are negligible in most retail settings. In many U.S. unionized settings, hard-pressed unions have accepted "two-tier" structures that offer lower wage and benefits for new hires while protecting incumbents.

Institutions and Gender Patterns

In all six countries, gender segregation of jobs remains a constant, and so do gender-specific patterns of mobility and compensation. In all six, it is difficult for women to break through the glass ceiling into management, especially in food retail. Women are also mostly excluded from electronics retail's big-ticket sales, which are often linked to commission pay. Equalizing institutions, such as those that ensure skill acquisition and credentialing for women as well as men (the German apprenticeship system, for example), or wage compression implemented through collective labor agreements do matter. However, they are significantly less effective when combined with exit options that build on women's secondary earner status in the household and labor market. Similarly, when exit options have fostered the competition of one vulnerable worker group against another, they have sometimes relegated women to secondary earner roles. In the recent price war in Dutch food retail, stable women workers were replaced by very young workers paid subminimum wage.

Institutions regulating the reproductive sphere also make a difference. Countries with accessible child care in some cases enable women with family responsibilities to access better job quality outcomes and avoid marginalization in very short part-time jobs. In France, the historical preference for full-time work, supported by the strong provision of child care options, has prompted policy action to set a minimum number of part-time hours.

Patterns and Prospects for Retail Jobs

Taking a step back from the details of job quality, what can we say about the overall production models in retail, particularly in European countries? With shared market pressures and similar technologies, retail industries in all six countries have moved in the same broad directions, developing options for using cheaper labor and deploying it only as needed. Across all six countries, the emerging combination of technology-enhanced high performance with low wages and worsening working conditions conforms with Bailey and Bernhardt's 1997 finding for the United States. In this sense, one may argue for a finding of broad convergence of intensified use of exit options to cut labor costs. Yet even amid this convergence, the *national* side of the national-sectoral model continues to matter. Retail retains national peculiarities with job quality consequences.

In the United States, as we saw in chapter 4, retailers are caught in a bind between service and efficiency goals, on the one hand, and a high-turnover, low-skill, low-commitment workforce, on the other. In Europe as well, questions arise about the sustainability of retailers' strategies to cut costs and maintain market share. For example, in Denmark and the Netherlands, competition for young workers with suitable attitudes and a high level of general skills may drive wages up, undermining the cost containment lever this workforce provides. Of course, change in state policy can alter worker decision terms and corporate strategies relatively quickly. In Germany and the Netherlands, recent increases in child care investment could alter the character of the labor supply of mothers. In the United States, pressures to raise the minimum wage have been growing.

Yet, because the six countries started in different places with respect to compensation, working conditions, and regulatory institutions for both product and labor markets, working in retail pays differently and is a different experience across countries. In U.S. retail, there has been a continuous, and rather uniform, erosion of compensation and working conditions. In Europe, the movement has been neither as continuous nor as uniform. New regulatory initiatives, such as higher minimum wages, have partially reversed trends toward falling compensation. Rather than uniform degradation of retail jobs, European countries have tended toward fragmentation via exit options: mini-jobbers in Germany, youths earning extra-low wages in the Netherlands, and involuntary part-time workers in France have taken the main hit. In all six countries, the retail industry has been a leader in such fragmentation and the experimentation with nonstandard hours, segmented work arrangements, and a variety of other exit options from institutions safeguarding job quality. Because of this trajectory of experimentation, retail developments may well point to the likely consequences of similar scheduling, recruitment, and compensation changes being considered in *other* industries. Alternatively, changes in policy environment and the strength of social movements may throw retail—with its emblematic "low-quality" jobs—into serving as a testing ground for novel collective action and regulatory strategies to bolster job quality for low-wage workers.

A QUICK DETOUR TO MEXICO

Chapter A1 (http://www.russellsage.org/publications/where-bad -jobs-are-better) expands this set of comparisons to a middle-income country by comparing retail jobs in Mexico and the United States. In brief, a head-to-head comparison of modern retail chain stores in the two countries (including a number of chains found in both) shows yet another set of differences in jobs, traceable to yet another set of institutional arrangements. The divergence in Mexican-U.S. work schedules provides the most striking contrast with the United States and the five European countries we just reviewed. Whereas in the United States and Northern Europe retail is distinctive for high rates of part-time employment, in Mexico part-time jobs in retail are rare; instead, Mexican retail workers' main scheduling issue is working unpaid overtime hours. The explanation lies in three very distinctive Mexican institutions. First, in Mexico, unlike the United States and its European counterparts, the minimum wage (and almost all other wages) is set by the *day*, which would make creation of short-hour jobs matched to peaks and valleys of consumer demand costly (since employers would be required to pay the daily minimum regardless of hours worked). By the same token, employers seek to extract as many hours of labor as possible for that daily wage, taking advantage of the fact that overtime premium provisions are poorly enforced. Second, in Mexico overtime pay kicks in at forty-eight hours, so retailers can readily cover weekends by overlapping six-day, eight-hour shifts. Third, in contrast with the United States but in step with Europe, employer-provided health and pension benefits are rare in Mexico, with most people relying on single-payer systems for both—so, as in Europe, Mexican retail enterprises have little incentive to bulk up on low-benefit or no-benefit part-time jobs to save on labor costs.

Mexican retail also differs from the United States in a number of other ways, reflecting broader differences in the two societies. Mexican women's retail career trajectories are far more often truncated, reflecting a norm that mothers will exit the workforce for an extended period to rear their children full-time. Top-to-bottom wage hierarchies in chain stores are markedly more unequal in Mexico—not surprising given that Mexico's economic inequalities are sharper overall. And retail-sector unions, which we have shown do manage to improve jobs for U.S. workers (though far less than in Denmark), are present but largely inert in Mexico.

In addition to these systematic U.S.-Mexico contrasts, ample variation in Mexican retail job quality also provides evidence of managerial discretion, as we have demonstrated for the United States. And in a further investigation that goes beyond the main arguments of the book, chapter A1 (http://www.russellsage.org/publications/where-bad-jobs-are-better) compares *informal* retail employment—that outside of the reach of labor standards—in the two countries, pointing out that although the scale of informality differs (in Mexico, the majority of retail workers are informal), there are U.S.-Mexico parallels in the growth of informal retail jobs. Mexico's heavy reliance on unprotected informal retail workers, chapter A1 concludes, holds cautionary lessons for the future direction of jobs in the United States.

CONCLUSION

In this chapter, we have analyzed the conditions that give rise to the variation in retail job quality and employment patterns across the United States and five European countries as well as among those European countries. This cross-national comparison brings out clearly the significant role that labor market institutions play in retailers' strategies and practices in labor deployment. Furthermore, and less predictably, the comparison also surfaces the significant role that reproductive institutions—education and training, family care policies—as well as product market regulations play in job characteristics and ultimate cross-national differences in job quality. The overall effect is a national-sectoral one: regulations, policies, and social norms in each country interact with each other and with global trends in retail in non-additive ways to yield national patterns of labor deployment and job quality in retail.

These national distinctions notwithstanding, in this comparison of six countries, the United States stands apart from European countries with regard to its thin labor standards regulation and remarkably limited product market regulation in retail. The lack of regulation of hours of operation and nearly complete absence of worker schedule regulation distinguish the United States. So do a low minimum wage and the abandonment of wage premia for "nonsocial" shifts (for example, holidays or Sundays). U.S. retailers' human resource strategies rely more extensively on labor turnover to keep wages low (workers churn out before accruing raises). Less-protective reproductive institutions also characterize the United States; workers' limited access to affordable child care options confines many caretakers (mostly mothers) to entry-level part-time retail jobs. While the United States is not unique, it marks one extreme along these dimensions.[49] These European comparisons hold lessons, then, for how the United States could improve retail jobs: a higher minimum wage, stronger unions, establishment of works councils, greater regulation of work schedules, and for that matter a more robust subsidized child care system could move U.S. low-wage work toward some of the more positive European outcomes.

6 / Cashiers in Large Supermarkets in France and the United States: The Role of Societal Effects

In the preceding chapter, we held the overall sector fixed and looked at the impact of six differing national institutional environments on retail jobs. But a true apples-to-apples comparison would look at the same subsector, and ideally the same job within that subsector. In this chapter, we get as close as possible to that ideal by comparing U.S. and French supermarkets, and in particular the cashier job in both. Again deploying a national-sectoral model, we trace several institutional effects on job quality differences between the two countries—including some touched on in chapter 5—but dig more deeply and broadly to unearth the full field of societal effects.[1] The powerful impact of this web of regulations, labor relations structures, and social norms once more helps make the case that changing the rules in the United States could improve retail jobs.

Continuing the sector-based approach in the previous chapter, we examine the interrelationships of markets, technology, work organization, and societal institutions in retail. The U.S.-France comparison is a natural next step. The United States and France are the home countries of the two largest retail multinationals, Wal-Mart and Carrefour, and as chapter 5 showed, France has the lowest share of low-wage workers in retail of any of the six countries surveyed.[2] The cashier job is likewise a natural choice because it is the largest category in the sector and exemplifies the problem of low-quality entry-level jobs. The focus on cashiers also has gendered import, since the job is disproportionately female. Limiting the comparison to two countries allows us both to consider competing explanations of some of the job quality disparities and to more fully flesh out just how differing U.S. and French institutions act—especially those institutions with less direct effects on job characteristics. We base our analysis on standard data sources and on company case studies— six large grocers in France and ten in the United States—that span stores with varied service levels, with over one hundred interviews in each country's set of companies.[3]

EXPLAINING DIFFERENCES IN PAY, PRODUCTIVITY, AND POSTURE

Panel 1 of table 6.1 compares absolute hourly pay levels between the two countries. French workers are on average more expensive per hour. However, the desirability of the cashier job to workers within a country depends primarily on the *relative* level of pay, in comparison with other alternatives. Using two-thirds of the median hourly wage in each country as a cutoff point for low wages, French retail workers are far more likely to be well paid in relative terms (table 6.1, panel 2).[4]

In order for French companies to profit comparably to their U.S. counterparts while paying more, they must reap higher productivity rates from their workers. And indeed they do (table 6.1, panel 3). Sales per square foot of selling area are, remarkably, nearly three times as high in large French retail establishments, bespeaking much more intensive use of space. Value-added per employee-hour is almost 12 percent greater in French retail. Zooming in on target item scanning rates, a key measure of cashier productivity in both countries, also reveals a higher rate in France. This higher productivity makes higher compensation economically sustainable for firms.

Another difference (not shown in the table) is that French cashiers sit whereas U.S. cashiers stand.

Table 6.1 / Profile of French and U.S. Retail

Gross Hourly Wages of Retail Workers in France and the United States

	France, 2006 (in 2007 Dollars)	United States, 2007
All retail	$16.91	$14.85
Large food stores (supermarket or larger)	16.49	12.31
Cashiers in large food stores	14.39	12.16
Cashiers from cases	11.51–14.96	Start at 5.15–10.00; top wage, 7.00–20.83

Workers Falling Below the Low Hourly Wage
Threshold in France and the United States, 2003

	France	United States
All retail	18%	37%
Food retail	19	48
Cashiers in retail	29	70
Cashiers in food retail	30	69

Retail Productivity Measures for
France and the United States

	France	United States
Annual sales per square foot of selling area (large food stores)	$1,348 (2007)	$582 (2007)
Annual sales per hour (large food stores)	$[260–290] (2007)	$139 (2007)
Value added per employee-hour (all retail)	$29.33 (2005)	$26.25 (2005)
Typical targets for items scanned per minute by cashiers	25 (up to 45)	20 (up to 25)

Sources: (1) *Gross hourly wages:* For France, all wages are from Institut National de la Statistique et des Études Économiques (INSEE, various years). For the United States, wages for "all retail" are computed from the March 2007 CPS; all other wages except sample wages are calculated by imputations combining March 2007 CPS data with 2004 and 2007 Current Employment Statistics (CES) annual averages (U.S. Bureau of Labor Statistics 2016a), along with weights from the 2007 Quarterly Census of Employment and Wages (QCEW) (U.S. Bureau of Labor Statistics 2008). In brief, we used the CPS to determine current wages and occupational differences and combined that data with CES data to determine subsectoral differences and weights. Imputation details are available upon request. The French consumer price index is from OECD (2008); the nominal exchange rate is from U.S. Federal Reserve Board (2009). (2) *Workers falling below the low hourly wage threshold:* France—INSEE (various years); United States—March CPS. (3) *Retail productivity measures:* For sales per square foot or per hour in France, estimations are based on Fédération du Commerce et de la Distribution (FCD 2008).
Note: French wages, sales, and value-added are converted to U.S. dollars at the nominal exchange rate. From the viewpoint of transnational corporations able to convert currencies and make global location choices, a nominal exchange rate conversion is most relevant.

CONTRASTS IN JOB CHARACTERISTICS ARE NOT ACCOUNTED FOR BY MARKET AND ORGANIZATIONAL DIFFERENCES

One possible source of difference in French and U.S. retail jobs is the national mix of food store formats. Perhaps the greater role played by large stores in France generates higher pay and productivity. Table 6.1 omits convenience and mom-and-pop stores, but even within large food stores, various formats coexist in both countries.

Category definitions differ across countries, making a head-to-head comparison difficult. Nonetheless, table 6.2 reveals broad similarities in store formats. In both countries, large outlets dominate food sales. (In fact, this dominance is somewhat more pronounced in the United States.)[5] France has a larger overall *average* store size, but the difference is small. Given similar store areas and France's greater sales per square foot (table 6.1, panel 3), average sales per store are considerably higher in France.

In brief, there is little to indicate that larger food stores in France explain the differences in pay and productivity. One must look elsewhere for an explanation of the differences found in pay, pace, and physical position of cashier jobs.

The mix of tasks bundled into cashier jobs is identical, for the most part, across the Atlantic. The French SBAM (sourire, bonjour, au revoir, merci) would be recognizable to any U.S. shopper (smile, hello, good-bye, thank-you). However, there are several noteworthy differences, which we alluded to in the introduction to this book. U.S. cashiers almost invariably identify and weigh produce, whereas in France consumers are often responsible for these tasks. French cashiers must remove anti-theft tags from liquor and clothing, whereas in the U.S. such tags are rare in the typical grocery order. U.S. cashiers usually bag groceries or at least assist the bagger and customer with bagging; in France, the customer is expected to bag. According to the researchers' observations, French cashiers typically do more to monitor for theft, including checking overhead mirrors and a panoramic lens at cash register level, checking goods on the belt (for example, examining multipacks of bottles for hidden small items) and checking inside customers' bags. French cashiers must count their cash at the end of a shift or when unloading a full register; in the United States, supervisors count cash.

The fact that U.S. cashiers stand is connected to bagging. A hu-

Table 6.2 / Profile of Large Food Stores in France and the United States

	France 2007	United States, 2002	United States, 2007[a]
Percentage of total food sales			
Supermarkets	33.1%	66.4%	70.8%
Hypermarkets/supercenters	33.0	15.1	24.1
All large food retailers	66.1	81.5	94.9[b]
Average square feet per store (in thousands)			
Supermarkets	11.7	11.8	12.5
Hypermarkets/supercenters	61.0	123.9	137.3
All large food retailers	18.9	16.5	20.2
Average annual sales per store (in thousands of dollars)			
Supermarkets	$12,239	$5,975	$7,186
Hypermarkets/supercenters	102,648	65,677	76,282
All large food retailers	25,482	8,492	11,443

Sources: French data are from FCD (2008) or INSEE (2009b). All U.S. data are from the U.S. Economic Census; 2002 sales are from U.S. Census Bureau (2005a), and area data are from U.S. Census Bureau (2005b); 2007 percentage of food sales is imputed as described in note a (food sales by format are no longer directly available); total sales and area are from U.S. Census Bureau (2015); 2007 count of establishments is from U.S. Census Bureau (2015).
Note: For the United States, "hypermarkets/supercenters" corresponds to the "warehouse stores and superstores" category. French sales are converted to U.S. dollars using nominal exchange rates.
[a] The U.S. percentage of food sales in 2007 is imputed as follows: percentage of food sales based on sales *i,2007* = sales *i,2002* x (establishments *i,2007* / establishments *i,2002*), where *i* denotes a size category.
[b] 2007 count of establishments from EC0744SXSB1 accessed through U.S. Census Bureau (2015).

man resource executive in a U.S. supermarket chain explained: "If you're sitting, it would be hard to swivel around and stand to bag. So that would be the most important reason that U.S. cashiers stand." And managers in stores held fast to the notion that cashiers "must stand." In contrast, French cashiers sit, at least in part because health professionals recommend it. France's compulsory industrial medicine system—an institution with no clear U.S. equivalent—has played a part in determining cashiers' physical position. Employer-paid medical personnel diagnose injuries and chronic illnesses, especially repetitive trauma disorders. Social Security (the national health system) monitors the incidence of reported job-related accidents and illnesses, in part because work-related sick leave and medical expenditures are covered by the national universal system. Social Security and the Ministry of Labor have safety overseers who may impose production process changes. Historically, because cashiers were full-time, these institutions weighed in on the physical stress related to standing for long hours. Retailers have followed their recommendations.

In the absence of an equivalent national system of industrial medicine, U.S. firms, retailers among them, react to the rising premia for private (but legally mandated) workers' compensation insurance, which covers medical expenses and lost earnings related to workplace injuries. Firms respond primarily to accidents with acute consequences and less so to chronic and stress-related conditions. Similarly, the national Occupational Safety and Health Administration (OSHA) inspection system is usually reactive rather than preemptive. Ergonomic concerns do not loom large for retailers.[6]

Interestingly for this contrast of two diametrically opposed practices, the ergonomic literature shows that both models—exclusively upright *and* exclusively seated postures—have negative health consequences. Ideally, workstations should accommodate both positions.[7] This literature also shows that productivity and satisfaction are not significantly different in the two positions. So standing versus sitting cannot explain differences in productivity and pay between the two countries.

As noted in chapter 5, cashier scan rates top out at twenty to twenty-five items per minute even in the fastest-paced U.S. retail settings, whereas French target scan rates go as high as forty to forty-five. Bagging by U.S. cashiers does not explain the difference in scan rates, which are calculated only for times when the register is online. A U.S. warehouse store cashier noted, "Like, if you're scanning things, you can hit 'total' between items and it'll stop the count." At first glance, U.S. cashiers' task of recognizing and weighing produce seems to explain the slower target scan rates, but this explanation is unsatisfactory. In French hypermarkets where cashiers are expected to weigh produce, fieldwork confirmed that scan rates remain very high. In fact, given French cashiers' expanded responsibilities for anti-theft monitoring, one might expect them to scan more slowly! A last source of productivity disparity could be the scan technology, but there is no evidence that French retailers use more advanced technology. Perhaps the difference stems from greater U.S. expectations for cashier interaction with customers; in any case, ergonomic evidence from the French cases documents that the faster pace takes a toll in repetitive motion disease.

Relatively small differences in the tasks of cashiers in France and the United States are consistent with the clear divergence between sitting and standing. But they do not explain the rather large differences in pay and productivity between the two settings.

Societal Effects with Direct Impacts: Labor Regulation

Both countries show direct institutional effects in the labor regulation sphere—that is, institutional features that affect job quality directly rather than, for example, by changing the decision terms of firms or employees. First and foremost, the sharp difference between the high value of the minimum wage in France and the low U.S. minimum wage plays a key role in the stark contrast in the incidence of low-wage work in retail. In France, a high national minimum wage (SMIC) relative to the national median wage contributes to the lowest incidence of low wages in retail of the six countries we compared in chapter 5. In 2006, the French minimum wage stood at 68 percent of the median wage. With low-wage workers defined as earners of less than two-thirds of the median net hourly wage, even with incomplete enforcement this law drove the proportion of low-wage workers below 20 percent.

In contrast, the U.S. minimum wage has lost real value over the past thirty years, under intensive lobbying by industries employing low-wage workers, particularly retail and food service. By early 2007, the real minimum wage had declined to only 30 percent of the median wage.[8] The U.S. Congress implemented a relatively small increase in 2007, with increments in 2008 and 2009. States may set a minimum above the federal level, and in 2007 thirty of fifty did so.[9] Where implemented, state minimum wages are about 20 percent higher than the federal wage.[10]

The minimum wage affects both entry-level wages and the reservation wage (the lowest wage prospective workers will accept). In France as in the United States, food retailers set entry-level pay at or slightly above the minimum wage. Using the nominal value of the U.S. minimum wage implemented in July 2008 ($6.55 an hour) as a yardstick, one in twelve U.S. retail workers—and one in five part-time, frontline retail workers—fell below the benchmark as of early 2007, while only one in nineteen other private-sector workers fell short.[11] Furthermore, the minimum wage's high relative value in France, combined with the guaranteed minimum income (RMI), contributes to a higher reservation wage economy-wide.

Second, the lack of mandated hourly pay and benefit parity between full-time and part-time workers in the United States contributes to the high incidence of low-wage work in U.S. retail relative to retail in France, which complies with a European Union directive on such parity. In 2007, part-timers in U.S. retail earned 67 percent of full-timers' hourly wages (and 31 percent of full-time weekly earnings), a disadvantage markedly exceeding that of part-timers economy-wide (77 percent of full-time wages).[12] Benefit exclusion is a liability and triggers dissatisfaction among part-time workers.

Third, unions' position in the labor relations system differs between the two countries. In France, collective bargaining influences retail wages through sectoral agreements with major chains that are extended to cover almost all workers regardless of union membership.[13] Actual membership is low—around 2 percent—and union power in stores is limited.[14] A hypermarket cashier's perspective is typical: "Few people join unions, because of fear. . . . Fear of losing your job takes people's spirit and consciousness away." Although the bargained starting wage is regularly set below the SMIC, the agreement includes seniority bonuses. In large chains, unions are able to secure additional advantages, including profit-sharing schemes. Consequently, in such chains, cashiers with one year's seniority can earn up to 125 percent of the hourly SMIC. U.S. retail unions have higher *membership* density—19 percent in grocery in the period under study—but a much lower share of the workforce is *covered by collective bargaining agreements*. U.S. unions do bargain for higher benefits and more predictable work schedules at unionized stores, but have little impact on compensation sectorwide.

Societal Effects with Indirect Impacts: Product Market Regulation

Though direct institutional effects explain much of the U.S.-French compensation difference, it is striking how much *indirect* effects matter for job quality disparities as well. Differences in the two national-sectoral models arising from contrasts in the regulation of shopping itself, part of the product market sphere, exert indirect effects on cashier job outcomes. French store opening hours, shopping cultures, and anticompetitive regulations induce concentrated peak hours with (exceedingly) high customer flows—with consequent pressures on cashiers.

In the near-absence of hours regulations, almost all U.S. food retail workers work one weekend day and often evening schedules. The impact on workers is clear, as a full-time supermarket cashier supervisor noted: "My shift starts at 2:00 in the afternoon and doesn't end until 11:00 at night. . . . You have to be able to be flexible with your hours. . . . You don't have a set schedule a week. . . . Sometimes I'll get a Saturday off, sometimes I'll get a Sunday off." In contrast, French food store hours are restricted by regulations and custom. French supermarkets are typically open from 9:00 AM to 8:00 PM, and hypermarkets close at 10:00 PM; both can open only five Sundays a year, with additional exceptions for tourist zones and, since August 2009, for some retail zones facing extreme customer flows. In central business districts or in tourist zones, stores can remain open sixteen hours a day. Despite a slight increasing trend—approximately an hour over a decade—shopping hours are concentrated. Still, even with these restrictions, retail workers frequently experience shift work because of the time involved in the setup and cleanup tasks that are necessary to meet EU food safety requirements.

In the two countries, store hours also reflect social schedules and rhythms of family life, which in turn strongly shape sharply contrasting shopping behaviors. French customers carry out only marginal purchases after dinnertime (7:00 to 9:00 PM), except for shift workers. Shopping hours are concentrated during the peak times of 5:00 to 8:00 PM on Monday through Friday and on Saturdays, largely as a result of the limit on Sunday opening. This limit constrains peak hours to about twenty to twenty-five hours per week (three hours a day Monday to Friday plus five to ten hours on Saturday), whereas U.S. stores typically have about thirty-six peak hours (four hours a day on weekdays and eight hours on each weekend day).

Moreover, France historically has had a Malthusian policy limiting the growth of local surface areas devoted to food sales. Restrictions were reinforced in 1996 and only partly removed in 2008. The policy was designed to shelter retailers in place from excessive competition. France has among the strictest zoning rules in the OECD competitive database.[15] By contrast, and consistent with a deregulation-prone economy, entry is almost free in the United States except for standard zoning requirements and some local ordinances that impose specific costs on big-box stores.

As a result, large food retailing sales areas reach only 3.2 square feet per inhabitant in France, as compared to 5.5 square feet in the United States.[16] This rate is even lower in France's largest metropolitan areas. The disparity is acute given a much larger at-home food consumption market in France: in 2006, food-at-home spending per capita was 2,600 euros ($3,300 at that year's average exchange rate), in contrast to $1,800 in the United States.[17]

The combination of these temporal and physical shopping limitations on such a large market dictates that French stores unavoidably experience massive customer flows during peak hours. The two studied hypermarkets welcome 10,000 visitors on weekdays and 25,000 on Saturday.

French regulations promote an organizational choice that maximizes the number of cashiers and warrants an intensive (and stressful) organization of work for cashiers.[18] In a hypermarket with a 100,000-square-foot sales area, fifty cashier stations can operate simultaneously. Sitting reduces the space per cashier, allowing stores to maximize the number of cash registers. High scanning rates keep checkout lines flowing briskly. Nonetheless, French shoppers often experience long waits during peak periods. This dramatically affects the relation between customers and cashiers. Said one hypermarket cashier: "As soon as five or six people are standing in line, people suffer. They don't understand, they see us as robots and not as individuals. You always have to work faster."

The U.S. focus on customer satisfaction has also generated regulations escalating the burdens on certain categories of workers—though not cashiers. Product labeling is the most striking example. In France, stockers simply mark prices not on the products themselves but on the shelves; digital posting is spreading and allows tens of thousands of price changes daily with negligible effort. In the United States, with some state exceptions, consumer information rules mandate the systematic (hand) labeling of all individual dry goods and some bulk produce items, generating a significant workload for stockers and contributing to lower measured overall productivity.[19]

More broadly, as seen in chapters 3 and 4, with few barriers to entry, large U.S. retailers face sharp price competition heightened by the aggressive expansion of Wal-Mart and the adoption of its practices by other retailers. Retailers' cost-cutting strategies increase downward pressure on wages. Pressures are particularly strong in regions with weak zoning regulations. In contrast, given barriers to entry in France, profits are simpler to extract. The pretax income of French supermarkets was 3.9 percent of sales in 2005, more than twice that of U.S. supermarkets (1.9 percent for fiscal year 2006–2007).

Indirect Societal Effects on Managerial Practice: Labor Supply

The level of the wage floor and the length of store opening hours both shape retailers' labor preferences. What employers want is only half the story, however. A set of institutions and norms also shape available labor supply. The meeting of labor demand and labor supply—each deeply influenced by institutions, regulations, and managerial strategy—generates differing outcomes in cashier jobs.

The overall rate of part-time employment in retail in the United States grew over time from the 1950s onward, reaching its current level (28 percent in 2014) by the end of the 1970s.[20] Retrospective accounts single out the extension of store hours as a precipitating event. "As hours started expanding . . . you couldn't efficiently staff without part-timers, unless you wanted to have overlapping schedules and redundancies," said the personnel director of a supermarket chain in the late 1980s.[21] As discussed in earlier chapters, in addition to allowing retailers to peg staffing to customer flows using gap filler and time adjuster part-timers, short shifts result in fresher, and thus potentially more productive, workers. U.S. retailers also offer lower wage scales and fringe benefits to part-timers. Management strategies—labor *demand*—thus drove the spread of part-time hours.

In France, in contrast, retailers' labor demand is shaped by the high minimum wage and the shorter store opening hours. Some higher-end supermarket operators signal their conviction that their image requires that their employees earn enough to shop in their stores. Regulations and norms drive retailers to extract higher productivity. Concurrently, like U.S. retailers, they aim to have part-time workers available for added hours as needed, but unlike their U.S. counterparts, they explicitly wish to deter employees from taking a second job. In addition, in their attempts to mirror a desired middle-class clientele, French retail managers seek workers with more polished social skills and reportedly prefer white, native-born workers. In summary, their strategies have led French retailers to design especially demanding jobs and to seek to be especially selective in filling those jobs.

What about the labor supply side? In both countries, the part-time workforce consists overwhelmingly of young workers and women of all ages. As retailers boosted part-time employment, they reached out to women and young people. U.S. labor market and welfare state institutions support the availability of these groups, particularly youth, to a greater extent than French institutions do. U.S. high school students generally have shorter school hours and years than their French counterparts—they are in school for about 799 instructional hours per year—leaving substantial afternoon and summer time available for work.[22] In France, in contrast, the typical fifteen-year-old receives 1,147 hours of instruction time per year.[23] It is also socially normal for a U.S. high school student to work; 35 percent of U.S. sixteen- to nineteen-year-olds were employed in the average month during 2007.[24] The French norm is quite different: only 9 percent of fifteen- to nineteen-year-olds were employed in 2006.[25] People younger than twenty-five, who make up 29 percent of the U.S. retail workforce, account for only 19 percent of retail workers in France.

It remains the norm in both countries that women are chiefly responsible for child care—but again, the institutional context differs dramatically. The United States lacks any national system of child care provision, in contrast with France, where almost half of two-year-olds and nearly all three-year-olds participate in a universal preschool system that extends to age six.[26] U.S. law requires only twelve weeks of *unpaid* maternity leave (and that only in 40 to 50 percent of the workforce, mostly in larger businesses), which is quite different from the minimum of sixteen weeks of maternity leave, paid at the normal salary, required in France. These distinct institutional constellations make for a larger pool of female part-time job-seekers in the United States and a considerably smaller such pool in France. Indeed, in French retail in 2007, more than 61 percent of part-time young workers and 46 percent of part-time women employees would have liked to work longer.[27]

A U.S. retail job is seen as a "good first job," as one manager put it. However, French earnings norms focus on the monthly wage package, in contrast with the United States, where, at least for supplementary earners, the hourly wage is most salient. Given this normative focus, French retailers offering low hourly wages in part-time jobs would be doubly cursed in the labor market, because low wages and short hours compound to a much lower total monthly pay. Instead of a "good first job," cashiering is often seen by the French as a job of last resort for the relevant populations.

Thus, U.S. employers seeking low-wage part-time workers, including a large contingent of short-hour workers, come face to face with students and mothers seeking part-time jobs, many of them willing to accept earnings that will supplement other family income sources. The French story is quite different. There, the net effect is that, as demand meets supply, French retail employers seek more from their employees, but the available French workforce is less disposed to work part-time jobs. Retailers are only able to square these two exigencies by offering an "efficiency wage" designed to attract and retain desired employees and elicit ongoing effort.[28] The alternative, as many managers pointed out, would be unmanageably high turnover, absenteeism, and pursuit of second jobs that would limit the scheduling availability of part-time workers.

Importantly, not all French institutions have the effect that might be expected. French retail unions have won a minimum weekly hour threshold of twenty-six hours. However, the policy is subject to exceptions for students and for those who "voluntarily" choose to work fewer hours. In practice, French field cases and standard statistical sources concur that the great majority of cashiers work fewer than twenty-six hours. Nonetheless, extremely short hours are less common in France than in the United States. Whereas 18 percent of U.S. retail workers usually work less than fifteen hours per week, and 34 percent work less than twenty, in France only 10 percent and 16 percent, respectively, do so.[29]

CONCLUSION

This comparison of supermarket and hypermarket jobs in France and the United States shows some common sectoral features. In retail, regardless of the national model, managerial imperatives include tight control of costs—particularly labor costs—the need for flexible deployment of labor, and the provision of adequate levels of service in the stores.[30] Though some have characterized these features as a "Wal-Mart effect," in fact they long predate Wal-Mart's rise to U.S. and international dominance.[31]

But as we have explained, there are also differences. This combination of similarities and differences reflects distinct national-sectoral models in the two countries. Each national-sectoral model is formed by the interaction of national institutions and sector-specific characteristics (notably the need to staff stores during long and nonstandard working hours), but not in additive fashion. Rather, the specific institutions that matter for each national-sectoral model do so in ways that are conditioned by the particularities of the retail sector. For cashier jobs, the lowest-paid category (other than U.S. baggers, who have no French counterparts), labor regulation such as the minimum wage is quite important. Low-wage jobs are those most likely to be protected by regulations that set a floor to the labor market.[32] And indeed, the higher minimum wage in France plays a significant role in accounting for the pay differential between the two countries. Higher compensation in France, in turn, underpins a faster work pace.

Nevertheless, other aspects of job quality that continue to differ across the two countries are not directly shaped by labor regulation but rather are affected by a cluster of other societal factors that, combined with product market regulations (restrictions on store hours and new store openings), result in different employment practices and outcomes. Most importantly, given retail's reliance on a part-time workforce, reproductive institutions shaping the labor force participation of mothers and youth loom large. These other societal factors have primarily indirect effects on managerial practice, which in turn has repercussions on job characteristics. The iterative effects cascade into differences in pay, productivity, and posture between the two countries.

A cautionary note is that though this chapter has compared

French and U.S. retail jobs as if they were fixed, in fact they are in flux. That flux reflects not just changing managerial strategies but also changing institutions. Today's U.S. retail jobs reflect a historically low minimum wage, declining union density in retail, and the demise of restrictions on store hours.[33] French retailers are currently pushing to liberalize store hours and reduce labor protection, and zoning policies are widely debated.[34] This mutability in institutions, and thus societal effects, points to the need for further historical as well as comparative research.

This chapter's findings resonate with both the literature studying dominance effects on managerial practices and the literature on spheres of influence shaping job characteristics. Like studies in those streams of work, this France-U.S. comparison examines the complex interaction between society, firm, and managerial practice, taking the sector as a mediating influence on national effects. The existence of distinct national-sectoral models points to the interdependent impact of societal and sectoral effects. The relevant societal effects in the case of retail are wide-ranging, embracing labor regulation via laws and collective bargaining, regulation of labor supply via schooling and care arrangements, and regulation of product markets via laws restricting store hours and the opening of new stores, along with a normative overlay in each domain—for example, a French norm that employees should be able to shop at the store where they work, norms about youth labor, and expectations about when one should be able to shop. Arguably, societal effects remain strong because shopping culture and consumption patterns are deeply embedded in social life. Thus, despite the global dominance of a small number of giant retailers, this comparison underlines once more that societal effects are likely to remain strong in the retail sector—and therefore that shifts in policy in the United States (and elsewhere) could improve retail jobs.

7 / The Surprisingly Changeable Wal-Mart Around the World

In one last comparison, we follow the world's largest retailer, Wal-Mart, around the globe to see whether the Blue Giant alters its practices in response to differing institutions—in this case holding the *company* constant as we look across countries. Wal-Mart sells both food and electronics, making it relevant for both our focal retail subsectors.

Popular discussions of Wal-Mart tend to present the giant corporation as both unique and uniform.[1] The widespread popular image is of a retailer that is uniquely big, uniquely unstoppable, and uniquely bad for labor and communities—in fact, bad in ways that are fundamental to its corporate identity, its core strategy, and its sweeping competitive success, and thus little susceptible to change. The academic literature also sometimes tends toward representations of Wal-Mart as monolithic and as a distinctive new model for doing business. Such representations can be found in critical accounts of Wal-Mart, such as Ellen Rosen's portrayal of the corporation as "the new retail colossus" or Nelson Lichtenstein's early description of Wal-Mart as the "template for twenty-first century capitalism," though his more recent work on the subject has been more nuanced.[2] But some laudatory accounts lean the same way, for example, McKinsey's 2001 report that attributes slow growth in retail prices in large part to a "Wal-Mart effect" accounted for by this one company's pricing policies.[3]

Part of the conventional picture is a Wal-Mart that is uniformly

replicating its U.S. model, including low-road employment practices, in country after country. That is, Wal-Mart's sectoral "dominance" effect as the most powerful multinational retailer over-
whelms nation-specific "societal" effects grounded in differing
institutions, deleting the "national" from our national-sectoral
model and spreading a lean, mean U.S. style of retailing around the
world.[4] If accurate, this picture challenges our contention that retail
jobs, and all jobs, are decisively shaped by their varying institutional environments—that national effects remain powerful. If Wal-
Mart's management model is muscular enough to override institutional differences among the twenty-seven countries where it
operates, it would appear to signal a global capitalism in which the
largest corporations are no longer effectively constrained by the
laws, customs, and systems that distinguish states and societies. Is
Wal-Mart indeed that mighty?

It is not. Like other large companies, Wal-Mart certainly puts its
strategic and cultural stamp on its subsidiaries around the world.
But a closer look at some of those twenty-seven countries (as well as
some countries where Wal-Mart formerly had a retail presence) reveals that the retailer adapts and adjusts to its environment, which
on the labor front can mean offering above-average wages and benefits and bargaining with unions. Thus, societal effects continue to
be enormously influential in the face of the multinational's home-
country effects (low wages, resistance to unions). But the Wal-Mart
example also illustrates that these societal effects are refracted in
distinct ways within the retail sector (as compared to auto manufacturing, telecommunications, or other industries) that lead us to
speak of national-sectoral effects. Retail is particularly susceptible to
the national side of national-sectoral effects because of deep national differences in the culture of shopping and consumption, but
it also presents an important case for the sectoral side, since a small
number of giant transnationals increasingly dominate retailing
worldwide.

In this chapter, we first put Wal-Mart in perspective with some
basic facts and comparisons, emphasizing that though Wal-Mart
may be the largest retailer in the world, it accounts for a small slice
of global retail. We then turn to how and why Wal-Mart's compensation levels and labor relations vary once our gaze extends outside
the United States. Next, we briefly point out that a global scan shows

variation in some other Wal-Mart characteristics that are often presumed to be fixed, and that Wal-Mart's changing corporate policies within the United States also reveal sensitivity to institutional pressures. We close by raising the question of whether *anything* about the Wal-Mart model has proven immutable. Throughout this series of global comparisons, we particularly draw on the case of Mexico, Wal-Mart's other great success story outside the United States and the other case we have studied most thoroughly.

PUTTING WAL-MART IN ITS PLACE

To start with, consider Wal-Mart's place in the world of global retail. Wal-Mart is indeed the world's largest retailer by employment and sales. But it is far from the most *global* retailer. Among the world's top six grocers, it sits in the middle of the pack in the number of countries where it has stores, and at the low end in percentage of sales coming from outside its home base (see table 7.1). There are two ways of framing this comparison: on the one hand, grocers from smaller countries (such as the countries of Europe) sell more outside their base; on the other hand, Wal-Mart is the biggest retailer in the world in large part because it dominates the biggest market in the world, the United States. The contrast is even more striking when looking at specialty stores, such as the fast-growing clothing chains H&M and Inditex (the company responsible for Zara, among other brands) and the home furnishings titan Ikea. The vast majority of sales for these companies come from far-flung networks of stores outside their birthplaces. Even Toys "R" Us, which shares Wal-Mart's U.S. base, is a far more globalized company.

U.S. observers' perspective on Wal-Mart's global heft is crucially influenced by its dominant position in the United States itself. Wal-Mart accounts for a stunning one-fifth of all the country's retail sales. Moreover, just to the south is Mexico, where Wal-Mart dominates the market more than in any other country, with nearly half of total retail sales. But Wal-Mart does not enjoy the same extreme market supremacy in other countries where it operates. Just to the north, in Canada, Wal-Mart accounts for 6 percent of food sales. In China, Wal-Mart sales are less than 1 percent of the total.[5] Although Wal-Mart is becoming increasingly global, it is far more entrenched in the United States, Mexico, and Central America than in the rest of the world.

Table 7.1 / International Operations of Wal-Mart and Selected Global Competitors, 2014

Company	Number of Stores, January 2014	Number of Countries Where Present, January 2014	Percentage of Sales Outside Home Base, Most Recent Year Available
Wal-Mart	More than 11,000	27	29%
Other grocery chains			
Carrefour (France)	10,102	34	54
Metro (Germany)	More than 2,200	32	60
Tesco (United Kingdom)	6,784	12	32
Ahold (Netherlands)	3,074	7	66
Aeon (Japan)	16,375	21	9
Other nongrocery chains			
Inditex (Zara, Spain)	6,249	86	79
H&M (Sweden)	About 3,000	54 (12 through franchises)	94
IKEA (Sweden)	345	42	95[a]
Toys "R" Us (United States)	1,764 (1,584 directly owned)	35	50[a]

Sources: Wal-Mart 2013, n.d. ("Company Facts"); Carrefour Group, n.d.; Metro Group website, available at: http://www.metrogroup.de/internet/site/metrogroup/node/9280/Len/index.html (accessed July 2017); Tesco PLC 2013; Ahold 2013; Ahold website, available at: https://www.aholddelhaize.com/en/about-us/ (accessed July 2017); Aeon, n.d.; Inditex Group 2013, n.d.; H&M 2013, 2014; H&M, store location list, available at: http://www.hm.com/entrance.ahtml?orguri (accessed July 2017); IKEA 2013; Inter IKEA Systems B.V., n.d.; Toys "R" Us, n.d.
[a]Percentage of stores (sales by country not available).

WAL-MART COMPENSATION IN PERSPECTIVE

Wal-Mart comes in for severe criticism for its low compensation levels in the United States. The chain's entry into a county lowers average retail wages in that county by 0.5 to 0.9 percent, with a larger 1.5 percent hit for grocery employees in particular.[6] But Wal-Mart does not occupy the same position in the labor market in other countries, as a close look at its Mexican subsidiary illuminates.

Wal-Mart Mexico is not a low-wage employer. One window on this (anticipating the next section on relations with unions) is Wal-Mart's union contracts. Comparing contractual levels of pay, which establish a lower bound for wages for Wal-Mart and the other Big Four supermarket chains for the same jobs in the same cities (Mexico City, Guadalajara, and León, Mexico's fifth-largest city), we found that Wal-Mex offered the same pay or slightly more (table 7.2).[7]

Table 7.2 / Contractual Biweekly Salary at Wal-Mart (in Pesos) Compared with Salaries Offered by Other Supermarket Chains, Selected Cities, 2004

	Wal-Mart (León, Guadalajara)	Comercial Mexicana (Léon)	Comercial Mexicana (Guadalajara)	Soriana (León)[a]	Gigante (Guadalajara)[a]
Security assistant	804	—	—	907	900
Salesperson, general merchandise	904	655	855	855	900

Source: Collective bargaining contracts from local labor relations commissions (juntas locales de conciliación y arbitraje), reviewed by Chris Tilly in 2004.
Notes: Employees work ninety-six hours per two weeks, so one can approximate the hourly amount by dividing by 100. The 2004 exchange rate was 11.3 pesos per U.S. dollar.
[a]Values imputed from 2002 pay levels—at four months of seniority at Soriana and six months at Gigante—by applying the percentage increase implemented by Comercial Mexicana in León. (The other chains do not set minimum pay levels by seniority.)

Table 7.2 establishes that Wal-Mex's pay is similar to that at other large supermarket chains. A second window is the actual pay levels of comparable employees in Wal-Mart and a wide variety of retail enterprises, including significantly smaller ones, in Morelia, the capital of the populous state of Michoacán (table 7.3). Again, Wal-Mex offered comparable or higher pay. The only exception is a market stand proprietress who employed a teenage assistant at a higher rate of pay than Wal-Mart. None of these salaries were handsome by Mexican standards: they far exceeded Mexico's ultra-low minimum wage, which amounted to about 500 pesos biweekly, but fell substantially short of the economy-wide average of 1,920 pesos. This is the pattern that we have flagged in the United States and Europe in the previous comparative chapters: retail jobs *as a whole* offer lower pay than other sectors.

In a number of other countries as well, Wal-Mart pays the going retail wage or better. China researchers have noted that "the wage, albeit low by Western standards, is usually slightly higher than the average paid by domestic retailers."[8] While Wal-Mart was in Germany, the company paid 3 percent above the collectively bargained level—presumably in part to deflect criticism for refusing to apply the sectorwide collective bargaining agreement.[9] In Argentina as well, Wal-Mart pays more than most of its competitors—nearly 40 percent more than one major competitor, according to a survey.[10] Wal-Mart operates in one of the lowest-wage sectors around the

Table 7.3 / Actual Biweekly Salary at Wal-Mart (in Pesos) Compared with Salaries Offered by Various Retailers in the City of Morelia, 2004

Jobs and Employer	Biweekly Salary	Comments
Cashier, Wal-Mart (Bodega Aurrera)	1,350	Bodega Aurrera is one of Wal-Mex's store types.
Cashier and clothing sales, department store chain	1,000–1,250	Includes bonus; salary for furniture sales is 1,450 pesos.
Cashier, gourmet store chain	1,200	
Assistant and cashier/ manager, corner store	1,166–1,348	Because hours differ from a forty-eight-hour week, we have calculated the ninety-six-hour equivalent.
Assistant, weekly street market produce stand	1,600	Pay is 100 pesos per six hours; we have calculated the ninety-six-hour equivalent.

Source: Interviews by authors, 2004.

world, but Wal-Mart as a low-wage employer *among retailers* appears to be a less than universal phenomenon.

In the United States, Wal-Mart also reduces labor costs by offering fewer benefits than many comparable retailers.[11] But as table 7.4 shows, in terms of benefits offered, Wal-Mex is in the mainstream of Mexican supermarkets. For the most part, all the major retailers offer only the fringe benefits required by Mexican law (although the law only requires a year-end bonus of two weeks' pay, and the retailers award twice that amount). The only outlier is Gigante, which offered more generous vacation benefits and a retirement plan to senior employees. But since retail is a high-turnover trade in Mexico as in the United States (the Mexican retailers' association estimated a turnover rate of 119 percent per year in large supermarkets in 2004), few employees could expect to last long enough to enjoy Gigante's generosity.[12]

How do we explain this variation in Wal-Mart's relative job quality? The underlying pattern is that Wal-Mart tends to offer labor standards above those of other retail counterparts where it is seeking to attract and motivate an above-average workforce because it is aiming at an above-average segment of the market. It tends to offer

Table 7.4 / Benefits Offered by Wal-Mart Compared to Other Mexican Supermarket Chains in Selected Cities, 2004

	Wal-Mart (León, Guadalajara)	Comercial Mexicana (León)	Comercial Mexicana (Guadalajara)	Soriana (León)	Gigante (Guadalajara)
End-of-year bonus (days of pay)	30	30	30	30	30
Paid vacation days after two years	8	8	8	8	10
Vacation pay as a percentage of regular pay	25%	25%	30%	25%, rising to 30% after two years	50%
Retirement plan other than social security	No	No	No	No	Yes

Source: Collective bargaining contracts from local labor relations commissions (juntas locales de conciliación y arbitraje), reviewed by Chris Tilly in 2004. Gigante went out of business in 2007.

standards below those of counterparts in countries where it is aiming at a below-average market segment. In short, the positioning of its job quality also depends on the market in which it is selling—very much in the same way that U.S. retailers selling to different market segments or using different strategies to distinguish their brand also adopt different labor strategies.

As with the varied U.S. company cases, this variation in Wal-Mart's relative job quality is not hard to explain. In Mexico and China, informal retailers (street vendors and the like) supply an important section of the consumer market. Wal-Mart could not reasonably hope to earn profits while underpricing these merchants, who tend to have no buildings and minimal infrastructure (a truck, a table); tend to avoid most enterprise taxes, health regulations, and labor laws; and tend to use unpaid family labor. Furthermore, Wal-Mart's long experience selling to U.S. residents with modest incomes would not translate well into selling to the much poorer people at the modest end of the income range in these countries, which are, after all, much poorer than the United States. To take one example, large stores in outlying areas accessed by car are *not* accessible to the large proportion of Mexican shoppers and the much larger proportion of Chinese shoppers who do not have the use of a car. Instead, Wal-Mart's formula for selling to a lower-end U.S. customer base translates best into selling to middle-class populations or higher in poorer countries. But to sell successfully to these middle-class customers, Wal-Mart must provide attractive, well-maintained stores (read: well-paid stockers), good customer service (read: well-paid cashiers), and workers who are from the middle classes or at least acculturated to interacting with middle-class customers (read: workers who are more expensive than average to attract and retain). On the other hand, in the United States and Canada, where Wal-Mart is aiming lower in the market, its wage and benefit package also aims below those of its major counterparts. Germany is the exception that proves the rule. As we mentioned, Wal-Mart in Germany *did* offer wages above the union scale, but only in an (unsuccessful) attempt to keep the union out.

Importantly, Wal-Mart's low U.S. and Canadian prices are made possible in part by their substandard compensation packages and labor practices, but also in part by their exceptionally well-developed logistical network underpinned by rapid growth. Wal-Mart was able to fairly quickly export this advantage to Mexico by piggybacking on the existing U.S. logistical infrastructure; acquiring the largest Mexican retailer at fire-sale prices in the aftermath of the 1994–1995 "Tequila Crisis," which led to massive devaluation of the peso; and expanding rapidly based on its First World deep pockets.[13] But in China and, indeed, in most other countries Wal-Mart has entered, it has not been able to purchase the leading company; nor (obviously) has it been able to take advantage of contiguity to the United States. These limitations on cost savings through logistical infrastructure, and thus on the ability to lower prices, have created one more incentive to target a middle-class clientele.

Taking this added variable into account complicates the analysis, but allows us to better explain some of the country-specific details. For example, in Mexico, Wal-Mart's logistical advantages plus the fact that the company it acquired, Cifra, already had a luxury banner (Superama) as well as a middle-class one (Aurrera), make Wal-Mex better able to target multiple consumer segments than would be the case in most other countries. In contrast, in Germany Wal-Mart entered without buying a chain and confronted the hard discounters Aldi and Lidl, which had brand loyalty among lower-income consumers, thorough geographic coverage (based in smaller stores), much better established logistical networks than the new entrant, and the sway with suppliers to make it hard for Wal-Mart to establish those logistical networks. So in Germany Wal-Mart tried to enter at the lower end of the market, but found this segment occupied by entrenched low-price sellers—as in Mexico and China—and ended up unable to make a go of it.

It is important to underline that we are *not* arguing that Wal-Mart offers "good" jobs in other countries. Again, retail tends to offer bad jobs in most countries. For example, in 2004, when we gathered detailed wage data on Wal-Mart in Mexico, the average Mexican retail wage was 66 pesos (about $6), little above the minimum wage of 44 pesos a day, which is generally acknowledged by Mexican labor researchers to be grossly inadequate.[14] Likewise, though Wal-Mart's Chinese wages may exceed the average for domestic Chinese retailers, Wal-Mart cuts corners on wages and benefits, skirting Chinese law.[15] Based on multiple country information available, Wal-Mart tends to fall in or near the mainstream of retail compensation practices wherever it goes.

A UNION-FRIENDLY WAL-MART?

Wal-Mart stores have [union-]affiliated personnel. Secondly, the company currently has thirty-one active union delegates. Third, far from not having unions, in our company two unions operate: retail and truck drivers.

—Wal-Mart spokesperson in Argentina[16]

Wal-Mart's energetic and well-documented resistance to unions in the United States has prevented the formation of a union in any part of the company's U.S. empire.[17] The same cannot be said in the rest of the world. Wal-Mart has union contracts in Mexico. In fact, to the extent we can determine, union contracts cover *all* Wal-Mex-owned stores, at least in Mexico City and the three other Mexican states where author Tilly has been able to review union contracts.[18] Wal-Mart also has union members and contracts at least in Argentina, Brazil, Canada, Chile, China, Japan, South Africa, and the United Kingdom, and the retailer had them in Germany before it exited that country.[19]

What's going on here? The legal scholar Kevin Kolben summarizes the pattern:

Wal-Mart is in fact highly responsive to local constraints and institutions that shape its behavior. While Wal-Mart might be the largest corporation in the world and is rapidly becoming more and more international in its scope, its conduct, at least with respect to freedom of association and collective bargaining, is embedded in the local—at least in the countries in which it currently operates.[20]

We would extend this account in a number of ways. First, to explain Wal-Mart's relationships with unions around the world, it is useful to map each nation's labor relations system across two dimensions: whether collective bargaining is required or at least strongly encouraged by key legislation, and whether unions are relatively independent and even adversarial or compliant and focused on cooperation with management (table 7.5). Two of the cells in table 7.5 are relatively unsurprising. In the upper right, countries where unions are independent but not required, including the United States, Wal-Mart has fought unions fiercely, though it has ended up compelled to accept them in every country listed except the United States.[21] In the lower left, countries where the law builds in an expectation of collective bargaining but unions are compliant, Wal-Mart has accepted unions—grudgingly in Argentina and China, but quite readily in Mexico, where a "paper" union typically serves as insurance against organizing by a more assertive worker organization.[22] The other two cells are more ambiguous. There are few if any countries where unions are compliant, not required, but

Table 7.5 / Mapping Labor Relations of Countries Where Wal-Mart Does Business

	Collective Bargaining Required or Expected	Collective Bargaining Not Required
Independent unions	Brazil, Germany	Canada, Chile, Japan, South Africa, United Kingdom, United States
Compliant unions	Argentina, China, Mexico	

Source: Authors' categorization.
Note: In Argentina and Mexico, unions are not compliant in general, but are very much so in the retail sector (Fernández and Benes 2009; Senén and Haidar 2009; Tilly 2014).

nonetheless widespread, so the lower right cell is empty.[23] Perhaps the most interesting category is the one that includes Brazil and Germany: in these countries, unionization is (more or less) required and unions are relatively independent and powerful. Wal-Mart did accept unions in both countries, although to the extent that we can tell, it pushed harder to keep them out in Germany.[24] John Peter Suarez, Wal-Mart senior vice president of international business development at the time, commented on the company's recognition of unions in Argentina, Brazil, and the United Kingdom: "We recognize those rights. In that market, that's what the associates want, and that's the prevailing practice."[25]

Second, besides the institutional environment mapped in table 7.5, an added overlay is whether Wal-Mart acquired a unionized company or not. In Argentina, Brazil, Chile, Mexico, and South Africa, Wal-Mart acquired companies with established relationships with unions and has sought to weaken them—but so far not to break them. In its China and Japan acquisitions, unions' status was relatively tenuous. In these countries, Wal-Mart has made more strenuous (though ultimately unsuccessful) efforts to exclude or marginalize unions, analogous to its approach in the United States.

Third, though Wal-Mart conforms with national institutional regimes around the world and is not dramatically out of step with other retailers, it does resist unions to the extent practical within those regimes. In Canada, for example, Wal-Mart simply shut down a store in Jonquière, Quebec, in 2005 when the workers succeeded in unionizing; Canada's Supreme Court later upheld the move.[26] We are not aware of other Canadian cases of retailers taking such a dramatic step. But Wal-Mart's competitors in Canada have hardly been union-friendly. Unionized Canadian grocery chains aggressively assaulted wages, hours, and working conditions in the 1990s, starting with market leader Loblaws in 1990, and the movement had swept up most union and non-union grocers by the time Wal-Mart entered in 1994.[27] Among Canadian-owned non-union companies, union avoidance strategies are ubiquitous and as well honed as in the United States. Indeed, a recent analysis finds that Canadian managers are *more* hostile toward unions than their U.S. counterparts.[28] Other U.S. retailers have been equally successful in avoiding Canadian unions; Wal-Mart's rival Target entered Canada by acquiring a unionized Canadian company (Zellers) and then successfully (and rather creatively) arguing that it should not be considered a successor company under provincial law and therefore was not obligated to recognize the union.[29] Efforts to unionize Canadian Wal-Marts have continued, and as we write, the United Food and Commercial Workers holds collective bargaining contracts with Wal-Mart Canada.[30] In short, Wal-Mart's practices are not far out of step with those of other companies in Canada, though it certainly has resisted unions more strenuously than most.

The Chinese case is similar, though the institutional setting is different. The All-China Federation of Trade Unions (ACFTU), the only legal union in China, generally pursues "harmonious" relations between management and labor by working closely with management, typically appointing managers to serve as the principal union officers.[31] However, Wal-Mart chose to avoid the ACFTU. In 2004, when the federation pressed Wal-Mart to recognize a union, Wal-Mart replied that recognition was only required when at least a small group of employees requested it, and no such request had been made. After repeated rebuffs, in 2006 the ACFTU undertook an uncharacteristic grassroots employee organizing campaign and employees requested unionization in store after store. Wal-Mart conceded defeat and recognized the union. At that point, since both Wal-Mart and the ACFTU had a shared interest in a nonconfrontational labor-management relationship, the ACFTU demobilized activist workers and leaders and went back to unionism as usual.[32] Chinese Wal-Mart workers have continued to mobilize, most recently forming a new "Wal-Mart China Staff Association" to pressure the official union to represent workers more vigorously.[33]

Even in labor relations systems that do not require union recognition, unions have at times been able to win significant gains for Wal-Mart workers. In the United Kingdom, the body of unionized Wal-Mart workers is growing.[34] In Chile, the sociologist Carolina Bank Muñoz reports, unions are "making strong and steady gains against this giant transnational corporation."[35] And though Argentina's retail union has historically tended to accommodate management, it has recently shown new militancy in putting pressure on Wal-Mart (so it may be migrating upward from the lower-left-hand corner in table 7.5).[36] Even in the union-unfriendly U.S. labor relations system, workers have organized and won concessions from Wal-Mart. The community group ACORN, which was shut down in 2010 after sustained attacks from the political right, built a Wal-Mart Workers Association (WWA) in central Florida that in 2006 claimed "a growing group of 300 current and former Wal-Mart workers in over 40 stores."[37] WWA came to an untimely end, but the model of an active "minority union" that presses Wal-Mart for changes even without union recognition was revived in 2011. In that year, the United Food and Commercial Workers (UFCW) launched OUR Walmart, with strikes in Wal-Marts across the country timed for the fall shopping surge; the organization continues to mount strikes and other actions, though the union slashed funds devoted to OUR Walmart in 2015 and the organization's future is unclear.[38] Wal-Mart publicly denies that the organization has had any impact on its corporate policies, but the multinational did adopt added accommodations for pregnant workers and a more worker-friendly scheduling system in 2014 following OUR Walmart strike demands and petitions on these issues.[39]

In sum, when it comes to labor relations as well as compensation, *societal effects overshadow dominance effects even in the world's dominant retail business.* This does not mean that Wal-Mart is a pushover for unions. As evidence of Wal-Mart's union relations in other countries attests, Wal-Mart has been a tough bargainer, tends to try to deal with unions as little as possible, and pushes hard to reduce labor costs. Where there are relatively more opportunities to avoid unions entirely (as in Canada and the United Kingdom), it does its best to exploit them. But even Wal-Mart does not get to rewrite or completely ignore the rules, and even where it fights unions hardest and most successfully, the company has at times made concessions.

OTHER CHANGEABLE ASPECTS OF THE WAL-MART MODEL

Other features of Wal-Mart in the United States that are often seen as part of the company's DNA are: underpricing of rivals, exceptionally hard squeezing of suppliers, and relentless expansion that can only be slowed via political opposition. But again, closer examination reveals that these features are part of the U.S. Wal-Mart phenotype, not the company's genotype.

In the United States, Wal-Mart is renowned for relentlessly pursuing everyday low prices (EDLP), which replace weekly sales on particular items with (at least in theory) consistently low prices on most items. Again, a look at Mexico is revealing. Wal-Mart introduced EDLP to Mexico in 1999–2000, nearly a decade after entering the country in 1991.[40] EDLP was not a practical mode of competition before then because high inflation made price comparisons difficult at best; Mexico finally tamed inflation in the late 1990s. Does this mean that Wal-Mex now undersells its competitors? In a word, no. The office of Mexico's attorney general for consumers tracks and reports prices on hundreds of items in Mexico's three largest cities, Mexico City, Guadalajara, and Monterrey. As of mid-2008, Wal-Mart held the low price title for 21 percent of items, but the highest price for 10 percent—hardly a decisive low-price advantage.[41] Indeed, according to *DSN Retailing Today*, "For the average Mexican consumer a trip to a Wal-Mart supercenter is a high-end experience."[42]

The Blue Giant fails to claim the low-price crown in other countries as well. Surveys of consumers in Shenzhen, China, depict a Wal-Mart clearly targeting middle-class Chinese.[43] When comparing Wal-Mart with its French rival Carrefour, which aims for a similar consumer niche, only 66 percent of Chinese consumers surveyed saw Wal-Mart as offering lower prices.[44]

For countries like Mexico and China where less formal retailers can underprice Wal-Mart, these findings are consistent with the same strategy of targeting a middle-class consumer stratum, as we noted with regard to compensation. But even in high-wage Germany, Wal-Mart, which entered in 1999, discovered that the domestic discounters Aldi and Lidl had beaten it to the punch. "The week Wal-Mart opened in Berlin," commented the geographer Susan Christopherson, "the Aldi across the street from the new superstore was offering for only thirty-four cents the same bread that Wal-Mart was selling for $1.13."[45] It is not surprising, therefore, that the "general consensus of the German consumers today [in 2006] is that Wal-Mart prices are neither necessarily nor significantly cheaper than those of their competitors." In the face of competition from German discounters, Wal-Mart even deviated from its EDLP gospel and advertised weekly specials to meet consumer expectations.[46]

Part of the lore of Wal-Mart are the cautionary tales of Vlasic Pickles and Rubbermaid, which became major Wal-Mart suppliers only to be driven into bankruptcy by Wal-Mart's constantly escalat-

ing demands for price cuts and just-in-time inventory, compelling
vendors to absorb the risks of demand fluctuations.[47] And not only
does Wal-Mart source from China, but it pits Chinese suppliers
against each other in what the *Wall Street Journal* describes as a
"scramble" to cut costs further.[48]

What do reports from other countries add? A Mexican supplier,
based on his experience of selling to all four major Mexican supermarket chains then operating, insisted that Soriana was squeezing
vendors hardest "right now" (in mid-2004). Around the same time,
a business consultant offered the opinion that Gigante was the most
aggressive in demanding discounts. The sociologists Rita Schwentesius and Angel Gómez's account of a cooperative of small agricultural producers that came to ruin in much the same way as Vlasic
and Rubbermaid demonstrates the difficulty of selling to *all* Mexican supermarket chains, not just Wal-Mart.[49] Similarly in China, a
number of foreign chains charge fees to Chinese suppliers; in fact,
"Carrefour was the most notorious," and Wal-Mart was slow to
adopt these practices.[50] In Germany, "domestic competitors, such as
Aldi and Lidl, [had] already negotiated rock-bottom prices from
suppliers."[51]

Thus, in the case of relations with suppliers, what we see is
"Walmartization without Wal-Mart," in the historian Nelson Lichtenstein's elegant phrase.[52] A substantial group of retailers has adopted pressure tactics toward suppliers. In part because Wal-Mart is
a recent entrant and in some countries (China and, while it was operating there, Germany) a smaller company than competitors, it
may not be the first or most relentless in squeezing vendors.

Wal-Mart has grown rapidly in the United States, and American
observers often assume that inexorable expansion around the world
can only be halted by a political counteroffensive. Indeed, Wal-
Mart's U.S. spread has been limited by a dozen years of "site fights"
that have greatly slowed the company's efforts to move into larger
cities.[53] But globally, economic challenges have posed obstacles to
Wal-Mart that are at least as great as the political resistance. Though
the Blue Giant has added countries of operation over time, it has
also subtracted them. It left Indonesia and Hong Kong (then still
independent of China) in the mid-1990s, pulled out of South Korea
in 2006, and the same year announced its decision to depart from
Germany—all of these departures due to inability to compete effec-

tively.[54] And despite discussing the possibility of opening in Russia as early as 2002, Wal-Mart has not yet succeeded in doing so.[55] Most recently, in 2013, Wal-Mart ended its India joint venture—in this case, because of political problems. Besides massive opposition in India to foreign ownership of retail stores, Wal-Mart was faced with Indian and U.S. government investigations of violations of foreign investment laws and corruption. (Wal-Mart does continue to operate the small number of wholesale outlets that were launched by the joint venture.)[56] Moreover, in most countries where it operates, and unlike in the United States and Mexico, Wal-Mart falls in the second tier of retailers; in some—Argentina, Brazil, China, Japan, the United Kingdom—the company continues to struggle to establish market share.[57] Certainly Wal-Mart is not alone in walking away from other countries: number-two global retailer Carrefour has left a series of countries. In short, Wal-Mart is in this, as in many other ways, a fairly typical global retailer.

If institutional differences around the world have an impact on how Wal-Mart behaves, we would also expect that the company would alter its behavior in the United States in response to heightened institutional pressure here. And in fact, it has. We have described how Wal-Mart has made changes in response to pressure from minority unions. But its responses to broad public disapproval have been even more sweeping. As public criticism of the company reached a crescendo in the mid-2000s, Wal-Mart announced an initiative that involved reaching agreements with major environmental groups, reducing packaging and waste, conserving energy, and shifting in part to more sustainably generated energy—though some environmentalists continue to criticize the changes as superficial.[58] Responding to criticism of inadequate employee benefits, in 2006 Wal-Mart altered its health plan to cover more employees, though it did so by shifting to a low-premium, high-deductible plan as it simultaneously increased its percentage of part-timers (who qualified for a more limited health plan); it scaled back health benefits a few years later, in 2011, as the post-2008 economic slump persisted.[59] Wal-Mart even joined unions in calling for a higher minimum wage in 2005 and a national health plan in 2007.[60] Wal-Mart has recently accompanied other retailers in pledging to improve base wages and schedule predictability. It won headlines for reaching an agreement with the Coalition of Imokalee Workers to pay a small premium to tomato suppliers that will be passed along to Florida tomato workers, as several restaurant chains have done.[61] Another article headlined "Wal-Mart Toughens Supplier Policies" refers to Wal-Mart's adoption of a "zero-tolerance policy" for violations of its global sourcing standards following a fire that killed 112 at a Bangladesh supplier to Wal-Mart—though it chose not to sign on to the more rigorous Accord in Fire and Building Safety agreed to by most global retailers following the even more deadly collapse of the Rana Plaza building that killed more than 1,100 a few months later.[62] None of this makes Wal-Mart a model employer or purchaser, but its responses to these institutional pressures signal that the massive corporation does respond to pressure in a variety of dimensions.

CHAMELEON OR VILLAIN? WAL-MART AND ITS CRITICS

If Wal-Mart generally conforms with local institutional norms around the world, we might expect criticism of the corporation to be muted, or at least not to be more pronounced than criticism of other global retailers. But in fact, Wal-Mart has come in for special criticism from labor advocates and others in Argentina, Canada, Chile, China, India, Mexico, South Africa, and the United Kingdom, in addition to the United States.[63] Why is this?

The critics do appear to be correct that Wal-Mart engages in widespread labor and human rights abuses in a number of countries, including Mexico, Canada, China, and Chile—along with the United States—as well as, at a minimum, strong antilabor practices in the United Kingdom. (So far, evidence is thin for the other countries where Wal-Mart operates.) But as we have documented, Wal-Mart's labor practices in these countries and others (Brazil and Germany when it operated there) appear to be fairly mainstream. Our own Mexican fieldwork and union contract analysis thoroughly document that on the labor front, Wal-Mart is quite unexceptional in its practices among large grocery chains in that country. So standard Wal-Mart critiques tell an important part of the story, but leave out another important set of facts. We can point to several reasons for this.

First, while Wal-Mart falls in the mainstream, it sits toward the anti-union end of the spectrum within the mainstream. But it does not uniformly occupy the lower end of the spectrum when it comes to compensation and labor standards, which generally are an important part of the critique.

A second rationale for the proliferation of Wal-Mart exposés is that Wal-Mart pioneered practices that have been broadly adopted by other large-scale retailers, leading to widespread "Walmartization without Wal-Mart"—a dominant firm effect. What qualifies as Walmartization? Three features of Wal-Mart do not vary across the world and have not varied over time, and all three are parts of its business strategy, not its labor strategy. First, and perhaps most important, Wal-Mart has developed highly automated logistical systems based on advanced information and communications technology to get products from supplier to store exactly when needed. Second, Wal-Mart sells based on a discounting strategy: it cuts consumer margins (markups on the wholesale price of goods) and makes profits on quantity rather than consumer or front-end margin. Finally, Wal-Mart *does* boost profits via a different margin: the "back-end margin," that is, price reductions from suppliers based on the huge quantities purchased, rather than adding large markups to consumer prices.[64]

Among these elements of "Walmartization," Wal-Mart was indeed a pioneer in linking point-of-sale data collection with a vast, highly coordinated logistical system, an infrastructure that all large retailers have emulated to one degree or another. But other practices sometimes attributed to Wal-Mart were well established long before Wal-Mart became large and influential. Wal-Mart certainly did not invent discounting: Sears and later A&P perfected the practice long before Sam Walton opened his first store, and European "hard discounters" such as Germany's Aldi and Lidl—for which the nearest U.S. equivalent is dollar stores—have discounted far more aggressively than Wal-Mart.[65] Squeezing suppliers was perfected by the Big Three automakers, and the strategy had rippled broadly through manufacturing by the 1980s. We are not aware of evidence that Wal-Mart took it to new levels or introduced it to retail. Most importantly, Wal-Mart's union avoidance techniques are adopted wholesale from a playbook with roots in the "welfare capitalism" of many large companies in the 1920s, which was later honed by a national network of management law firms and consultants in the 1970s.[66]

Third, it can be argued that comparing Wal-Mart with its major local competitors is not the only legitimate framing of Wal-Mart's labor practices. An extensive literature argues that foreign direct investment by multinationals is likely to *raise* labor standards in the countries of the global South—because the multinationals will seek a workforce above average in skill and stability, because they will press host governments for a stronger rule of law in order to reduce risk to their investments, or because they will transfer more enlightened labor practices from their home country to the host country.[67] Therefore, demonstrating that Wal-Mart's global labor practices are *no better* than typical home-country retailers offers a useful corrective to the generalization that multinational investments will lead to higher labor standards. In addition, in multinationals' home countries, including the United States, there is a powerful normative proposition that multinationals *should* respect human and labor rights wherever they operate, as even a cursory examination of the website of United Students Against Sweatshops or a variety of other antisweatshop nongovernmental organizations (NGOs) and advocacy organizations reveals. The power of this norm to fuel successful labor advocacy campaigns has been argued in a growing body of research.[68]

Fourth (and linked to the "higher standard" argument), for reform campaigns directed at business practice, it makes sense to target a single corporate offender to make the issue easier to understand and demands more winnable. This typically means painting that one offender as a particular villain—an approach that, for example, the United Farm Workers perfected in their boycott campaigns.[69] In the 2000s, that is precisely what the UFCW did with its "Wake Up Wal-Mart" campaign, and the Service Employees International Union (SEIU) did the same with "Wal-Mart Watch." Their two websites are no longer active, but the current "Making Change at Wal-Mart" and "OUR Wal-Mart" campaigns are similar. However, taking a focus on a singular villain to a global level requires appreciating local conditions around the world. Failure to do so can lead to some peculiar global dynamics. For instance, at a 2005 Buenos Aires convening of retail unions from across the Americas attended by author Tilly, the agenda of the conveners (UNI Global Union, a global federation of unions in services, including retail) was clearly to mobilize Latin Americans against Wal-Mart. A representative of the United Food and Commercial Workers, whose members are retail workers in the United States and Canada, spoke at length about Wal-Mart's antilabor practices in those countries and around the world. But the Latin American union officials did not seem completely convinced by the catalog of Wal-Mart's behavior. As one somewhat puzzled Chilean unionist put it, "The practices you're describing sound just like the practices of companies in our country" (not including Wal-Mart, which only entered Chile subsequently in 2009). The campaign to build a common front against Wal-Mart across the Americas ran into a similar problem in Brazil, as an observer noted:

> In Brazil, however, the American [anti-Wal-Mart] activists face a major obstacle: the lack of criticism of Wal-Mart. "We have a good relationship with Sonae [a company acquired by Wal-Mart]," admitted [São Paulo retail union president] Patah. Wal-Mart in Brazil adopts the same labor practices as its [Brazilian] counterparts.[70]

Even UNI Global Union's own 2005 report on Wal-Mart around the world acknowledged Wal-Mart's generally good relations with Brazilian unions and compliance with the country's labor regulations.[71] At the Buenos Aires meeting, after some sputtering, the discussion shifted to why it could be productive to particularly target Wal-Mart—because it is the largest of a handful of global retailers expanding rapidly around the world, and because a singular target makes a campaign more intelligible—even if Wal-Mart does *not* have uniquely harsh antilabor ways. In the years since, Latin American retail unions' alertness to Wal-Mart's corporate practices in a broader global context has led, among other things, to vigorous anti-Wal-Mart protests in Argentina, Brazil, and Chile.[72]

Finally, we would suggest that both the high global profile of U.S. scholarship and resentment of the United States as the global hegemon also fuel the volume of criticism directed at Wal-Mart. U.S. researchers tend to dominate global scholarly discussions, and unsurprisingly, the biggest-in-its-industry, rapidly expanding, and now globalizing Wal-Mart looks to U.S. researchers like the main story about global retail. Resentment of U.S. economic and geopolitical hegemony, on the other hand, can make it appealing for observers in other countries to point to U.S.-based global corporations as the leading threats to labor rights and economic justice around the world. This alignment creates a feedback loop between criticisms of Wal-Mart that originate in the United States and those originating elsewhere.

Critics of Wal-Mart's practices in its U.S. home market *also* tend to overstate the case spotlighting Wal-Mart. First of all, while it pays well above the minimum wage in some parts of the country (helping account for the Wal-Mart CEO's call for support of a higher minimum wage in 2005), many smaller retailers pay less and do not even offer the benefits in Wal-Mart's limited package.[73] Of course, it is reasonable to expect corporate giants to adhere to higher standards than smaller businesses, but even in the arena of retail's titans, Wal-Mart is not as distinctive as is commonly presumed. Consider Target, Whole Foods, and Trader Joe's, three Wal-Mart rivals that generally enjoy much more positive public images. A quick scan of the "Target Sucks" website populated by disgruntled workers or a review of Target's hard-hitting approach to defeating a 2011 unionization drive in New Jersey reveal the kind of policies and actions for which Wal-Mart is frequently excoriated.[74] The same is true for Whole Foods, where management has struck hard against attempts to unionize and settled a lawsuit over overtime premium violations.[75] And the cheery employee mien that is part of the Trader Joe's "brand" turns out to be a scripted act.[76] Even at Costco, the poster child for employee-friendly retailing, union gains only go so far. According to a union source, the company has concertedly, and so far successfully, opposed the spread of unionism beyond the stores that were unionized at the time they were acquired, and only one Costco worker in eight was in a unionized store as of 2005.[77]

Arguably, the strategic targeting argument has particular force in the United States, since Wal-Mart is the largest retailer, the one that has expanded most aggressively over the past thirty years, and the one that, given its scale and geographic reach within the country, poses the greatest competitive threat to unions' foothold in urban grocery stores. We find that argument less compelling on a global scale, but there are certainly legitimate reasons to spotlight Wal-Mart's practices, notably Wal-Mart's degree of antilabor extremism in some settings and its tendency to match rather than raise standards abroad. However, to address the debate over the relative weights of corporate dominance effects (Wal-Mart as a global vector of U.S. low-road retailing around the globe) and societal effects (national institutions as determinants of feasible corporate strategy and of job quality), we must look more closely at Wal-Mart's practices around the world. This chapter's closer look makes it clear that societal effects are alive and well—consistent with other findings throughout this volume. Wal-Mart's treatment of labor is not the same all over the world—and is not likely to become so soon.

8 / Conclusion

We have now completed our tour of retail jobs around the world, starting in the United States and finishing up with the variegated global footprint of Wal-Mart as an employer. We launched this voyage to challenge what we call the "myth of inevitability": the notion that retail jobs are constrained to be bad—and worsening—jobs, as they mostly are in the United States, by the fundamental economic realities of the sector. We have focused on the retail sector, a large and in many ways archetypal low-wage employer in the United States, as a window into low-quality service jobs in general. We chose to examine jobs in grocery and consumer electronics stores, which represent "old" and "new" retail, capture the breadth of job arrangements, and present striking gender contrasts in employment.

To mount our theoretical and evidentiary challenge, we deployed comparisons of retail jobs *within* countries (chiefly the United States) and *across* countries (including five European counterparts and Mexico).[1] We aimed to parse out economic imperatives from the effects of distinct national institutions and social norms (what we and others call societal or national effects) and from the impacts of discretionary managerial decisions and strategies at varying levels from the corporate headquarters to the sales floor. The evidence we have amassed makes a strong case that, because of the significant impact of institutions ranging from labor relations systems to gender norms, little about the quality of retail jobs is inevitable. This, in turn, points to promising possibilities for economic change in the United States (as well as elsewhere) that would upgrade jobs in retail and other "bad job" service sectors, and we discuss these possibilities in the last section of this concluding chapter. But before turning to those positive prospects, we summarize our argument in more detail and briefly sketch new developments in U.S. retail since we completed our fieldwork.

WHAT WE HAVE LEARNED

Investigating two exemplary sectors—food retail, emblematic of "old" retail and the omnipresent face of the industry, and consumer electronics, dominated by big-box formats—we asked two questions about what makes retail jobs better or worse:

• What national institutional settings make a difference in job quality?

• What room for maneuver do retailers have, within a country, to manage for better jobs? Under what circumstances do managers make "better job" choices?

To answer these questions we drew both on detailed investigation of U.S. retail job quality and on cross-national comparisons. In U.S. field studies, we explored the factors of variation in retail job quality within the country and within given product markets. We emphasized the "left side" of our framework for the determination of job quality laid out at the beginning of chapter 3, which focuses on the interconnections among economic forces (mainly competitive pressures), management's product and labor strategies, and job outcomes (see figure 3.1). How much leeway is there for variation in retailers' labor strategies, and what are the implications for job quality? What is the relationship between following a high-road product market strategy, and following a similarly high-road labor strategy? We found that there is *some* room for variation due to distinct managerial orientation (selection of market segment but also investment in the workforce), ownership (privately held, nonleveraged firms have more managerial autonomy), and within-country regional differences in market regulation, this last instance implicating the institutional context. A high-road market orientation seems necessary, but not sufficient, for improving jobs.

We then studied sources of variation across five Western European countries and the United States, all sharing a similar stage of economic and industrial development and similar modern retail formats. Thus, we stressed the role of institutions, broadly defined to include regulations in employment and reproduction spheres as well as social norms (shopping culture, gender roles). In these comparisons, we emphasized the "right side" of figure 3.1's analytical framework, underscoring the institutional influences on management strategies, workforce options, and resulting effects on job quality. The point of entry into these comparisons is the notion of a national-sectoral model for retail that incorporates country effects on employment *as they are mediated* by retail's distinctive role as a leader in using exit options from national (institutional) regulatory settings. We drew upon findings from a multinational study that involved country-level retail studies by others.[2] We find that several national institutions do have direct effects as well as indirect effects that bear upon managerial decisions and have implications for workers. These cross-national differences in job outcomes occur *even within* a retail industry that in all of these countries benefits from numerous exit options from the regulatory framework for employment. In the United States, price- and cost-cutting pressures have almost automatically translated into a squeeze on hourly wages and total labor hour budgets, which have become the primary focus of store managers. These pressures, in turn, have generated patterns of thin staffing, hours rationing, and, as a result, declining job quality and inordinate pressure on managers as well as threats to service quality. In five European countries, similar pressures have played out differently, with less dire outcomes for job quality.

Given that we and others found that institutional differences matter for job quality, we then traced exactly how their effects play out by looking at two contrasting cases: French and U.S. supermarket cashier jobs, a position through which women and young workers enter retail. We delved into webs of national institutional effects. Here we conclude that, indeed, the multidirectional interactions among product market rules (zoning, opening hours), labor regulation (minimum wage), and reproductive sphere policies (child care, family leave, school schedules), combined with social norms ("workers should be able to afford prices in the stores where they work") and shopping patterns, lead to very different jobs. U.S. cashiers are in low-pay, low-productivity (as measured by checkout speeds), and nearly universally part-time jobs with high turnover. French supermarket cashier jobs are relatively high-pay, higher-productivity, and mostly full-time, with lower turnover.

Modern retail also has migrated massively to lower-income countries, including settings where a principal or at least significant form is informal retail—smaller operations that often are not registered as businesses. Mexico offers such an example, discussed briefly in chapter 5 and at length in online chapter A1 (http://www.russell sage.org/publications/where-bad-jobs-are-better). Mexico's location adjacent to the United States, the dominant role of Wal-Mart in retail sales in both countries, and the massive migration and investment flows across the border all suggest that we might expect very similar retail jobs in the two settings. But once again, this is not the case, and once again, key explanations lie in institutional divergences.

Women workers in retail share similar fates, relative to men, throughout this cross-country exploration. Social norms deem them to have an "innate" ability to relate to people and therefore to be good at customer service. Norms also facilitate employers taking this ability for granted and therefore not compensating it when it is manifest. Moreover, social norms compel women to respond to the social and institutional context by interacting with the job market in limited ways (part-time) and sometimes episodic ways (built around care responsibilities). These patterns enable women's confinement to jobs that, for the most part and across countries, lie below the regional director level—at least in the two subsectors in which extensive fieldwork was conducted, though we would *not* expect a rosier diagnosis in other subsectors.

With all these comparative patterns in mind, we then took a deep dive into the cross-national practices of the prime mover of retail markets, Wal-Mart, in its multiple incarnations in twenty-seven countries. Again, even this behemoth and setter of retail trends behaves differently, in terms of both choice of market segments and labor strategies, across countries. Outside the United States, Wal-Mart is neither uniformly a low-price seller nor uniformly a low-wage retailer, and in many countries it plays ball with labor unions, contrary to its zero-tolerance stance toward U.S. unions. Wal-Mart does export some core strategic elements around the world, showcasing the vigor of its "dominance" effects. But its behavior is also constrained and shaped by national laws, labor relations systems, and norms, as well as by economic differences such as the teeming informal competitors in Mexico or China. In short, Wal-Mart is not the exception to the influence of societal effects around the world but rather demonstrates that influence in one country after another.

In the remainder of this concluding chapter, we examine "what's new"—the recent competitive and public policy trends in retail (in the two subsectors and beyond)—and also "what's next"—the likely future developments in retail job quality. We also discuss possible strategies for generating better job outcomes.

WHAT'S NEW: RECENT CHANGES IN RETAIL AND ITS CONTEXT

Trends in the U.S. retail sector over the last several decades have had a certain depressing sameness when it comes to job outcomes: jobs started out "bad," for the most part, and have gotten worse. But the mighty forces of American consumerism and corporate strategy aimed at harnessing it never stand still, and neither does retail. In the relatively small number of years since we completed our field research, retail has continued to mutate, in the United States and elsewhere. New business models have advanced and old ones have struggled, and in reviewing what is new, we devote the lion's share of the update to these shifting competitive processes. Policymakers and grassroots organizers have altered the institutional environments in which retailers—and low-wage service businesses in general—employ their workers. In this section, we review significant changes in retail's competitive environment and the pressures and constraints that retail chains face as employers, largely limiting our attention to the United States. We caution at the outset that those expecting us to herald the end of store-based retail will be disappointed. We are convinced that, despite the dramatic inroads of online sales, store-based retail will remain widespread for the foreseeable future, for reasons we explore in the following section, "What's Next."

National and global market consolidation

Consolidation and the Role of Private Equity Investment   Over several decades, food retail has consolidated from independents to chains, to regional chains, to multiregional and national chains. Wal-Mart is making the most serious bid for the national market, though Kroger, Costco, Safeway, and Target are all pushing in the same direction. In consumer electronics, a more recent form of retail, national chains quickly achieved domination and absorbed independent consumer electronics retailers or drove them out.

Consolidation has continued in the years since we completed fieldwork, driven by the desire to head off market threats from Wal-Mart's expansion into groceries as well as from discounters (in both food and consumer electronics) and membership warehouse formulas. Relatedly, the industry has been reshaped by private equity investment, which figures in a spate of supermarket and general merchandise chain mergers and acquisitions in the past decade in particular. A peculiarity of retail that appeals to private equity investors is that store chains own real estate (stores and warehouses): the equity funds can strip and sell off this real estate to generate return for investors, lease back the buildings to the retail operation, and later sell the corporation, yielding still more gains for investors (while often leaving the retailer saddled with additional debt).[3] In many cases, the real estate alone is sufficient to make a chain attractive.

Following purchase by an equity investor fund or consolidation, chains are divested of lesser-performing stores and jobs in remaining stores often are cut. The push to yield high returns to equity investors and the accompanying debt service usually squeeze stores' finances, compounding existing pressures on labor costs and, some research finds, depressing inventory availability, thus affecting the goods on offer.[4] In the case of consolidations, the goal is both to expand one's market presence and to boost economies of scale and scope. To avoid having stores from formerly separate chains "cannibalize" each other's market, the newly merged company thins out stores located near each other.

In food retail, the most visible recent example of these developments is the $9.6 billion 2014 buyout by Cerberus Capital Management that merged Safeway supermarkets with New Albertsons Inc. (The latter combined companies that Cerberus purchased in 2006 from SuperValu.) Safeway itself had had a spell of private equity ownership in 1986 that came with significant job cuts.[5] The attractiveness to investors of the merged companies' retail real estate can be seen in the blend of ownership, which included real estate investment firms, trusts, and money managers along with equity fund and hedge fund investors.[6]

The consumer electronics subsector, for its part, has witnessed continued erosion of profit margins, rapid encroachment of online retailers (initially Dell for computers, later Amazon), and a wave of bankruptcies or restructurings. Falling margins create inordinate pressure on full-line big-box electronics stores. An industry observer noted in 2012: "Today, retailers have to sell almost twice as many TVs as five years ago to achieve an equivalent amount of revenue— and even more than that to match past profit levels. The average price of a TV has fallen 40 percent since 2007 even as screen sizes have increased, while gross profit margins have tightened from about 30 percent on upper end models to the low teens."[7]

Consumer electronics bankruptcies along with continued acquisitions have accelerated consolidation in consumer electronics. The closing of Circuit City left Minneapolis-based Best Buy as the main bricks-and-mortar consumer electronics chain left standing. Similarly, Office Depot's absorption of OfficeMax thinned the ranks of chains in the office supply–cum–electronics category, and the proposed merger of Office Depot with Staples, pending as we write, would leave only one major player in this subsector. The serial bankruptcies and restructurings of Radio Shack Corporation ushered in a different kind of store with a much narrower range of product offerings and eventually ended in a final bankruptcy and liquidation in 2017. Bankruptcies have not necessarily helped alleviate competitive pressures because of the concurrent growth of online retailing (addressed later in this chapter); the liquidation of Circuit City in 2009 was expected to relieve pressure on surviving electronics retailers, but Amazon and Apple gobbled up much of the company's former market share.[8]

Global Consolidation   Global consolidation of retail has also advanced over the last decade, but at a slower and more uneven pace than some predicted twenty years ago.[9] Global retailers' expansion has indeed encountered significant roadblocks. We have already noted in chapter 7 how Walmart's incursions into a number of countries failed to take root. France's Carrefour, the second-largest global retailer, has also scaled back its global ambitions in recent years, exiting India and Colombia and spinning off its holdings in Indonesia, the Middle East, North Africa, and Central Asia to franchisees.[10] British retail giant Tesco withdrew from the United States after a bruising rollout of the Fresh & Easy Chain; it also pulled out of Japan and Korea and downscaled its China operation to a joint venture with a Chinese retailer.[11]

But amid all these setbacks, global retailers continued widening their global reach on other fronts: Walmart bought chains in Chile and South Africa, Tesco expanded in Thailand while Casino bought up Carrefour's holdings in that country, and Carrefour and Japan's giant retailer AEON accelerated their investments in other Asian countries.[12] The global giants' retreats have been to some extent reactions to recession in their home markets in the United States and Europe and should prove temporary to the extent that these economies restore growth. Overall, however, global retail consolidation is looking more like a slowly, sometimes haltingly rising tide rather than an unstoppable steamroller.

Competitive Responses in Food: New Formats

U.S. supermarket chains have pivoted toward urban locations and smaller formats, both as a proactive response to the saturation of suburban areas as well as competition from other store formats and as a reactive strategy driven by shifts in shopping patterns that may have consolidated after first emerging during the Great Recession. These pivots merit a closer look.

Experimentation with Food Store Formats   In developing more varied store formats, most notably smaller stores, grocery chains aim to address several competitive challenges and stem the loss of supermarket market share—down 15 percent since 2005—to smaller markets, convenience stores, farmers' markets, and dollar stores.[13]

First, full-service supermarket chains have bumped up against the limits of food retail markets in suburban areas. Basic saturation of the market compounded by pressure from restaurant trade (with the resulting decline in meals eaten at home) creates roadblocks to growth. Expanding supermarket chains seek new markets in central cities. In these areas, they aim to capture market share from the remaining urban independent or regional chains and small stand-alone stores—what remains of mom-and-pop and ethnic neighborhood stores. However, limited parking availability, zoning regulations, and other constraints make it a challenge to open a conventional full-service supermarket, particularly as standard supermarkets have grown in size and evolved toward supercenters selling general merchandise—hence the chains' move toward smaller store formulas.

Second, supermarket chains seek to preserve "walk-through" snack and meal purchasing, a particular piece of the market that is under threat from convenience stores, which have increased their fresh food offerings, and a whole array of other (mostly packaged goods) food vending activities carried out by gas stations and other kinds of retailers (for example, office supply stores and multiproduct chain drugstores).[14] They also seek to make inroads into the fast-food segment of the restaurant industry by increasing offerings of prepared, made-to-order takeout foods in conventional supermarkets.

Competitive pressures have occurred in tandem with shifts in consumption patterns: consumers increasingly purchase food through a variety of outlets (including online) and store formats. Sometimes described as a "millennial" phenomenon, this behavioral change, while not ubiquitous, has compelled supermarket chains to vary their approach to food retail and offer multiple "channels" for purchasing food.[15]

Conventional chains such as Wal-Mart, Target, and Giant Foods have thus opened smaller stores that carry a far narrower range of products and are located in central cities or where a convenience store might have located otherwise.[16] Smaller chain stores "stand" between convenience store and full-service supermarket. Unlike most convenience stores, they do sell fresh produce along with basic, often discounted, dry goods and sometimes fresh dishes.

These small-store formats also may enable chains to carry out their expansion into central-city areas while also mitigating resistance from local communities and development actors. Aldi reportedly faces significantly less resistance to its urban stores than Wal-Mart, perhaps because the discount chain mostly has smaller stores, whereas Wal-Mart is known for its supercenters.[17] Smaller stores can specifically address competition from dollar stores, which are sometimes used as convenience stores by middle-income customers.[18]

A significant concomitant of smaller stores is the narrower range of goods on offer. In this way, supermarket chains imitate "targeted-market" competitors such as Aldi and Trader Joe's, whose business models are built around limited product ranges; both chains did well during the recession.[19] Smaller stores address customer expectations of convenience—walking through a full-range supermarket's wide selection can be a hindrance. The favoring of convenience also happens to coincide with what some observers deem a narrowing of the breadth of products on offer across *all* formats.[20] Wal-Mart began in early 2015 to narrow the range of products in stores in order to control costs and facilitate inventory management and shelf restocking. As of October 2015, the average supercenter, with about 120,000 products, had experienced a drop of 2,500 total items in less than a year—and had slashed the number of items on display even more dramatically, by 15 percent.[21] A narrower product range enables the retailer to focus a greater share of the customer's attention on the products on offer.[22]

With the development of small-store formats, national grocery chains also try to leverage competitive advantage by addressing local differentiation in consumption patterns. They attempt to tailor assortment across city types and to address culturally specific preferences. Advances in logistics technologies and practices facilitate this adaptation. For example, Safeway and Wal-Mart have adopted hybrid distribution systems that allow for customizable selections in local markets.[23] Local sourcing becomes an additional marketing tool, communicating to consumers that the company is no different from a regional or local store.[24]

If fully and successfully implemented, this geographical differentiation of grocery stores—historically the province of independents or regional chains—is likely to result in further encroachment by national and multiregional chains. To the extent that regional chains and local supermarkets are more likely to be privately held, the potential for preserving "islands" of autonomous labor deployment strategies that are less driven by the imperatives of stockholder or private equity returns—as discussed in chapters 3 and 4 on the U.S. company cases—is likely to decline.

Heightened Low-Cost Competition: Legacy of the Recession?

Since the 2007–2008 recession, supermarkets have had to contend with customers' heightened cost awareness as well as what appears to be a longer-term trend toward polarization of spending patterns and a thinning of middle-income customer ranks. Supermarkets have addressed this shift by emphasizing private-label offerings and driving harder bargains with suppliers, practices started before the recession as a means to address Wal-Mart's low-price competition. Nevertheless, one recession-induced consumption change has been a shift from supermarkets to dollar stores by low-income customers and even middle-income ones.

The term "dollar store" actually covers a small range of diverse store formats with slightly different customer targets. Dollar General and Family Dollar compete as general merchandisers, selling a relatively greater share of items priced around $10. In contrast, Dollar Tree and 99¢ Only sell a greater share of $1 items.

For decades, dollar stores were found overwhelmingly in rural areas, in the poorest city neighborhoods, and in the South. But since the recession hit in 2007, they have grown nationally in urban centers like Chicago and Los Angeles, and in a wider range of neighborhoods. Each of the major dollar store brands saw strong profits in the recession years, and they channeled these profits into expansion.[25] Dollar General doubled its number of stores from 2000 to 2010.[26]

Dollar stores themselves started to encounter economic headwinds in the post-recession years. As of early 2012, dollar store shoppers began to cut down on discretionary purchases. As a result, big dollar store chains experienced slower growth and posted earnings reports that were disappointing to investors.[27] Dollar stores also seem to have difficulty handling inflationary pressures: Dollar General CEO Rick Dreiling observed: "We have 228 items that are priced at $1 that we think are incredibly important to our customers that we elected not to take price increases on [as of June 2012]. This sounds almost silly, but a $1 item going to $1.15 in our channel is a major change for our customer."[28] But even with new challenges, dollar stores are maintaining market share, just not growing as fast as in the first decade of the century. These merchandising patterns create competitive threats for conventional supermarket chains.[29]

The Changing Dollar Store Customer . . . and the Changing Dollar Store Job?   The traditional dollar store consumers have been low-income earners, and their numbers increased during the recession: workers earning less than $35,000 increased by 1.8 million between

2007 and 2010.[30] About one-quarter of dollar store customers qualify for food stamps; as food stamp rolls swelled with the recession, dollar store demand did as well.[31]

During the recession, dollar stores made gains with earners above low income; as of this writing, it is unclear whether this behavioral shift will continue past the sequels of the recession. Generally, "middle-priced" consumer brands have seen sales declines as brands at either end of the price distributions have seen gains.[32] Some observers credit sales growth among middle-income earners with propelling dollar store growth overall; these shoppers may use dollar stores' greater accessibility for "fill-in" trips.[33] Half of Dollar Tree's new customers have incomes over $70,000.[34]

To remain competitive as an employer with rival discount retailers such as Target and Wal-Mart, some dollar store chains have increased hourly wages.[35] Wal-Mart's February 2016 wage and benefits increases for hourly workers have surely increased hiring competition among large discounters.[36] Partly in a bid to retain its workers and in order to improve the "quality" of store service, Dollar General will also increase the base hours allocated to employees in a "large group" of its 11,800 stores.[37] The implications for job quality are likely to be mixed. The growth of smaller stores in urban settings may generate greater ethnic diversity in the workforces, depending on their distribution across neighborhoods. However, longer commutes in urban areas may make it difficult and hardly worthwhile for workers to keep part-time jobs or to accommodate unpredictable schedules. Part-time gap fillers may find these jobs less amenable to combining with family care responsibilities or study. The growth of dollar stores, if sustained, may trigger growth in the relative share of entry-level and most likely low-wage jobs. These stores' small scale and narrow product range provide few midlevel jobs, although some dollar store chains' recent addition of fresh produce may alter this pattern because of the management requirements for maintaining fresh produce departments.

E-commerce and "Clicks-and-Mortar" Formats

E-retailing in Food Retailing   Until quite recently, online food retailing (including sales via smartphone and other mobile devices) has been a relatively underused format.[38] The industry and its analysts distinguish between "online" (computer) and "mobile" (phone) sales as two distinct sales channels. Though there are important differences between a cell phone and a computer as sales portals, both differ far more markedly from bricks-and-mortar stores than they do from each other, so for simplicity we combine the two under the heading "online."

E-retail's impact has grown, driven above all by Amazon. Still, as of 2013, e-retail had made limited inroads into the food retail market; it was estimated to account for only 0.9 percent of all food and beverage sales, and as of 2016, it had only reached 2 percent.[39] Of course, Amazon's recent purchase of Whole Foods (along with Wal-Mart's recent acquisition of online seller Jet.com) signals a serious attempt to greatly expand that share.

Younger customers' propensity for online ordering, even of groceries, has prompted and accelerated a set of changes in grocery retailing that have been long afoot but had not taken hold in significant ways until very recently. Home delivery has long been heralded as the "next-generation" service improvement for grocery stores, though one difficult to achieve within the constraints of affordability for customers and cost control for supermarket chains. Over the past fifteen years, a number of grocery chains have thus either run their own home delivery system coupled with online ordering (Ahold–Stop & Shop's PeaPod) or connected with online preorder, shopping, and delivery systems that achieve a similar result.[40]

A hybrid service formula consists of online preordering with the possibility of drive-by store pickups. This formula is far more manageable cost-wise for grocery chains because the logistical challenges of efficiently conducting scattered home deliveries and keeping orders refrigerated during a home delivery route are offloaded onto the customer, limiting the supermarket's responsibility to keeping a refrigerated chamber for orders ready for pickup. With this hybrid online-order–cum–in-store-pickup formula, supermarkets follow the practice of general merchandise and department stores (Wal-Mart, Home Depot, and Macy's), which have found that ordering online for in-store pickup has proven popular.[41] Some chains have partnered with Internet-based, storeless companies to address the home delivery conundrum; this partnership reconciles supermarkets' competitive need to provide delivery service and Internet service companies' desire to avoid inventory costs.[42] Google

Shopping Express lets customers place orders online for products from physical stores run by retailers including Costco, Staples, and Walgreens.[43] Whether this formula developed as a proactive strategy to meet customer demand or as a defensive strategy in the face of expansion of online food retail is not clear.[44]

In a reverse move, Amazon, which primarily delivers dry goods through conventional home delivery services, has recently sought to enter the fresh grocery delivery business, first by opening its own bricks-and-mortar stores and more recently by acquiring Whole Foods. The stores are meant to support and expand the reach of Amazon Fresh, its same- and next-day delivery service, into major metro areas. Amazon piloted physical stores, starting in 2014 with a New York City location, to provide "face-to-face experience," allow customers to pick up online orders, serve as a distribution center for couriers, and test the viability of the model.[45] Amazon added several more "convenience stores," then in 2017 purchased Whole Foods with 450 stores, not long after a report, so far unconfirmed, surfaced that Amazon was considering adding over 2,000 store locations, which would place it among the top bricks-and-mortar retailers.[46] Physical pickup locations could help Amazon Fresh solve the "last mile" problem—the cost and complexity of getting perishable goods to consumers—by "having consumers come to Amazon," thus addressing the same challenge that supermarkets aim to solve with drive-up services.[47]

Online ordering combined with drive-up pickup or home delivery most likely will have several implications for within-store job configurations. Reduced cashier staffing, greater reliance on scanning devices by staff who collect items and pull together grocery orders, and increased staff at pickup locations and for deliveries all seem likely. Whether delivery staff will be employees of grocery chains or Internet-based delivery companies is not clear. The impact on the gender mix of the workforce is difficult to predict. Also still unclear are the potential size of the selling channel and the implications for the volume of jobs in the average store over time.

E-retailing and Consumer Electronics   When we conducted our U.S. retail field study, consumer electronics had already experienced a significant loss of market share in the PC business to Dell. Both electronics and office equipment and supply stores noted that profit margins on PCs were thin and falling. Each of these subcategories had gravitated toward other sources of higher margins: large flat-screen TVs and home installation services for electronics big-box stores, office supplies and photocopying and design services for office equipment stores. Electronics retailers also relied on PC technical support units as well as extended warranty/service contracts, although, as we discussed earlier, these warranty services had begun to experience low-price competition from Wal-Mart and other discounters.

During and since the U.S. study, big-box consumer electronics chains have experienced softer demand owing to the Great Recession and heightened competition from online retailers—in both e-commerce from Internet-based firms, such as Amazon and Apple, and in click-and-mortar online sales from general merchandise discounters, such as Wal-Mart.[48] As of 2013, e-commerce was estimated to account for a substantial 33 percent of sales of computers (hardware and software), 18 percent of electronics and appliances sales, and 17 percent of office equipment and supplies.[49] Margins have continued to decline for PCs and even flat-screen TVs, products that earlier had come to the rescue of consumer electronics chains.[50] In addition, consumers seem to conduct online information searches about products and to rely less on in-store guidance from staff, a trend that could further change the nature and composition of sales staff jobs.

To navigate a retail world with growing online retail options, big-box general merchandisers like Wal-Mart and Target have sought seamless integration between online and bricks-and-mortar environments.[51] Consumer electronics big-box chains are similarly engaged in enhancing the "virtual" presence of their brand and making shopping easy and accessible through all channels, not only physical stores. Meanwhile, as in groceries but at a more accelerated pace, Amazon is rolling out up to 400 bookstores to complement its online sales platform—no word yet about whether literal showrooms for other goods such as consumer electronics will follow, but the possibility seems real.[52]

In coming years, increased customer access to and use of information sources outside stores (online) are particularly likely to affect the "service-driven" competitive strategies adopted by consumer electronics chains (described in chapters 3 and 4). For single items (TVs, PCs), in-store guidance from sales associates is likely to decline. Sales attention and customer service are more likely to be further focused on the packaging of home entertainment and home-office systems and on design and installation services as well as service contracts for these complex systems. Thus, the move of large chains to differentiated service levels with a service- and knowledge-intensive "store-within-a-store" approach is likely to continue and to be considered a way to maintain a competitive edge.[53] Chains may also seek new services to add: the office supplies giant Staples recently announced a plan to add yet another store-based service: providing office-sharing space for freelancers,[54] and Best Buy has added "home advisory" services in which employees visit customers' homes to advise them on tech.[55] The implications for labor deployment and jobs are ambiguous. There is likely to be demand for sales associates with higher skills relative to those who answer basic product information questions—a trend well under way over the past ten years.

Store Automation   Related to e-commerce trends are moves to further automate store staffing. Self-scanning, which originally sparked predictions of the elimination of the cashier, has had a relatively modest impact on the front end of grocery stores (and other retailers). The current landscape has contradictory signals about how dramatically automation will change store staffing in the near future. On the one hand, Amazon's new "Amazon Go" convenience store format has customers make purchases on their phones and then pay online as they leave.[56] Panasonic, meanwhile, has introduced a "smart" shopping basket that scans purchases as they are placed into the basket, then dumps them into a bag at a checkout pay station.[57] Around the same time, however, the grocer Albertson's has reported that eliminating self-scan and self-checkout altogether resulted in higher customer satisfaction![58] What is not ambiguous is that the logistical "back end" behind both stores and direct-to-customer shipping will continue to see further automation.[59]

POLICY-RELATED CHANGES IN THE UNITED STATES

As we write, the U.S. policy environment has been dramatically altered by the results of the 2016 elections. These outcomes are likely to close off worker-friendly policy options and open up worker-unfriendly ones at the federal level for at least the next several years, and possibly considerably longer. Spillover into state and local policies, in ways that we cannot fully anticipate at present, also seems likely. Nonetheless, we focus on the progressive elements within the most recent wave of policy changes—and later in the chapter, in contemplating future policy directions, we similarly focus on upside possibilities.

Potential Implications of the Affordable Care Act

Our optimistic slant starts here: repeal or at least non-implementation of the Affordable Care Act of 2010 appears imminent as we write, but we believe that it is still useful to discuss what the ACA's effects would be if it were fully implemented. The universal coverage goal of the ACA could lessen the harmful implications of retail part-time employment under the pre-reform system because part-time workers would gain access to basic health insurance through insurance exchanges and, if eligible, federal or state subsidies for the premium. Some possible effects also include more voluntary worker job quits or hours reductions among those covered by employer plans prior to the ACA.[60]

Questions have been raised about the effects on the part-time/full-time ratio of the part-time weekly hours threshold (thirty hours) in the ACA's employer mandate, which requires large employers (over fifty workers) to offer *affordable* health insurance to their full-time workers or pay a penalty.[61] The full-time threshold for the employer mandate is thirty or more weekly *average* hours over the year or 130 hours per calendar month, including vacation and paid leaves of absence.[62] This mandated threshold may raise implementation issues for retailers who routinely schedule ostensibly "part-time" workers for hours over thirty. It remains to be seen whether this clause compels de facto eligibility for these workers.[63] We also do not yet know whether—with the gradual reduction of the full-time standard to thirty-five and even thirty-two hours among retailers—some may simply devolve the bulk of their workforce to usually scheduled hours below thirty in order to avoid having to provide coverage or pay the penalty.[64] Prior to health insurance reform, health coverage for full-timers was discretionary and thought to induce retention and commitment; once turned into a mandate, it may lose its appeal as a human resource management tool. In this latter case, the mandate could again be argued to foster short-hours (under thirty) staffing practices. At the very least, it may stunt an incipient trend among a few large retailers to cover part-timers in their company health plan because part-time workers can now access insurance exchanges and Medicaid subsidies where available.

Drawing upon similarities with the earlier Hawaii and Massachusetts health insurance reforms with similar but not identical employer mandates, the economist Marcus Dillender and his colleagues have estimated that 5 percent of workers currently without employer-based insurance would be potentially eligible for employer coverage under the mandate (a number that would be halved were the full-time threshold set at forty hours).[65] Over half report working in retail, accommodations, or food service.[66]

While cautioning that many of the data necessary to answer the questions of numbers of workers affected and changes in costs and benefits to employers and workers are not yet available, and after developing estimates for the U.S.-wide impacts of the ACA based on the contrast between the U.S. mandate and the Hawaii experience with a more stringent mandate, the Dillender team projects a possible two- to three-percentage-point increase in involuntary part-time employment in retail and accommodation and food services, about 600,000 to 900,000 jobs.[67] Again, the prospect of repeal or failure to implement the ACA places all of this in question.

Minimum Wage and Hours Activism

Activism on the Rise The issue of retail's low wages and problematic work schedules has blended with similar concerns in other low-wage customer service work, notably fast-food work. In recent years, activism on low-quality jobs has built momentum and crystallized around concerted action on wages and, since 2014, on unpredictable schedules.[68] The "Fight for $15" movement of fast-food workers has garnered the most attention, but it has been accompanied, less visibly to the public eye, by similar arguments for improving retail jobs, such as those advanced by New York City's Retail Action Project (RAP).[69]

Local wage activism has yielded a new burst of local- and state-level increases in the workforce-wide minimum wage. About twenty cities and counties passed minimum wage ordinances between 2012 and 2015.[70] Laws raising the minimum to $15 over time were passed in SeaTac and Seattle, Washington, and in San Francisco (2014) and Los Angeles (2015).[71] New York State's governor announced a similar minimum for fast-food workers in early 2015, then for state employees late in the year, and in 2016 Oregon adopted a minimum climbing to $14.75 in cities by 2022.[72] These laws have three- to five-year lags in implementation. Whether city-level ordinances can sustain challenges from some state legislatures that are hostile to the policy and pass preemption laws that prohibit their mandates is unclear.

Following close on the heels of minimum wage bumps have been local laws requiring large retailers to give employees two weeks' advance notice of work schedules. San Francisco passed such an ordinance in 2014, with Seattle following suit two years later. As of early 2017, New York City has been weighing a similar plan, but one limited to fast-food workers (with the somewhat dubious rationale that retail workers are sufficiently protected by unions).[73] At the state level, New York attorney general Eric Schneiderman in 2015 announced an investigation of the scheduling practices of thirteen retail clothing chains, leading a string of national chains to announce two-weeks'-notice policies.[74] Schneiderman later joined with attorneys general from several other states to challenge "on-call" scheduling, in which employers call workers one or two hours before the shift to see if they will work.[75] California legislation mandating advance notice was introduced in 2016, but not adopted. Oregon passed a 2017 law mandating retail, hospital, and food service companies with over five hundred workers to provide written notice of schedules a week in advance, starting in July 2018, as well as ten-hour breaks between work shifts or provide a pay premium. By 2020, the mandated schedule notification will expand to two weeks.[76]

Corporate Responses?   Retailers and fast-food chains have aimed to head off mandated increases, and to respond to those in place, by announcing their own entry-level increases. It is unclear to what extent these steps have been taken as a response to activism or because of the general economic improvement that necessitates raising base wages to address incipient recruitment and hiring difficulties. Given its size, visibility, and market dominance, Wal-Mart was singled out for militant action as early as 2012.[77] In February 2015, the retailer announced that it aimed to increase minimum wages for entry-level and long-term hourly employees to at least $10 a year later—and in implementing the change in 2016, Wal-Mart broadened pay raises to encompass almost its entire U.S. hourly workforce and also provide free short-term disability insurance.[78] OUR Wal-Mart, the pressure group of company employees, complained, however, that wage increases came coupled with hours cuts so that many employees ended up with little or no increase in take-home pay.[79] Throughout 2015, the clothing discounter TJX, the big-box discount retailer Target, and others announced similar bumps in their base wage. In early 2016, Costco shored up its reputation as a higher-paying retailer by raising its minimum pay rate to $13 an hour.[80]

Retail and fast-food chains have also adjusted schedules in reaction to activism and adverse publicity about short-notice scheduling and short-hour shifts.[81] Wal-Mart's 2015 wage announcement also included a policy to offer workers "more control over their schedule." The company followed up in 2016 by adding new "fixed shifts" and "flex shifts" (the latter allowing employees to build their shifts from blocks of time needing coverage) with greatest access to desirable shifts for more senior employees, to existing "open shifts" (in which managers can freely set each week's shifts within workers' stated availability).[82] An example from fast food calls for caution. Starbucks' stated intentions of providing advance notice ran into difficulty with implementation in 2015. It appears that at least some managers continued the practice of short notice partly because their incentives and performance rating (minimizing labor hour usage) compelled them to avoid risking "overscheduling" when implementing advance notice.[83] Interestingly, the *Wall Street Journal* in 2016 highlighted a mini-trend toward heavier retailer reliance on full-time workers. (With the emphasis on "mini": the *Journal* identified only one example, the convenience store Sheetz, which has increased its full-time percentage only to 53 percent.)[84] However, as author Tilly has noted, retailers always tend to adjust their percentage of full-timers upward when labor markets tighten—as was occurring in 2016.[85] All may not be well or simple if retail employees must wait for voluntary employer human resource policy changes to resolve pressing labor issues.

Possible Implications   Incumbent retail workers will reap immediate benefit from minimum wage increases. The staged increases—

giving retailers and other employers time to plan for adjustments—aim to minimize impacts on staffing levels. The fact that these wage raises will affect almost all employers of low-wage workers should "level the playing field" and reduce the competitive pressures from lower-cost operators. Low-cost competition effects are most reduced where statewide, or even countywide, minimum wage laws—rather than city-level ones—are implemented. Still, business-level impacts and employment levels will be affected differentially across retail subsectors. Contrast the situation of grocery stores, for which most shopping is local (though not entirely immune to price competition from online retail), with that of big-box electronics stores, which already are in direct competition with online and other mail-order retailers. We leave the discussion of how wage increases interact with retailers' decision-making on technology use, staffing mix, skill development, and labor deployment to later in the chapter.

WHAT'S NEXT: LIKELY FUTURE DIRECTIONS FOR RETAILERS AND RETAIL JOBS

What's next for retail? In seeking to answer this question, we take another, future-oriented look at two sources of ongoing change that are likely to critically affect the character of jobs in retail in the coming years. We start by looking at the technological and competitive dynamics that are shaping retail as a business, holding the institutional and regulatory environment constant for the sake of argument. We then explore what institutional and legal changes might be mobilized to improve retail jobs. This latter exploration is necessarily more speculative, though we hope not completely fanciful. Importantly, most of the steps we consider in this second "what next?" scan hold potential not just for bettering retail employment but for *improving a wide range of bad jobs*. Retail, being a leader in exit options and emblematic of low-quality jobs, is our entry point and lens for thinking about varied ways to make bad jobs better.

Throughout, we continue to focus primarily on the prospects for retail jobs in the United States, though we comment briefly on likely outcomes elsewhere. However, in weighing ameliorative options for retail jobs in the United States, we also point to the institutional and legal frameworks that this book has analyzed in Western Europe and Mexico.

Future Retail Trends and Their Implications for Jobs

In looking at technological change and competitive strategy in retail, two recent trends seem likely to continue. More retail activities will shift from store-based to online. And the tug-of-war between reducing costs and enhancing quality, variety, and service is likely to continue vexing retailers. These two ongoing tendencies will affect both the mix of jobs and their quality. It is risky to hazard predictions for the rapidly transforming retail sector, but in this discussion we court risk, offering a few predictions about retail futures.

The Future of Stores and the Future of Retail Jobs   As Internet and mobile phone technologies evolve, they generate ever easier and more reliable ways to search for online shopping opportunities, make informed choices, succumb to bargain shopping, and carry out purchases. Already, retailers are dealing with what they call an "omnichannel" retailing environment.[86] In this context, we can expect continued shifts of consumers away from stores and toward online sales (with a combination of delivery and on-site pickup).[87]

Jobs will follow. Retail jobs will shift away from customer interaction and cashiering and toward warehousing and delivery tasks. In some ways, the change is analogous with the catalog sales revolution launched by Montgomery Ward, Sears, and others in the late nineteenth century: tasks that have been performed face-to-face become more footloose or are stripped down to a quick delivery or pickup transaction. This change in itself does not dictate a particular quality trajectory for the jobs involved. For instance, author Tilly and his coauthors have argued that the recent restructuring of the food service sector that shifted food preparation from decentralized on-site work to centralized, factory-based work actually led to average improvement of jobs on some indices.[88] Nevertheless, recent research suggests that most warehousing jobs are poorly paid temporary jobs brokered through staffing intermediaries and that short-haul truck drivers like those in delivery tend to be misclassified as independent contractors and therefore receive neither employer-provided benefits nor statutory employee rights (unemployment insurance, minimum wage, overtime, occupational safety and health, collective bargaining, and more).[89] In this context, shifts away from in-store retail may actually lead, on net, to worse jobs— or at least jobs that are not much better.

Despite retail's brave new technological world, stores are not going to disappear anytime soon. As of 2014, nonstore retail employed only 3 percent of retail workers (with online electronics sales comprising just over one percentage point of that total), and store-based retail employed more than five times as many people as *all* nonstore retail, warehousing, and trucking combined.[90] Several major factors will keep stores necessary, relevant, and a greater sales channel and larger employer than online sales for some time to come:

- High-end stores typically sell not just high-end goods but the experience of being waited on. They sell idiosyncratic goods and services that may require explanation by staff, and they stand to gain significantly by "upselling" to well-heeled consumers. Jobs are unlikely to change in this sliver of the market.

- We have argued that service is an important differentiator for stores in the midrange as well, but in this stratum the ambiguous term "service" more likely translates into answers to simple questions and getting checked out quickly, rather than personal attention. To provide this kind of midrange service, new technology will increasingly be deployed to emulate a Bargain Warehouse executive's dictum that "the best service is self-service"—that is, enabling customers to make their desired purchases with minimal interaction with staff.[91]

- At the opposite end of the spectrum, very low-end stores seek to make goods available at the lowest cost possible. They are more likely to serve the shrinking group of people who lack online access or savvy and customers who would choose lower prices over delivery and convenience. Such stores are particularly likely to persist in rural areas and low-income urban neighborhoods.

- There is still a continuing need for showrooms across a variety of merchandise. The list includes goods for which fully assessing quality requires looking and perhaps touching (large-screen TVs, beds, but also ripe fruit and fresh fish) and ones for which design is key and styles vary widely (such as some varieties of hardware). Reinforcing the importance of the showroom experience, a recent study found that online grocery purchases from *bricks-and-mortar retailers* are larger on average than purchases from "pure play" online retailers such as Amazon and FreshDirect—perhaps part of the reason that Amazon has captured only 1 percent of the grocery market and now seeks to rapidly add physical stores.[92] In some parts of retail, there is some convergence as many store-based retailers in subsectors like consumer electronics have begun to scale stores back to showrooms in order to support online sales, and online sellers add physical showrooms for the same reason. In both cases sellers are harking back to an earlier dry goods sale model of displaying "one of each" in the store, with stock warehoused for delivery or pickup.[93]

- Sociability can be a sought-after coproduct, even at the expense of convenience. This is certainly a factor in farmers' markets and corner stores in which the same salesperson staffs the counter year after year, but not in most chain stores with their sky-high labor turnover rates. In the long run, then, sociability seems likely to protect selected islands within retail, but not the mass store-based retailers most directly threatened by online sales of standardized goods. However, some experts expect the desire for human contact to limit online grocery sales quite dramatically. "The whole premise is that you're saving people a trip to the store, but people actually like going to the store to buy groceries," according to the retail analyst Kurt Jetta.[94]

- Finally, having physical stores adds logistical advantages to online selling. Customers often prefer "click-and-collect," when they can buy online and pick up at a nearby location at their convenience. And stores can double as mini-warehouses that can speed up deliveries to consumers. By leveraging these aspects of stores, Best Buy is "turning its cavernous stores from a potential drag on its business into a way to fend off Amazon," according to a recent *Wall Street Journal* article;[95] Amazon's purchase of Whole Foods implicitly acknowledges the continued importance of physical store locations.

With these factors at work, improving jobs in store-based retail—this book's main focus—will remain a critically important agenda. But job quality in warehousing and delivery will also loom as an increasingly important concern. So will potential further technological transformation of warehouse and delivery jobs—two sectors that have already been radically transformed, deskilled, and sped up in recent decades. Two technological shifts that may be on the near horizon are robotized stock-picking and delivery by drone.[96]

The future of stores outside the United States looks different for richer countries than for poorer ones. In wealthy countries like Japan and most of Europe, employment shifts will look similar to those in the United States. Highly wired populations will buy increasing amounts of goods and services online, and storage and delivery jobs will grow at the margin. In poorer countries, high-income, urbanized populations will similarly shop increasingly online. During the last decade in Mexico, for example, credit card use has become widespread, and goods delivery services have markedly expanded coverage and reliability, opening the door to online sales.[97] But in most of the poorer two-thirds of the world, the shift from street vending and mom-and-pop stores to "modern" retail formats and consolidation of national and global chain dominance dwarfs the shift to e-shopping. As a result, in the near future retail in *these* countries will look *more* like pre-Amazon U.S. retail than it does today.

Will these changes have the same impact on retail job quality in other countries as in the United States? If we have argued one thing in this book it is that offering a general answer to this question is not possible. Country-specific institutions—societal effects, more broadly—crucially determine how job quality plays out, and institutions are a moving target, with new exit options constantly being explored. We can cautiously venture that the big retail shift toward "modern" store formats in lower-income countries will on the whole improve jobs by shifting them from undercapitalized self-employment and informal sector employment to higher-productivity jobs in chain store formats where labor standards are more easily monitored and policed. However, we know from the United States that higher productivity does not necessarily translate into better compensation or more humane scheduling. Moreover, the finding from our longitudinal study of retail workers in Mexico (see online chapter A1 at http://www.russellsage.org/publications /where-bad-jobs-are-better) that *nonsupervisory workers in chains earned pay comparable to those in informal sector retailers* underlines the caution with which we venture this hypothesis.

Competitive Trade-Offs and Job Outcomes   A near-universal in our U.S. retail case studies is a challenging tension between staying competitive by keeping costs low and staying competitive by offering some combination of greater quality, variety, service, or convenience. We have argued that when retailers lean toward the cost-cutting side of the trade-off, lower job quality typically follows. Does our analysis tell us anything about likely future changes in the mix of "cost-cutting first" as opposed to "a superior offering first" retailers?

To some extent, the intensity of the tug-of-war results from income polarization and the resultant polarization of consumer buying power. Most U.S. retailers once sold to a slice of the large U.S. middle class, but stagnant or falling earnings for most and galloping income gains at the high end have eroded that middle class and the mass markets it generated. Retailers that are not firmly anchored at the low end, with Wal-Mart and the dollar stores, or at the high end, with Whole Foods and specialty stores, have struggled to retain an adequate customer base.

Thus, the main result of the segmentation of consumers has been growing segmentation of retail into higher-end and lower-end chains. And on the employment front, that has translated, at least to some extent, into segmentation of retail jobs. But the sizes of the segments differ markedly. Most U.S. workers and households are garnering incomes that are stalled or declining relative to their counterparts from one or even two generations earlier. They might prefer to access better service, higher quality, and stimulating variety, but they can ill afford to—so lower-priced options will appeal to them most.

So far, policy responses to growing inequality have been small compared to the scale of the processes generating income disparities. For this reason, we expect U.S. income polarization to continue to grow for some time to come, and with it stratified consumption and the resulting segmentation of retail jobs.

In our current institutional environment, having few high-end stores implies few high-end jobs. We hasten to add that the inverse is not true: in the U.S. institutional and competitive context, the presence of many high-end stores would *not* imply many high-end jobs. As the sociologists Bailey and Bernhardt observed years ago, retail that presents as high-road in terms of innovation, style, and customer service may nonetheless offer low-quality jobs.[98] We *would* expect retailers that offer more to consumers to generate somewhat better jobs, simply to dampen worker turnover and assure a baseline of customer service, and some of our field cases confirm this. But on the whole, our case-study evidence concurs with Bailey and Bernhardt's findings, suggesting that dramatically better compensation or other job features are rare indeed in the U.S. chain retail landscape and, where they occur, are the result of considered management commitments, albeit supported by market segment targeting. It is also important to note that segmentation of customer offerings and job quality can be carried out within a single company (grocery chains with several banners catering to different consumer strata) and even within a single store (as in electronics stores with a store-within-a-store targeting high rollers).

We have hedged this job quality prediction by locating it "in our current institutional environment." This caveat deserves much closer attention. As we have emphasized throughout the book, retailers (and other employers) face a variety of choices regarding how to manage and deploy labor. Employers choose between motivating workers with carrots (good jobs) or with sticks (surveillance and punishment). They choose between keeping operating costs low by investing in productivity-enhancing technology, on the one hand, and keeping wages and benefits low and using intricate just-in-time scheduling to keep staffing to the bare minimum, on the other. And all of this takes place in the context of the choice we have been foregrounding here—between competing on low prices or competing on a superior mix of goods and services. But the viability of each of these choices depends crucially on the constellation of policies and institutions governing employment and product markets. To the extent that institutions block the option of sweating workers, companies will be more likely to choose good jobs, investment in technology, and upgrading the consumer offering—think Denmark or France. But if the low road is wide open, retailers will tend to choose it, or else they will have to contend with being undercut by their low-road competitors.

The U.S. institutional environment is not fixed. The Progressive Era, the New Deal, the Great Society, and the neoliberalism ushered in by President Ronald Reagan's "morning in America" have marked major changes of direction, all with momentous implications for labor and job quality. And though the corrosive antigovernment views and suspicions of unions that bolster the recent neoliberal U.S. policy regime seem deeply entrenched, the norms embodied in these attitudes are mutable as well. In a shifting environment of policies and norms, the future is not simply dictated by technological trajectories, consumer preferences, and business imperatives, but depends on choices made by a variety of actors in the polity, economy, and society. With this in mind, we turn in the next section to key choices in U.S. public policy that could shift retail jobs, and other bad jobs, onto a different track.

Before looking at these policy choices, a word about likely futures in other countries. Not surprisingly, our view is that those futures likewise depend on institutional choices. In wealthy countries like the five European nations we examined, the future mix of lower-cost and better-offering stores, as well as the future contours of retail job quality, depend on the contest between regulatory institutions and the exit options that offer escape from those institutions. In the recent playing out of this contest, institutions have limited exit options in French and Danish stores, but Germany's potent mix of exit options, notably the part-time mini-job with favorable tax treatment, has seriously eroded retail job quality. This does not mean that German retail jobs are indistinguishable in quality from those in the United States—there is still a strong apprenticeship infrastructure that nurtures retail multiskilling, as well as universal health coverage and a voice, however reduced, for retail unions. We would note as well that the European versions of the high road do *not* foreclose the possibility of low-price models: the "hard discounters" Aldi and Lidl, which underpriced Wal-Mart in Germany, are flourishing in all five of the European countries with which we compared the United States.

In middle-income countries such as Mexico, and even more so in low-income countries, the "supermarketization" trend has not yet run its course. As supermarketization advances, policies framed as defending worker interests, like Mexico's daily minimum wage, *could* be strengthened, extended, and more adequately enforced. Or they could instead simply channel worker exploitation in different ways, as when the daily minimum incentivizes employers to extract unpaid overtime, rather than limiting workers to skimpily compensated part-time jobs, as in the United States.

Possible Institutional Changes

As forecast earlier in the chapter, notwithstanding the current political conjuncture, we choose to focus here on optimistic possibilities rather than pessimistic ones. We frame U.S. policy choices that could improve retail jobs in terms of four objectives: (1) improved compensation, (2) sustainable scheduling, (3) discouraging overuse of part-time employment, and (4) skill-building and upward mobility. In addition, we consider broader policy changes that could (5) encourage high-road employment and (6) increase worker bargaining power. The policy proposals we review range from ones that are highly politically feasible (in some cases just incremental extensions of existing policies) to ones that are currently more remote possibilities. We have not included in this list options that strike us as utopian and not achievable in the medium term. Very few of these policies specifically target the retail sector, or to put it more positively, most would help improve jobs across the board. We also distinguish between *mandates* that would directly require improvements in the terms and conditions of employment and *incentives* that would work mainly by changing employers' decision-making calculus. This discussion overlaps to some extent with the rundown on recent policy developments earlier in the chapter, but here we focus more on what is *likely* to happen, or at least what *could* happen, in the medium to longer term given a bit of political will.

Improved Compensation   Policies to boost compensation are among the most politically accessible in the United States today, and in fact this agenda is already in motion. The "Fight for $15" as a minimum wage has moved from a rallying cry to legislation in a growing number of settings, as described earlier in this chapter, and is likely to spread further. There is overwhelming support for a generous increase in the minimum wage, even among Republican voters. Most likely minimum wage increases will continue to spread across municipalities and states, which will in turn ramp up the pressure on Congress—even a Republican-controlled Congress—to enact some kind of increase in the federal minimum.

The other key front for minimum wage and similar laws is beefing up enforcement, since such labor standards are poorly implemented at the low end of the labor market.[99] The recent Los Angeles minimum wage ordinance builds in new enforcement provisions, and a variety of proposals to strengthen monitoring of employers and sanctioning of offenders have been advanced—notably measures to more formally integrate unions, worker centers, and community-based organizations in these processes.[100] The U.S. Department of Labor's Wage and Hour Division has in recent years taken a leading role in foregrounding enforcement, exploring alternative methods of monitoring, and prompting interagency collaboration approaches and federal-state collaboration to achieve higher compliance and better settlements for workers. Though we can be confident that these advances will soon be rolled back with the change in federal administration, in the longer run they continue to hold promise. As we saw in the case of France, a high and well-policed minimum wage can help shift the entire compensation structure of an industry like retail. On the flip side, the case of Mexico reminds us that a low and poorly enforced minimum—the predominant direction of U.S. federal minimum wage policy over the last forty years—paves the job quality low road.

One other enhancement to compensation that has proven popular with policymakers (including quite a few Republicans) is federal and state Earned Income Tax Credits (EITCs). The federal EITC, and state programs based on it, offer a tax credit to low-wage earners with children. The tax credit is *refundable,* meaning that even if it exceeds taxes owed—indeed, even if the tax filer owes zero in taxes—the credit is "refunded" so that the lowest-wage workers get a bonus. The EITC has garnered bipartisan support, like the minimum wage, because it is framed as rewarding work.[101] EITC expansions implemented by President Obama during the late 2000s recession were even made permanent in the contentious 2016 budget, with Republican majorities in both houses of Congress.[102] The credit enables workers to hold part-time jobs when they must for personal reasons. The effects on managerial decision-making are ambiguous; many debate whether substituting public subsidy for high wages is a desirable incentive for market-leading retailers.

Sustainable Scheduling   The unsustainable elements in current U.S. retail scheduling practice include variability and unpredictability in both shifts worked and number of hours per day or week. (We consider *insufficiency* of hours, in the form of a surfeit of part-time work, as a separate problem, though of course the issues are closely related.) In the extreme, some workers experience literal "just-in-time" scheduling that can involve being called into work or sent home without warning (all "voluntarily," of course). How can we get retail employers to schedule sustainably, at least at the basic level of providing workers with their schedule a decent interval in advance, and sticking with those scheduled hours?

A new wave of local laws requiring advance notice of work schedules has put sustainable scheduling squarely on the public policy agenda, as we reported earlier.[103] But even before that, "reporting pay" laws were in place as another important tool to moderate employer abuse of just-in-time scheduling.[104] At the time of writing, seven states and the District of Columbia require employers to provide some minimum number of hours of pay to workers who report to work (with the minimum ranging from one hour in New Jersey to four hours in New York and D.C.). This creates an incentive to avoid very short shifts and to only call in workers for unscheduled hours when they are needed for a substantial block of time. Twelve states *without* reporting pay laws (along with California, which does have such a law) have "call-back pay" laws that require a minimum payment or the overtime rate for times when employees are called in outside their regular schedule. Colorado and the District of Columbia even mandate a low base rate of pay (below the minimum wage) for time spent on-call *offsite*.[105] Extending these incentives to more states or even to the federal level would help to tame the worst scheduling excesses.

A number of recent policy steps toward sustainable scheduling have not sought to regulate day-to-day scheduling, but rather to simply introduce a measure of workers' control over their work time when confronting extenuating life circumstances—expanding U.S. workers' access to paid leave, which is skimpy relative to other wealthy countries.[106] The Clinton administration, which shepherded the Family and Medical Leave Act, also encouraged the establishment by states of temporary disability insurance programs, which can cover pregnancy, among other conditions, and many states have adopted TDI systems. California and New Jersey go beyond the federal Family and Medical Leave Act (which mandates unpaid leave) by requiring paid parental leave, supported by a separate insurance fund paid for by employer and employee contributions.[107] Massachusetts has a pending bill funding paid leave exclusively through an employer mandate. As we write, President Trump's budget proposes instituting six weeks of paid parental leave funded by state Unemployment Insurance systems and following Unemployment Insurance eligibility rules; the proposal may not survive the budgetary process.[108] As of December 2015, twenty-six states and localities had passed laws mandating paid sick days.[109]

Another policy direction that could further tame out-of-control work schedules would be the reimposition of "blue laws" limiting store opening days and hours. France is a global example of a country that has generally held the line on unlimited opening hours, but as we noted in chapter 6, recent policy reforms have relaxed some of those restrictions.[110] Meanwhile, in the United States, where old-fashioned store hours are a distant memory, recent voluntary action by retailers has begun to deescalate the opening hours "arms race." In 2015, a number of smaller retailers won applause from employees for announcing that they would remain closed on "Black Friday," the day after Thanksgiving, the biggest shopping day of the year, and make it a paid holiday for workers.[111] Codifying into law renewed restrictions on hours—or at least limitations (for example, limiting hours of large stores, or reducing store service levels to skeleton levels during some periods)—could further cool out competition via extended hours.

Discouraging Overuse of Part-Time Employment   Part-time work is a necessity for some who are balancing paid work with family responsibilities, studies, or partial retirement. But in the retail sector in particular, and to some extent in the economy in general, high levels of part-time employment come with two negative pieces of baggage. First, a substantial minority of part-time employees would rather be full-time. In 2014, more than one part-timer in four would have preferred full-time hours.[112] Second, as we have stressed, part-time employment often (very often in retail) comes with a lower hourly wage and almost always offers a much-reduced benefit package. This inferior compensation essentially exploits the constrained schedules of women with young children, students, and others. The two negatives are connected, since lower hourly wage and benefit costs create an incentive for employers to proliferate part-time jobs beyond the level desired by job-seekers—perhaps even beyond what is desirable for the longer-term interests of the business. We focus here on part-time work as a distinct employment arrangement rather than a mere schedule characteristic, which is a particular issue in retail, but it is important to note that there are analogous problems with other forms of nonstandard work in other sectors: independent contractor status in construction (and increasingly in passenger transportation, thanks to Uber and its peers); temporary agency employment in warehousing and less-skilled manufacturing; franchising in fast food; freelancing in technical jobs; and so on.

To curb abusive overuse of part-time hours, the key is removing the economic incentives for it. Here a sensible policy proposal has been circulating since the 1980s; it was proposed by then-congresswoman Patricia Schroeder as early as 1993, though it has not yet developed enough political traction to be enacted anywhere in the country: part-time parity, a requirement to pay the same hourly wage to part-timers and full-timers doing the same work and to offer part-time workers an appropriately prorated set of benefits that meet a minimum floor of protection. Universal and uniform health care coverage, such as a single-payer system, would likewise remove the current major cost advantage (per hour) of using part-timers. We observed in chapter 5 that, as is well known, Western European countries have such universal and uniform health systems. We also pointed out in that chapter the less-known fact that a European Union directive calls for part-time compensation parity; implementation across Europe remains uneven.

Skill-Building and Upward Mobility   Feasible policies on education and training all fall into the category of incentives rather than mandates, and they touch on both the supply of skills and the demand for them. The Obama administration's Department of Labor, following up on earlier George W. Bush and Bill Clinton administration initiatives, made major investments in supporting the expansion of apprenticeship and certification programs.[113] U.S. federal and state programs on this front do not approach the level and systemic effect found in Germany, but they do mark significant steps toward rebuilding the apprenticeship tradition in the United States, which had been reduced to a few beachheads, primarily in the building trades. Increasingly, mobility paths in retail do not involve upward mobility with a single employer, so portable certifications would be particularly useful there. Many of the skills involved are more broadly applicable ones, such as customer service, that could be applied in hospitality or other service industries.

Public policies can also create an incentive acting on the demand side, stimulating employers to provide training to incumbent workers. In the mid-1990s, then U.S. labor secretary Robert Reich proposed a small "training tax" on employers that would be refundable to reimburse them for training offered to nonmanagement employees; his proposal was based on a similar, more ambitious, French policy. Reich's proposal went nowhere at the federal level, but half a dozen states did adopt similar policies. The largest such program, in California, assesses an employment training tax of one-hundredth of a percent on the first $7,000 paid to each employee in a calendar year; the tax has generated more than $1 billion in training expenditures.[114]

Managing for High-Road Employment   In addition to mandates and incentives to promote specific human resource practices, new programs could inform and prompt employers to move to high-road employment more generally. This approach is appealing, but it is difficult to find instances where it has achieved scale. Restaurant Opportunities Centers United (ROC-U), a network of worker centers deploying advocacy, organizing, training, and public education to improve low-end restaurant jobs, has for years featured a high-road restaurant program.[115] High-road examples are important for making ROC-U's case for better jobs in the sector. But our observation of the small number of high-road restaurants repeatedly featured by ROC-U and some use of its Diner's Guide "app" suggest that the actual number of restaurateurs involved is small at present.

Our reading of the evidence is that while informing employers of win-win opportunities and celebrating high-road operators are helpful actions, large-scale change depends more on using *policy* to pave the high road and especially to close off the low road—in other words, to alter managerial incentives and thus decision making. We found variation in pay, benefits, use of part-timers, and so on, in our U.S. sample, but mainly within a fairly narrow band. As noted in earlier chapters, some private rather than corporate retailers have greater managerial autonomy, but even this latitude is limited. Our "higher-road" case studies—the privately held Homestyle and The Market in food retailing, Tech Source in consumer electronics—differ from their competitors, but in limited ways in terms of job outcomes. Like every company in their sectors, they are continually looking over their shoulders at low-cost competitors, and that creates tensions between cost management and strategies headlining quality, variety, and service. Costco, often touted as the "anti-Wal-Mart," has successfully achieved distinct job outcomes, but its sales are only a bit over one-third the size of Wal-Mart's (and it has only one-seventeenth the number of stores and other units).[116] Differences among U.S. retailers are dwarfed by the differences between U.S. chains and similar ones in France, where a whole ensemble of laws and norms underpin better jobs. These patterns point us back to *policies* that mandate, or incentivize, or render economically feasible the creation of better jobs and *grassroots strategies* to accomplish the same thing, to which we turn next.

Before we consider mobilization strategies that help close off the low road, there is one more general high-road paving policy initiative worth considering: providing technical assistance to small businesses with owners who are interested in shifting to the high road (either on their own initiative or because they are facing penalties for employment law violations) but cannot see how. The prospect would be to explore whether such approaches are suitable to address challenges within the scattered sites of retail chains, many of which leave store managers to wrestle with cost control without full understanding of the ramifications for job quality and future productivity. Research on business inspection systems in Central America, the Caribbean, and Brazil indicates that inspectors with the skills and mandate to advise businesses on upgrading, rather than just imposing penalties, can facilitate sectorwide shifts toward higher-road labor strategies.[117] Revamping inspection systems to build in this kind of "tutelary" role might be difficult to achieve in the U.S. policy regime, but federally funded Small Business Assistance Centers could be made loci for investment in technical assistance *linked to improvements in job quality*.

Making such an approach relevant to larger chains would require some compulsion on their corporate calculus to alter managerial goals within stores and support managers in making the shift. One lesson we learned from Europe is that high labor turnover is a central concern *in the corporate boardroom* as a threat to firm profitability, not a secondary issue to be simply "managed" by store managers. Currently, instructions from U.S. national chains' headquarters to store management ("Reduce labor hours!," "Do not authorize overtime!") often induce these individuals not only to downgrade job quality with erratic scheduling and low pay but also to violate basic labor standards such as minimum wage and overtime hours laws—as evidenced by the large number of lawsuits against Wal-Mart and other big-box chains. With these actors—separate from small shops—policy actions, such as Department of Labor guidance, advisories, and systematic enforcement where violations are egregious, are necessary to move the focus from local managers to corporate managerial incentives and their consequences in practice and to change the signals being sent to stores.

Increasing Worker Bargaining Power   Underlying bad jobs in retail are starkly unequal power relations between large retailers and workers, at least in the ubiquitous non-unionized environments. Possibilities for rectifying this imbalance include both public policy proposals and labor movement strategy initiatives.

A first, and quite important, power-balancing policy would be using federal fiscal and monetary policy to reduce unemployment further and keep it low. Retail jobs were better in 2000 when unemployment was at a thirty-year low of 4.0 percent than in 2014 when, despite significant recovery from the late-2000s recession, unemployment stood at 6.2 percent. Discussing the policies necessary to drive unemployment down falls outside the scope of this book, but any plan for improving jobs needs to note this crucial pressure point.

A next set of strategies involves facilitating conventional unionization and moving the United States a bit closer to Denmark in this regard. Of course, comprehensive U.S. labor law reform could simply render a card check[118] sufficient for union representation (as proposed in the Employee Free Choice Act, first introduced in 2008), but this and similar proposed reforms have faced fierce employer opposition since at least the 1970s, and none have been passed.[119] Recent national political changes offer virtually no hope in this domain.

Other approaches encompass mobilizing unionized retail workers and their allies in ways that boost their clout and, more importantly (given shrinking union density), using new approaches to representation campaigns. To start with, there are *traditional union activities:* strikes, such as the 2003–2004 Southern California supermarket strike, and boycotts, like the UFCW's boycott of the southwestern El Super chain to pressure the company to negotiate a contract. A more recent innovation is the *corporate campaign,* which attempts to mount pressure by reaching out to various company stakeholders—consumers (exposing problems with merchandise quality), financiers (spotlighting weaknesses in company performance), regulators at the federal, state, and local levels (including authorities with permitting power over localized expansions), and so on.[120] The UFCW, and in particular its Retail, Wholesale, and Department Store Union (RWDSU) subunit, have also made some effective use of *community unionism*—geographically clustered organizing that incorporates community involvement and support. In Bushwick, New York, RWDSU worked in coalition with Make the Road by Walking, a community group, to successfully unionize a number of small local retailers.[121]

Retail globalization has also opened the door to new kinds of labor strategies. Swedish apparel merchandiser H&M signed a global framework agreement, specifying certain company labor practices, with its powerful home union in 2004. When H&M expanded to the United States, RWDSU and other UFCW locals leveraged this agreement to get H&M to accept card check union elections and rapidly won the right to represent a set of stores in the New York City area.[122] This victory illustrates the multinational "home-country" effect, in this case (albeit an uncommon one) operating toward job improvement rather than deterioration.

Indeed, as some of the foregoing examples suggest, trade unions and other grassroots labor organizations in the United States have experimented with strategies that depart ever more dramatically from union representation campaigns and collective bargaining under the terms of the National Labor Relations Act. The retail sector has been one major locus of such experimentation, and Wal-Mart has been the principal target. The UFCW started out organizing for traditional union representation elections at Wal-Mart, but when the company responded to a 2000 vote in favor of union representation by meat-cutters at a Texas store by shutting down the meat-cutting department, the union turned to other options.[123] One line of union activity simply consists of compiling and disseminating negative publicity about the Blue Giant. Wherever the UFCW has localized strength, it has also mounted "site fights," building coalitions to block or place conditions on Wal-Mart store openings. In line with corporate campaign strategies, the retail union has also produced financial analysis reports directed at investors, arguing that Wal-Mart's stance toward labor and job quality has hurt firm performance—for example, they point out that the disorderly stores, empty shelves, and lack of basic service that result from this stance are all dimensions that hurt store sales.[124] These campaigns have indeed helped constrain Wal-Mart's growth and compel it to institute widely publicized improvements in wages and benefits, though these fall far short of what union representation has obtained for workers.[125] The UFCW has also attempted to use pressure from unionized Wal-Mart workers in the United Kingdom, Argentina, and Chile to influence the company's U.S. practices, though the impact of these efforts is unclear (see chapter 7).

The U.S. labor experiments that diverge furthest from traditional union strategies have been a set of ventures into "minority unionism," in which an organization mobilizes workers and makes demands on an employer *without* seeking to demonstrate majority worker support or win a representation election, at least in the short to medium term. The Wal-Mart Workers Association and OUR Walmart have rolled out this strategy, as discussed in chapter 7. RWDSU launched the New York City–based Retail Action Project, a worker center for retail workers. RAP engages in the wide range of activities characteristic of U.S. worker centers: advocacy, training, research and publicity, and leadership development, in addition to carrying out and supporting direct retail worker organizing.[126]

Unlike other avenues to institutional change, when it comes to grassroots organizing strategies directed at retail, the United States may not have a great deal to learn from other countries because it has been such a fertile seedbed of organizing innovation itself. In contrast, we find that European retail unions have been able to make more straightforward use of their countries' labor relations structures, especially at the national level, which are in general friendlier toward labor rights, rather than resorting to new strategies. As we pointed out in chapter 7, Wal-Mart workers *have* launched organizing campaigns that departed from the standard union playbook in Argentina and China, and Mexican community and human rights organizations have unleashed investigative research and publicity campaigns and site fights akin to those in the United States.[127] But U.S. organizing among retail workers currently appears to be the source of the most creative alternative strategies in the world.

In summary, the landscape of possible institutional change to improve retail jobs in the United States presents varied approaches. Targets for improvement include compensation, scheduling, skill development and mobility, and overall high-road employment. Modalities of reform include mandates but also incentives directed at employers. Solutions can hew to a "French" (state regulatory) approach or a "Danish" (organizing and bargaining) approach. We have identified many frontiers on which to advance. But we close this book with a reality check on how likely it is that we will see an overall improvement in U.S. retail jobs.

IN CLOSING: IS THERE ANY REALISTIC HOPE FOR BETTER RETAIL JOBS?

Can U.S. retail jobs be better anytime soon? We break this question down into an economic question and a political one, and address each briefly. The economic question stems from that old chestnut, the "job-killer" thesis: won't improving retail jobs lead to higher retail prices, imposing costs on the rest of society, dampening demand, and depressing the number of retail jobs? Our reply is that yes, prices will almost surely rise (compared to what they would have been), but four factors mitigate the worry about this.

First, boosting the quality of jobs in retail will help a large chunk of the low-wage workforce and either directly (for many of the policies) or indirectly (for organizing approaches, for instance) affect substantial numbers of other low-paid workers. The net effect will be redistribution from higher-income consumers (who can readily absorb a price increase) to lower-income consumer-workers (who will get a wage increase).

Second, the short-run macroeconomic impact of redistributing resources downward will be to stimulate overall consumption because those at the low end of the income spectrum spend, rather than save, most of their income.

Third, an increasingly common view among labor economists is that labor markets are *monopsonistic*—that is, buyers (employers) hold market power based on segmentation in the labor market, paying "below-market" wages but employing fewer workers. To the extent that this view is correct, as we believe it is, compelling wage increases may actually lead to *expansion* of hiring, just as setting a price ceiling will lead ex-monopolists to produce more. (It only makes sense to restrict hiring if it has the desired effect of reducing the going wage.)

Fourth, a potential positive long-term effect will be to induce retailer investment in increased productivity (thus further moderating price increases) through both technological improvements and investment in worker skills. This *would* reduce retail employment relative to the level that would prevail "all else equal"; schematically, it would move low-wage, labor-intensive U.S. retail closer to high-wage, capital-intensive French retail. However, this change would most likely occur at a gradual pace that would allow workers to seek other employment options, especially in U.S. retail with its high turnover and elevated concentrations of youth.

All of these arguments have recently been thoroughly reviewed in the exploding research literature on the impacts of minimum wage increases.[128] Of course, these adaptive processes would probably unfold differently across retail subsectors.

The political question is in many ways more challenging: are any of these institutional changes achievable in the United States of today and in the next decade or so? We would emphasize again, of course, that institutions, including deeply held norms, *do* change. Laws regulating the minimum wage, social insurance, collective bargaining, workplace safety and health, and workplace discrimination and diversity are concrete accomplishments from change efforts that are widely accepted in much of the world—though aspects of existing laws are constantly being questioned. It is plausible that growing public concerns about inequality and economic immobility could translate into deeper shifts in norms regarding work and the proper ways to regulate it. Moreover, some of the proposals we list are clearly achievable because they are already in motion— notably minimum wage increases and the Affordable Care Act— though again, as we write, at least some of these advances are about to be reversed. Other reforms proposed here could gain widespread appeal akin to that currently enjoyed by the minimum wage, since they can similarly be framed as rewarding hardworking people who are not getting a fair shake.

On the grassroots organizing front, labor law reform to level the playing field for unions—that is, to restore to workers reliable and fair access to representation and bargaining—has been a tough sell since the 1940s, and unionization has trended downward since the 1950s. However, we have been here before. The U.S. trade union movement was largely given up for dead by the early 1930s, but then the industrial unionism of the Committee for Industrial Organization (the CIO's original name) erupted, contributing to the political preconditions for the adoption and implementation of the National Labor Relations Act *and* generating by far the largest increase in union density the country has ever seen. It would be foolhardy to predict a repetition of that history, but the current ferment of organizing innovation and the highly visible "Fight for $15" movement—which few would have predicted as late as 2011—could certainly lead to the consolidation of new models of worker organization and quite possibly laws to institutionalize them in the longer run.

The main point is not that change is unstoppable but rather that the institutional reforms and reinventions needed to upgrade retail jobs in the United States *are worth achieving*. Achieving them will be a matter of political will, devotion of financial resources, and ingenuity in coming up with new approaches. But this is precisely the story of where European labor market and labor relations reforms came from, where Mexico's strong-on-the-books labor law also came from, and indeed where the U.S. institutions that do protect workers effectively came from. If there is any lesson to be learned from our in-depth analysis of the nature of U.S. retail jobs and our far-ranging tour of their counterparts around the world, it is that the problems with these jobs are many and deeply tenacious, but that possible solutions are likewise numerous and well worth the attempt.

Notes

CHAPTER 1: INTRODUCTION

1. U.S. Bureau of Labor Statistics 2016a; Institut National de la Statistique et des Études Économiques 2016. Ratios calculated from 2013 annual averages (most recent year of data available for France). "Nonmanagerial" also excludes professionals. The two ratios are not strictly comparable because the U.S. data compare retail wages with all private-sector workers, whereas the French data compare retail wages with all employees, both private- and public-sector. (However, this disparity should not greatly affect the ratios.)

2. On the "1 percent," see Milkman, Luce, and Lewis 2013; Piketty 2014. On the middle and bottom, see Kalleberg 2011; Mishel et al. 2012.

3. Molyneux 2015.

4. De la Garza 2012; Gautié and Schmitt 2010; Kuruvilla, Lee, and Gallagher 2011; Warhurst et al. 2012; Evans and Tilly 2015.

5. Chirino 2015. For the U.S. Chamber of Commerce position on labor, see the statement on its website at: https://www.uschamber.com/labor. The pro-business Employment Policies Institute (https://www.epionline.org/) should not be confused with the pro-labor Economic Policy Institute. For academic backing of pro-business positions, see, for example, Neumark, Salas, and Wascher 2014.

6. Osterman 2012.

7. On U.S. trends, see Appelbaum, Bernhardt, and Murnane 2003b; Kalleberg 2011. On global trends, see Carré et al. 2012; Evans and Tilly 2015.

8. Freeman 2007a; Friedman 2005.

9. Evans 2010; Ritzer 1998; Royle 2006.

10. Appelbaum and Batt 2014.

11. Harvey 2007.

12. Freeman 2007b; Kalleberg 2011; Solow 1990; Tilly and Tilly 1998.

13. We address our reasons for focusing on retail later in the chapter. It is important to add that our choice of the retail sector, most aspects of our study design (except in Mexico), and the opportunity to carry out comparisons with five similar European studies resulted from participation in a six-country comparative research project on low-wage jobs funded by the Russell Sage Foundation; for a summary, see Gautié and Schmitt 2010.

14. For work focusing on the United States, see Appelbaum, Bernhardt, and Murnane 2003a; Appelbaum and Batt 1994; Doussard 2013; Herzenberg, Alic, and Wial 1998. For research on other countries, see Bosch and Lehndorff 2005; Gautié and Schmitt 2010; Holtgrewe, Kerst, and Shire 2002; Maurice, Sellier, and Silvestre 1986; Smith and Meiksins 1995; Warhurst et al. 2012.

15. The chapter on Mexico is omitted from the print edition but is available as an online supplement.

16. Company identities are confidential, and we identify them by pseudonyms throughout the book.

17. This study was conducted with support from the Russell Sage Foundation as part of the "Low-Wage Work in the Wealthy World" project. Fieldwork was facilitated in some cases by the National Retail Federation. Philip Moss of the University of Massachusetts Lowell contributed to some of the site visits.

18. Marc Maurice, François Sellier, and Jean-Jacques Silvestre (1986) elaborated the concept of a national or societal effect in their landmark study of manufacturing plants in France and Germany that were closely paired in product, market, and technology but had different job outcomes. In the words of Janice McCormick in her introduction to their study, Maurice, Sellier, and Silvestre contributed to developing a theory of "how a nation's major social institutions decisively coordinate and structure work relations." Three sets of factors—the educational domain, the business organizational domain, and the industrial relations domain—determine how "work and society are inextricably connected." Furthermore, they place the development of the employment relation in "its national societal and cultural context" (viii). Perhaps most succinctly, Maurice, Sellier, and Silvestre state that their intent is "to analyze the firm not as a universal institution but as a social con-

struct" (195). On the national-sectoral model, see Askenazy et al. 2012.

19. Bosch, Mayhew, and Gautié 2010.

20. A short summary of the key findings reported in the online chapter A1 is included in chapter 5.

21. Greenhouse 2005; Ton 2012.

CHAPTER 2: NUMEROUS, YOUNG, FEMALE, AND POORLY PAID: A PROFILE OF THE U.S. RETAIL WORKFORCE AND ITS CONTEXT

1. U.S. Bureau of Labor Statistics 2016a.

2. Statista 2015.

3. Hortaçsu and Syverson 2015.

4. All real wages are adjusted for inflation using the Consumer Price Index for All Urban Consumers (CPI-U).

5. U.S. Bureau of Labor Statistics 2016c.

6. Mishel, Bernstein, and Allegretto 2007, table 3.27. More recent editions do not include this analysis.

7. Authors' calculation from June 2014 Current Population Survey (CPS).

8. Mishel, Bernstein, and Boushey 2003, table 3.13. Again, this analysis is not available in more recent editions.

9. See online table 2A.2 (*source:* U.S. Department of Labor, Bureau of Labor Statistics, "Productivity and Costs," available at: http://stats.bls.gov/lpc/home.htm#data, accessed August 2015, with added calculations by authors).

10. Johnson 2002.

11. On negative productivity growth in the first period, see Tilly 1996.

12. U.S. Census Bureau, "Community Facts," American FactFinder, available at: http://factfinder.census.gov (accessed July 2015), table EC0744SSSZ2.

13. Lebhar 1952, 63.

14. U.S. Bureau of Labor Statistics 2014a.

15. See online figure 2A.6. For this and all online figures and tables based on our own data analysis, sample sizes are also reported online.

16. The electronics subsample is too small for a reliable comparable estimate.

17. Frazis et al. 1998.

18. Burns 1982.

19. Moss and Tilly 2001.

20. Richardson 2005.

21. Unionstats.com, n.d.

22. U.S. Bureau of Labor Statistics 2016a. The difference is sixteen percentage *points*—50 percent versus 34 percent. These percentages differ from those reported in online appendix 2A and discussed later in this chapter, because they are from a different source that has adequate sample sizes to generate reliable estimates for the much smaller electronics sector.

23. For a review of this research, see Warhurst, Tilly, and Gatta 2017.

24. When comparing the large states, there appears to be a positive correlation between union density and the union wage premium, but no such relationship is apparent across the larger regions. Analysis of grocery workers in the fifty states plus the District of Columbia actually yields a small *negative* correlation between density and the payoff to unionization (not shown). The correlation is −0.24, significant only at the 10 percent level. Adding controls for the square of union density and/or the right-to-work status of the state to a regression of premium on density diminishes the significance of estimates well below standard levels without altering the sign of the effect. This negative correlation suggests that the main impact of higher levels of unionization on the union wage premium in grocery stores is a "union threat effect": where there is higher union density, non-union employers are more likely to raise wages closer to union wage levels, narrowing the wage gap between union and non-union workers. In any case, whether owing to differences in competitive environment, union strategy, or the level of political support or hostility for unions, there are large disparities in unions' impact on grocery wages across the United States.

25. The source for all demographic statistics, unless otherwise specified, is the authors' calculations from the June 2014 Current Population Survey. The universe is all privately employed wage and salary workers. Frontline jobs include cashiers, clerks, and baggers.

26. Carré, Holgate, and Tilly 2006.

27. Lambert, Haley-Lock, and Henly 2012.

28. Jayaraman and Food Labor Research Center 2014.

29. Cohen 2017.

30. Tilly 1996.

31. The Bureau of Labor Statistics defines part-time work as less than thirty-five hours a week, unless the job is defined by the respondent as full-time. Because in our fieldwork we encountered full-time workers working as few as thirty-two hours, we chose a thirty-two-hour cutoff. We use the "usual hours" variable from the CPS, which allows us to use the same variable across the time series. This method underestimates the rate of part-time employment because average hours worked in a week for each person can include more than their primary job (which is retail in this case).

32. The electronics percentage is not a reliable estimate, since it is based on a very small number of observations. However, data for the last twenty-five years consistently show a gap of twenty percentage points or more in the percentage of unionized workers between grocery and electronics frontline workers.

33. Specifically, 36.8 percent for women versus 20.7 percent for men.

34. It is possible that black and Latino workers stay in retail for lack of access to higher-paid and more desirable job opportunities elsewhere in the economy. With seniority, retail workers tend to move to full-time work, and thus blacks and Latinos are less likely to be in part-time jobs than others. Data reviewed here do not prove this point but indicate a different pattern for these groups than in the economy overall.

35. The figure for women with dependent children working part-time is 31.5 percent, versus 37.6 percent for those without children.

36. Among retail workers, 6.4 percent work short hours, versus 4.3 percent for all private workers. See online tables 2A.6 and 2A.7.

37. Among retail workers, 22.3 percent work sixteen to thirty-one hours a week, versus 15.0 percent for all private workers.

38. U.S. Bureau of Labor Statistics 2015a.

39. Holzer et al. 2011, 133.

40. This may be due in part to the greater vulnerability of manufacturing businesses and jobs to economic cycles.

41. Andersson, Holzer, and Lane 2005. Because of their data source, these authors use the old Standard Industrial Classification (SIC) definition of the retail industry, which includes eating and drinking places. Employees in eating and drinking places account for 52 percent of their group of low earners in retail (table 3.4).

42. Ibid., tables 4.6, 4.7.

CHAPTER 3: CHANGE AND VARIATION IN RETAIL JOBS IN THE UNITED STATES: A VIEW FROM CASE STUDIES

1. A "banner" is a brand of store within a company. For example, Sam's Club is a Wal-Mart banner, as is (confusingly) Wal-Mart.

2. Appelbaum, Bernhardt, and Murnane 2003b; Osterman 1982.

3. Batt 2000.

4. Appelbaum, Bernhardt, and Murnane 2003b. On FedEx and UPS, see Cappelli and Crocker-Hefter 1996.

5. Bailey and Bernhardt 1997.

6. Grimshaw and Rubery 1998; Moss, Salzman, and Tilly 2008. The relationship between the product and labor strategies is most visible when market shifts precipitate a change in product orientation, which then requires an adjustment in the labor approach. This adjustment must be compatible with the HR practices already in place and must also build on these in such a way as to avoid tensions among goals (Cappelli and Crocker-Hefter 1996).

7. We also completed three serendipitous interviews with one electronics retail employee and two grocery union representatives at companies to which we were not able to secure access.

8. See chapter 8 for a more complete (and referenced) discussion of these recent trends.

9. On private equity's impact on labor costs and staffing reductions, see Matsa 2010. On other impacts, see Appelbaum and Batt 2014.

10. See, for example, Martin 2009.

11. Carré, Holgate, and Tilly 2009.

12. Although the data reported here come from individual stores, they follow the guidelines from the banner and higher-level corporation with regard to wage scales and the allocation of benefits.

13. We use turnover figures reported by company representatives or calculated from data conveyed in interviews. We were not able to persuade company representatives to give us their operational definition of "turnover," so we cannot be confident that all the numbers they gave us are fully comparable.

14. We explore the continued expansion of delivery options in food retail in chapter 8, though our assessment is that it is not yet a major competitive differentiator.

15. Though we did not study such cases, it is conceivable for a company to run convenience, discount, and full-service store formats to tap into distinct customer segments.

16. Turnover is four times higher, however, for short-hour part-timers—those working less than twenty hours a week.

17. *Business Week* 2006; see also *Discount Store News* 1998.

18. Berner 2005.

19. Ibid.; *Digital Home* 2008.

20. Goldstein 2007.

21. Birchall and Allison 2008. The only post-2009 reference to consumer electronics installation and repair at Wal-Mart that we have been able to find is a 2015 move to host MyTech USA repair service shops in a small number of supercenters; see the MyTech USA website at: http://mytechusa.com/ (accessed December 2015).

22. A Bargain Warehouse appliance clerk commented, "We don't necessarily get training on all the products. Other stores, electronics stores, they give them a lot of training, especially with their sales. But since we don't have any commission or anything like that, we don't necessarily get as much training."

23. Grugulis and Bozkurt 2009.

24. Carré, Tilly, and Holgate 2007; Carré et al. 2010; Jany-Catrice and Lehndorff 2005; Lambert, Haley-Lock, and Henly 2012.

25. This threshold is subject to change as retailers implement the Affordable Care Act (still in effect as we write, though efforts to repeal it continue) and its mandate on employers to provide insurance for workers regularly scheduled to work over thirty hours or pay a fine.

26. These patterns have been exacerbated in recent years by the use of software that enables retailers to slice patterns of customer flow into ever-finer segments. In 2014, these issues came to the fore in the news accounts of the complaints and militancy of fast-food workers and retail workers (Center for Law and Social Policy, Retail Action Project, and Women Employed 2014; Miller 2014) and Starbucks' announcement that it was changing its scheduling practices and providing one week's advance notice of schedules. We discuss the policy implications in chapter 8.

27. The economist Claudia Goldin made this point most recently for a number of service occupations (Miller 2014).

28. Full-timers in grocery stores can sometimes request a schedule that meets their constraints in exchange for flexibility about working during "unsocial" hours. "That's what I told them," said a cake decorator. "That's the only thing I ask. And they're very accommodating on that. I said, 'I'll work whatever days you need, whatever hours you need me, but I just need to leave by 3:00 or 3:30.'"

29. Some have argued that women, particularly mothers, are confined to gap filler status even if they think of themselves as time adjusters and aspire to be considered for full-time status; thus relegated to gap filler status by supervisors who do not see them as flexible, they miss out on promotion opportunities (Ruan and Reichman 2014).

30. Occasionally, workers reported "solving" a difficult schedule by swapping shifts with colleagues and then seeking authorization from their manager for the switch.

31. Recent news accounts (Greenhouse 2014; Miller 2014) stress the complications of variable schedules for parents, particularly single parents.

32. Clawson and Gerstel 2002; Gerstel, Clawson, and Zussman 2002.

33. Some also note that the combination of fluctuating and nonstandard work hours (such as evenings and nights) with family responsibilities appears to put women retail workers at greater risk of sleep disruption than is the case for male retail workers (Maume, Sebastian, and Bardo 2009).

34. Lambert and Henly 2009, 2010. In their studies of the scheduling practices of a clothing retailer, Julia Henly and Susan Lambert (2014) noted similar difficulties with the short and erratic scheduling experienced by frontline workers.

35. Center for Law and Social Policy, Retail Action Project, and Women Employed 2014; Schneider and Harknett 2017.

CHAPTER 4: COMPETITIVE AND LABOR STRATEGIES: ADDRESSING SUSTAINABILITY

1. Our findings are generally consistent with those of Jayaraman and Food Labor Research Center 2014.

2. Ton 2012; Center for Law and Social Policy, Retail Action Project, and Women Employed 2014. Since our field work was carried out, Wal-Mart has announced some improvements (see chapter 8).

3. Carré, Tilly, and Denham 2011.

4. Turnover, at 60 percent, is high by historic standards for the company.

5. Peter Cappelli and Anne Crocker-Hefter (1996) note that a firm's history shapes the tools at its disposal to adapt to rapid change in competitive conditions. "Mature" firms with fairly stable internal labor markets turn into "defenders" of their market. They may experience difficulty moving to a different market segment. The dis-

tinction is useful even for retail, where "stability" in the workforce is far lower than in other sectors.

6. Appelbaum and Batt 2014.

7. A third formula is a higher-end supermarket encompassing a few stores.

8. The Consumer Price Index can be found at the U.S. Bureau of Labor Statistics web page http://www.bls.gov/cpi/.

9. Another consumer electronics chain in the study, High Fidelity, offers only the upper segment of services, and thus it does not experience job segmentation. The entire chain—and other specialist companies like it—differs from large chains in the sector in that the entire staff, including most managers, consists of high-level salespeople paid on commission.

10. As noted earlier, the third and final warehouse case in our sample, Village Voice, has retained regional primacy thanks to its location in rural areas not reached by the giant discounter Wal-Mart.

CHAPTER 5: COMPARING RETAIL JOBS IN THE UNITED STATES AND WESTERN EUROPE

This chapter draws on writing and analysis shared with several other colleagues, all of whom participated in the Russell Sage Foundation's "Low-Wage Work in the Wealthy World" project. The comparative analysis of job outcomes in the United States versus five European countries draws extensively on analysis and writing shared with Dorothea Voss-Dahm and Maarten van Klaveren, and that analysis itself rests on analyses prepared by national retail research teams in the "Low-Wage Work in the Wealthy World" project in Denmark, France, Germany, the Netherlands, and the United Kingdom, organized and funded by the Russell Sage Foundation. Parts of this chapter are excerpted verbatim from the resulting chapter (Carré et al. 2010). This work draws extensively on research summarized in the retail chapters of the "Low-Wage Work in Europe" national monographs (Askenazy, Berry, and Prunier-Poulmaire 2008; Esbjerg et al. 2008; Mason and Osborne 2008; van Klaveren 2008; Voss-Dahm 2008). Unattributed European interview quotes come from these chapters or the underlying case studies.

1. "Exit options" consist of gaps or weaknesses in institutions bolstering job quality, or they result from deliberate evasions of or "top-down" exemptions from regulation.

2. Gautié and Schmitt 2010.

3. Ferner 1997; Maurice, Sellier, and Silvestre 1986; Meardi et al. 2009; Royle 2006; Smith and Meiksins 1995.

4. Gadrey and Jany-Catrice 2000, 26.

5. Bailey and Bernhardt 1997.

6. Jany-Catrice and Lehndorff 2005.

7. Baret, Lehndorff, and Sparks 2000; Bosch and Lehndorff 2005. See also Lloyd and Payne 2016.

8. Maurice, Sellier, and Silvestre 1986. See chapter 1, note 18.

9. Bosch and Lehndorff 2005. See also Gadrey, Lehndorff, and Ribault 2000 for another synthesis and a slightly different formulation, though the implications are similar.

10. Chris Smith and Peter Meiksins's (1995) framework recognizing broad system effects (the dynamics of capitalist production relations), societal effects, and dominance effects brings similar dimensions to bear on, first, organizations' choices and, second, employment systems.

11. Coiling and Clark 2002.

12. See note 9.

13. Whitley 1999.

14. Tilly 1996; Jany-Catrice and Lehndorff 2005.

15. Streeck and Thelen 2005.

16. For more on French and German retailers' exploitation of exit options, see Jaehrling and Méhaut 2013.

17. In the United States, the immigrant share in retail (13 percent), and in cashier/stocker jobs in particular (12 percent), is lower than for the private sector as a whole (18 percent) (authors' calculation from March 2007 CPS). The Danish figure of 4 percent (Esbjerg et al. 2008, 157) compares to 5.8 percent of foreign-born workers for total employment (Gautié et al. 2009). Germany's 5.5 percent share relates to the 7 percent of the German workforce who are non-German citizens. In the United Kingdom, the 8 percent of cashiers and 9 percent of sales assistants who are immigrants compare to the 6 percent of the U.K. labor force who are immigrants (Mason and Osborne, 2008, 135–36, compared to Gautié and Schmitt 2010). For privacy reasons, exact figures are missing for France and the Netherlands, but case-study data suggest for both countries an overrepresentation of immigrant workers or workers from ethnic minorities in low-end/hard-discount food retailing, notably in the large urban areas.

18. Tijdens 1998; Voss-Dahm 2003.

19. On German and Dutch retailers, see Voss-Dahm 2000.

20. Samuel 2015.

21. Inman 2016. U.S. cities and states have also begun adopting new controls on scheduling, as explored in chapter 8.

22. According to the French fieldwork, exceptions to this minimum are often negotiated.

23. European data are from the 2006 Labour Force Survey; U.S. data are from the 2007 CPS.

24. On strategic segmentation in the call center sector, see Batt 2000.

25. Europaeisches Einzelhandelsinstitut 2006, 91, 92.

26. Moss and Tilly 2001.

27. Abernathy et al. 2000.

28. These within-country differences are partly due to a research design that split the company samples between "high-end" and "low-end" service levels, although there is not a perfect match between service level and degree of use of highly automated high-performance business systems.

29. Autor, Levy, and Murnane 2003, 132.

30. Marsden 1999, 37.

31. Lehndorff and Voss-Dahm 2005.

32. The Baccalauréat is the national diploma that students have to earn at the end of high school in order to gain access to tertiary education.

33. Marsden 2000, 344.

34. Streeck and Thelen 2005, 29.

35. Andersson, Holzer, and Lane 2005.

36. The five-country correlation coefficients (omitting the United States) are −0.72 and 0.91, respectively.

37. See Gautié and Schmitt 2010, ch. 2.

38. Other European countries have store size regulations, but they are less stringent and in flux; these regulations have had the greatest impact in France.

39. Tijdens et al. 2007. The law mandates only that the CLA be in force if 50 percent of workers in a workplace are members of the main union.

40. Westergaard-Nielsen 2008, 38.

41. Unionstats, n.d.

42. The number of mini-jobs in retail increased by 20 percent from 1999 to 2007. Their share of total employment rose from 21.7 percent to 23.3 percent; every fourth job in retail in 2007 was a mini-job.

43. Chubb et al. 2008; van Klaveren, Tijdens, and Sprenger 2007.

44. Carré, Holgate, and Tilly 2006.

45. Authors' calculations from 2006 data in StatBank Denmark 2007.

46. We have data for three countries only: the U.S. and Danish figures are sales per employee-hour because value-added data are not available for these subsectors. The U.S. figure uses sales from the 2002 Economic Census, employment and weekly hours from Current Employment Statistics (CES) (Bureau of Labor Statistics 2016a), and an economy-wide average of weeks per year from Hyde (n.d.) and Raines (2007). The Danish figure uses data from StatBank Denmark, except hours per full-time-equivalent (FTE), which are from the European Foundation for the Improvement of Living and Working Conditions, and the economy-wide average of weeks per year is from Hyde (n.d.). Dutch figures are from Industrial Board for Retail Trades (2005, 8), based on value-added per hours worked per year.

47. Unemployment insurance benefits are based on the fixed part of pay only. Thus, low bargained wages have an impact on unemployment benefits.

48. Short-hour part-time work has had this effect particularly because it is combined with the problems of union organizing in numerous small workplaces. For a discussion of Germany, the Netherlands, and the United Kingdom, see Dribbusch 2003.

49. It is important to note that less-protected, objectively lower-quality jobs do not necessarily imply that U.S. workers are less satisfied with their jobs than their European counterparts. Past research has shown that U.S. workers have lower expectations than workers in other wealthy countries (Frege and Godard 2014; Lincoln and Kalleberg 1985; Przeworski and Teune 1970), most likely owing to a combination of social Darwinist ideology and simply being accustomed to a low-regulation, low-rights work environment.

CHAPTER 6: CASHIERS IN LARGE SUPERMARKETS IN FRANCE AND THE UNITED STATES: THE ROLE OF SOCIETAL EFFECTS

This chapter is based on a joint analysis with Philippe Askenazy, Jean-Baptiste Berry, and Sophie Prunier-Poulmaire that resulted in the coauthored paper "Working in Large Food Retailers: A France–United States Comparison," which was published in a slightly different version as Askenazy et al. (2012). Parts of this chapter are excerpted verbatim from the paper and the article.

1. Maurice, Sellier, and Silvestre 1986.

2. For comparative purposes, "low-wage" is defined as an hourly wage that falls below two-thirds of the economy-wide median.

3. For details on the French grocers, see Askenazy, Berry, and Prunier-Poulmaire 2008.

4. Higher hourly pay in France does not necessarily imply *adequate* pay, both because of a higher French cost of living and because of the part-time employment that is common in retail in both countries.

5. The larger share of hypermarkets in France than of supercenters and warehouse stores in the United States is primarily an artifact of a lower selling area threshold for the French category. Hypermarkets are defined as stores over 2,500 square meters; therefore, the French hypermarket category includes stores that would be classified as supermarkets in the United States. The much greater floor area of U.S. supercenters compared to French hypermarkets stems in part from this definitional difference, but also presumably reflects the more recent rollout of supercenters and hypermarkets in the United States and the well-known lower density typical of U.S. development.

6. Vega 2005.

7. Lehman, Psihogios, and Meulenbroek 2001.

8. Authors' calculations from U.S. Department of Labor (n.d., "History of Federal Minimum Wage Rates"); U.S. Bureau of Labor Statistics (2016a); and the Consumer Price Index for All Urban Consumers (CPI-U).

9. U.S. Department of Labor, n.d. ("History of Federal Minimum Wage Rates").

10. Dube, Lester, and Reich 2010.

11. See chapter 2; see also Carré and Tilly 2008.

12. Carré and Tilly 2008.

13. These sectoral agreements are administrative extension of the basic terms of the collective bargaining agreement between major retailers and major union federations.

14. Union membership is distinct from coverage by the terms of a collective bargaining agreement.

15. Boylaud and Nicoletti 2001.

16. Square footage for French food retailing spaces includes classic supermarkets, hard-discount stores, and hypermarkets. The figures for France in this subsection are estimated using the Fédération du Commerce et de la Distribution (FCD 2007) and INSEE

(2008a) databases. U.S. figures (from 2007) come from Food Marketing Institute (n.d.). A supermarket is any full-line self-service grocery store generating sales volume of U.S. $2 million or more annually.

17. INSEE 2009a.

18. Silva 2016.

19. NIST 2010.

20. Tilly 1996, table 2.5.

21. Ibid., 146.

22. Silva 2007, table 1.

23. OECD 2007, table D1.1.

24. U.S. Bureau of Labor Statistics 2008.

25. INSEE 2008b, T207.

26. On child care in the United States, see Albelda 2008. On the French universal preschool system, see Kamerman et al. 2003.

27. INSEE 2008a.

28. Akerlof and Yellen 1986.

29. U.S. numbers (for 2007) were computed by authors from March 2007 CPS; French numbers (for 2006) are from Esbjerg, van Klaveren, and Voss-Dahm (forthcoming).

30. Mathieu Hocquelet and his colleagues (2016) provide an overview of these pressures in the French context and their consequences for worker experiences.

31. Lichtenstein 2009.

32. Gautié and Schmitt 2010.

33. Carré and Tilly 2008.

34. Askenazy, Berry, and Prunier-Poulmaire 2008; Samuel 2015.

CHAPTER 7: THE SURPRISINGLY CHANGEABLE WAL-MART AROUND THE WORLD

Parts of this chapter are adapted from Tilly 2007.

1. See, for example, Dicker 2005; Norman 2004; Quinn 2000.

2. Rosen 2006; Lichtenstein 2004, 2009.

3. Lewis et al. 2001; see also Ghemawat and Mark 2006.

4. These terms are adopted from Ferner 1997; Maurice, Sellier, and

Silvestre 1986; Meardi et al. 2009; Royle 2006; Smith and Meiksins 1995; and others.

5. These estimates involve various sources and imputations. All sales are net sales. *United States:* Comparison is for 2011. Total retail sales are taken from U.S. Census Bureau (2014), net computed as (retail sales – retail purchases). U.S.-based Wal-Mart U.S. sales and global Sam's Club sales are taken from Wal-Mart (2011). U.S. Sam's Club sales are imputed as six-sevenths of the global total, based on Wal-Mart (n.d., "Our Business") statement that Sam's Club has opened "more than 600 clubs in the U.S. and 100 clubs internationally." To-tal U.S. Wal-Mart sales are computed as the sum of Wal-Mart U.S. sales and imputed Sam's Club U.S. sales. *Mexico:* Comparison is for 2009. The Mexico total is the "gross margin on purchase-sale of merchandise" from INEGI (2010). Mexico Wal-Mart sales are from Wal-Mart México (2009). *Canada:* We are only able to compare food sales; see USDA (2013), 1, 23. *China:* Comparison is for 2012. Retail sales per capita are from Euromonitor International (2013), multi-plied by the China population from World Bank (n.d.). Wal-Mart's 2012 China sales estimated at $10 billion based on Loeb (2013).

6. Dube, Lester, and Eidlin 2007.

7. In 2007, subsequent to the gathering of these data, one of the Big Four, Gigante, declared bankruptcy and went out of business. Co-mercial Mexicana sought bankruptcy protection to reorganize its debt in 2008, was denied it by the courts, but ultimately struck a deal with its creditors in 2010, retired its debt in 2012, and contin-ues to operate as the fourth-largest retailer in Mexico (González 2008; Planet Retail 2010c, 2012). Soriana has grown aggressively.

8. Lo, Wang, and Li 2006, 310.

9. Christopherson 2006; Landler and Barbaro 2006.

10. Abal Medina 2004, 120, 127.

11. Carré, Holgate, and Tilly 2006; Lichtenstein 2009; Rosen 2008.

12. The reported estimate of 119 percent is based on multiplying the association's reported third-quarter turnover rate by four.

13. Though the revelation of bribery by Wal-Mart's real estate division in Mexico may also help to explain the exceptional rapidity of its rollout of new stores there (Barstow 2012; Guthrie 2012; Viswa-natha and Barrett 2015).

14. Bortz and Aguila 2006.

15. Unger, Beaumont, and Chan 2011.

16. Quoted in Trigona 2007.

17. Featherstone 2004; Lichtenstein 2009, ch. 5.

18. Out of thirty-one states plus the Federal District; see Tilly 2014; Tilly and Álvarez-Galván 2006. Contracts were obtained from the local labor relations commission archives.

19. For Argentina, see Carbajal 2007; Eidelson 2012; Trigona 2007. For Brazil, see Observatorio Social 2000. For Canada, see Mui 2008. For Chile, see Álvarez-Galván and Tilly 2011; Figueroa Cerda 2009; Schnitzer 2011. For China, see Chan 2011b; Lague 2006. For Japan, see UNI Global Union 2011. For South Africa, see Gedye 2013. For the United Kingdom, see Timmons 2006. For Germany, see Christopherson 2006. See also Kolben 2007 and Human Rights Watch 2007, 27, for (incomplete) lists of countries where Wal-Mart has union representation.

20. Kolben 2007, 330–31.

21. Bank Muñoz 2011 (Chile); Lichtenstein 2009 (United States); Mui 2008 (Canada; see also the discussion later in this chapter); Taal 2012 (South Africa); Timmons 2006 (United Kingdom); UNI Global Union 2011 (Japan).

22. Tilly 2014.

23. UNI Global Union 2011.

24. Christopherson 2006; Kolben 2007; Lichtenstein 2009.

25. Mui 2011.

26. Kary and Deslongschamps 2009.

27. Kainer 1999, 2002.

28. Campolieti, Gomez, and Gunderson 2013.

29. Lancaster House 2012, Strauss 2011.

30. Featherstone 2009; Mui 2008; UFCW Canada, n.d.

31. Tilly and Kennedy 2010; Tilly et al. 2013.

32. Chan 2011b; Unger, Beaumont, and Chan 2011.

33. Van der Horst 2015.

34. Mui 2011.

35. Bank Muñoz 2011.

36. Logan 2013.

37. Robinson 2006; see also Nesius 2005.

38. Dwoskin 2012; Greenhouse 2011a; Greenhouse and Clifford 2011; Logan 2013; Moberg 2015; Olney 2015; OUR Walmart, n.d.

39. Depillis 2014; OUR Walmart 2014.

40. *DSN Retailing Today* 2001; Luhnow 2001.

41. Álvarez-Galván and Tilly 2011.

42. Braine 2004, 43.

43. Lo, Wang, and Li 2006.

44. Ibid.

45. Christopherson 2006, 69.

46. Aoyama and Schwarz 2006.

47. Fishman 2003; *Frontline* 2004.

48. Wonacott 2003.

49. Schwentesius and Gómez 2002.

50. Wang and Zhang 2006, 308.

51. Aoyama and Schwartz 2006, 80.

52. Lichtenstein 2009.

53. O'Connell 2013; Roberts 2015; Warren 2005.

54. Burt and Sparks 2006; Ramstad 2006; Landler 2006.

55. Berfield 2013; Kiselyova 2012; *Reuters* 2012.

56. Berfield 2013.

57. See, for example, Carew, Abkowitz, and Nassauer 2016; *Newsmax-Finance* 2015; Pearson and Nassauer 2017.

58. Berner 2005; Goldberg 2007.

59. Barbaro and Abelson 2007; Greenhouse and Abelson 2011; Joyce 2006; Mui 2006.

60. Maher 2007; Zimmerman 2005.

61. *Supermarket News* 2014.

62. Banjo 2013; Clean Clothes Campaign, n.d.

63. For examples from Mexico and Argentina, see Campaña Internacional contra los Contratos Colectivos de Protección Patronal en México 2012; Carbajal 2007; Hernández 2008; ProDESC 2008.

64. Vorley 2007.

65. Satterthwaite 2001; Planet Retail 2010a.

66. Jacoby 1997; Levitt 1993; Logan 2006.

67. For an excellent review of this literature, see Mosley 2011, 40–41, 50–63.

68. See, for example, Anner 2011; Anner and Evans 2004.

69. Bardacke 2011; Ganz 2009.

70. Facchini 2005, authors' translation.

71. UNI Global Union 2005, 11, as cited in Kolben 2007.

72. Bank Muñoz 2011; Trigona 2007; UNI Global Union 2014.

73. Zimmerman 2005.

74. Target Sucks, n.d.; Berman 2011; Greenhouse 2011b.

75. Bates 1998; Nathans 2003; Paumgarten 2010; *Wall Street Journal* 2000.

76. Scheiber 2016.

77. Greenhouse 2005. Dividing Greenhouse's 2005 figure of 14,000 unionized employees by the current U.S. employment total—found at Costco (n.d.)—we estimate that the current level is more like one in ten. We are not aware of any additions to the number of unionized workers.

CHAPTER 8: CONCLUSION

1. See online chapter A1 (http://www.russellsage.org/publications /where-bad-jobs-are-better).

2. The Russell Sage Foundation project on "Low-Wage Work in the Wealthy World" yielded five European studies, each including a retail trade case study.

3. Appelbaum and Batt 2014; Gelles, Jopson, and Chassany 2013.

4. Matsa 2010.

5. De la Merced and Alden 2014.

6. Jacobius 2014.

7. Zimmerman 2012.

8. Ibid.

9. Reardon and Berdegue 2002.

10. Esposito and Ulmer 2012; Planet Retail 2012, 2013, 2014.

11. Chaudhuri and Carew 2015.

12. Planet Retail 2010a, 2010b; Vidalon 2010. Also, European and Japanese clothing retailers such as Zara, H&M, and Uniqlo entered the U.S. market.

13. Barclay 2015.

14. Horovitz 2015.

15. Ibid.

16. Even IKEA furniture warehouses, renowned for being perhaps the biggest box of all, are experimenting with small, in-city stores as well as facilities dedicated only to pickup of online orders (Milne

2015). In 2016, Wal-Mart retreated on the small store front, closing down all 102 Wal-Mart Express stores (its smallest format, launched in 2011), while stating plans to continue expanding its somewhat larger Neighborhood Market stores (Nassauer 2016a), but in 2017 the company piloted an even smaller convenience store format (Neiswanger 2017).

17. Clifford 2011.

18. Bustillo 2010; Hitt 2011; Natunewicz 2011.

19. Clifford 2011; Kowitt 2010. Another example in the pipeline is the German retailer Lidl, which is expected to open U.S. stores in 2018. Lidl operates with single-label products, small stores, and goods displayed on pallets. It requires customers to bring their own shopping bags and to bag their own groceries. It is expected to have an impact on the small-format stores of large discount retailers, such as Walmart Neighborhood Markets and Trader Joe's (Peterson 2015).

20. Roberts 2009.

21. Nassauer 2015.

22. Wal-Mart shoppers spend an average of twenty-two minutes per visit; a customer would need to view seventy-five items per second in order to see the 100,000 items in the store (Roberts 2009).

23. Zimmerman 2008.

24. Conlin 2009.

25. *The Economist* 2009; Murphy 2011; Natunewicz 2011.

26. Tuttle 2012.

27. Zimmerman 2012.

28. Ibid.

29. Hikes in gas prices have been mentioned as a contributor to the growth of dollar stores because they offer proximity in urban areas (Kadet 2011).

30. Eaton and Zimmerman 2010.

31. Zhao 2009.

32. *Wall Street Journal* 2012.

33. Hitt 2011; Natunewicz 2011.

34. Zimmerman 2011.

35. Ziobro 2015.

36. D'Innocenzio 2015; Nassauer 2016b.

37. Ziobro 2015.

38. Russolillo 2016.

39. Hortaçsu and Syverson 2015, 24, table 1; Jargon, Gasparro, and Haddon 2017.

40. Ahold acquired Peapod in 2001 (Peapod, n.d.).

41. Bensinger and Morris 2014; Nash 2016.

42. Whole Foods and Ralphs have partnered with start-up Instacart (a "sharing economy," Internet-based food delivery company in which individuals bid to do others' shopping) to deliver groceries to shoppers' residences (Li 2014).

43. Barr and Winkler 2014.

44. Nearly $4 billion was invested in food-related tech companies in the first half of 2014, more than double the $1.6 billion invested in 2013, according to the food consulting firm Rosenheim Advisors (Li 2014).

45. Bensinger and Morris 2014.

46. Bensinger and Stevens 2016b; Stevens and Safdar 2016; Hufford, Gasparro, and Stevens 2017. Amazon has also started opening bookstores (Van Grove and Li 2016) and has announced plans to open stores selling furniture and consumer appliances as well (Wingfield 2017).

47. Donato-Weinstein 2015.

48. For example, the big-box chain Best Buy has engaged in cost-cutting (layoffs, store closures, thinning management) since 2012. The company's 2014 second quarter same-store sales declined 2.7 percent. Meanwhile, Amazon's quarterly sales of electronics and general merchandise for North America (a broader category) were estimated to have grown by about 30 percent (Ramakrishnan 2014).

49. The authors draw upon the U.S. Bureau of the Census definition of e-commerce as "transactions sold online over open networks such as the Internet or proprietary networks running systems such as Electronic Data Interchange (EDI)." Transactions over the Internet are those business-to-consumer transactions that define retail (Hortaçsu and Syverson 2015, 7, and 24, table 1; Lieber and Syverson 2012).

50. Cognizant Reports 2011.

51. O'Donnell 2011; Planet Retail 2011.

52. Bensinger 2016.

53. Cognizant Reports 2011.

54. FitzGerald and Kapner 2016.

55. Safdar 2017.

56. Stevens and Safdar 2016.

57. Mochizuki 2016.

58. Springer 2016a.

59. Bensinger and Stevens 2016a; Kitroeff 2016b.

60. Dillender and Houseman 2015.

61. Two thousand dollars per year per uncovered worker after the first thirty plus $3,000 for each employee who signed up for subsidized coverage.

62. Employers covered by the mandate must make coverage available to full-time employees and eligible dependents after ninety calendar days of employment. (Coverage is effective on the ninety-first day.) If there is a gap in employment, a new ninety-day waiting period does not begin unless the employee has been absent for at least thirteen weeks.

63. As of 2015, when a large employer could not "reasonably determine" whether the worker met the thirty-weekly-hour threshold, a "look-back" rule allowed the company to measure their full-time status over a measurement period up to twelve months during which they were not counted for the purpose of offering health insurance or calculating penalties. Variable-hour workers found to be working full-time during the look-back period would be considered full-time for a following "stability period" regardless of whether their hours went below the thirty-hour-per-week threshold.

64. Retail industry groups have advocated, with success in the U.S. House of Representatives, for the full-time threshold to be set at forty weekly hours, nearly ensuring that most retail workers in large chains with a full-time standard at thirty-two to thirty-five weekly hours would be ineligible for coverage under this mandate (Hamstra 2014).

65. Dillender, Houseman, and Heinrich 2015; Dillender and Houseman 2015. The Hawaii mandate is more stringent. The Massachusetts mandate applied to smaller employers but was removed in 2013.

66. Dillender, Houseman, and Heinrich 2015, 3–4.

67. In an analysis of the Massachusetts health insurance reform's impacts, Dillender, Houseman, and Heinrich (2015, 38) report that "the Massachusetts health reform modestly increased part-time employment among low-educated workers, and the structure of incentives under the ACA, along with the current economic and political environment, arguably could induce relatively greater

shifting of workers into arrangements not covered by the mandate."

68. Massey 2011; Rampell 2013.

69. Luce and Fujita 2012; Ruetschlin 2014.

70. National Employment Law Project 2015.

71. When a Service Employees International Union campaign to unionize all 4,000 food service workers at the Seattle airport in SeaTac, Washington, and set a wage floor encountered the refusal of employers to bargain, it morphed into a drive for a legislative ballot question for a $15 minimum wage in SeaTac. As one news report noted: "The SEIU had assumed that, when confronted with such a measure, the airport would begin bargaining in exchange for having the measure withdrawn. It didn't. Instead, SeaTac voters approved the measure, and the cause of the low-paid so dominated the local media that the following year, the city of Seattle raised its minimum to $15 as well, increasing the incomes of 100,000 workers" (Meyerson 2015).

72. Lazo 2016; McKinley 2015.

73. Chandler 2016.

74. Levey 2016; Horowitz 2017.

75. Manatt Phelps & Phillips LLP 2017.

76. Leyva 2016.

77. Logan 2012.

78. Ziobro and Morath 2015; D'Innocenzio 2015; Nassauer 2016b.

79. Lauer 2016.

80. Nassauer 2016a.

81. Greenhouse 2014a.

82. Ziobro and Morath 2015; DePillis 2016.

83. Scheiber 2015; Sen and Gleason 2015.

84. Feintzeig 2016.

85. Tilly 1996.

86. Chao and Norton 2016.

87. Baker and Martinez 2015.

88. Lane et al. 2003.

89. Allison, Herrera, and Reese 2015; Halvorsen 2015; Johansson 2007; Smith, Bensman, and Marvey 2012.

90. U.S. Bureau of Labor Statistics 2016a.

91. See, for example, Taylor 2015.

92. Banjo 2016; Springer 2016b.

93. Kapner 2015; Lee 2015.

94. Soper and Zaleski 2017.

95. Safdar 2017.

96. Soper 2015; Nassauer and Nicas 2015.

97. However, online sales remain quite limited in Mexico, amounting to only about 2 percent of annual retail sales as of 2015 (Harrup 2016).

98. Bailey and Bernhardt 1997.

99. Bernhardt et al. 2009.

100. Fine and Gordon 2010.

101. Sykes et al. 2015.

102. Levey 2016.

103. An experimental study with an unnamed retail chain found that store-level managers who had been assigned a policy of posting the work schedule one month in advance in fact posted schedules significantly earlier (Lambert 2015).

104. Alexander and Haley-Lock 2014.

105. Society for Human Resource Management 2015.

106. Ray, Sanes, and Schmitt 2013.

107. Gault et al. 2014.

108. Feintzeig 2017.

109. Family Values at Work, n.d.

110. *The Economist* 2013.

111. FitzGerald 2015. In 2016, more stores stayed closed on Thanksgiving proper, but apparently most stores backed off the Black Friday closing experiment (Kapner 2016; Peltz 2016).

112. Calculating those working part-time for economic reasons as a percentage of the total of (part-time for economic reasons + usually works part-time) among those at work in non-agricultural industries. Calculated from U.S. Bureau of Labor Statistics 2014b.

113. U.S. Department of Labor, n.d. ("Apprenticeship USA").

114. Olson-Kenney 2014.

115. ROC-U, n.d.

116. Ratios based on Costco's 2014 annual report (reporting results

through August 31, 2014) and Wal-Mart's 2015 annual report (reporting results through January 2015).

117. Pires 2008; Schrank and Piore 2007.

118. A card check union election requires only that a union demonstrate that a majority of employees wish to be represented by that union. This dispenses with the standard secret ballot election, a process that in practice has afforded U.S. employers expansive opportunities to run devastating anti-union campaigns.

119. Weil 2008.

120. Jarley and Maranto 1990.

121. Hetland 2015.

122. Coulter 2013.

123. Human Rights Watch 2007.

124. Marshall 2012.

125. Roberts 2015.

126. Retail Action Project, n.d.

127. Chan 2011a, 2011b; Medina 2009; van der Horst 2015; Hernández Castro 2008; ProDESC 2008.

128. For recent reviews, see Belman and Wolfson 2014; Doucouliagos and Stanley 2009; Reich et al. 2015, appendix B; Schmitt 2013.

References

Abal Medina, Paula. 2004. "Los dispositivos de control como inhibidores de la identidad colectiva: Un estudio de caso en grandes cadenas de supermercados" ("Control Devices as Inhibitors of Collective Identity: A Case Study in Large Chain Supermarkets"). In *El trabajo frente el espejo: Continuidades y rupturas en los procesos de construcción identitaria de los trabajadores* (*Work Before the Mirror: Continuities and Ruptures in the Workers' Identity Construction Processes*), edited by Osvaldo R. Battistini. Buenos Aires: Prometeo Libros.

Abernathy, Frederick H., John T. Dunlop, Janice H. Hammond, and David Weil. 2000. "Retailing and Supply Chains in the Information Age." *Technology in Society* 22(1): 5–31.

Aeon. N.d. "About Aeon." Available at: http://www.aeon.info/en/about aeon/ (accessed July 2014).

Ahold. 2013. *Annual Report 2012*. Available at: https://www.ahold delhaize.com/media/1417/ahold-full-ar-2012.pdf (accessed July 2017).

Akerlof, George A., and Janet L. Yellen, eds. 1986. *Efficiency Wage Models of the Labor Market*. Cambridge: Cambridge University Press.

Albelda, Randy. 2008. "Why It's Harder (and Different) for Single Mothers: Gender, Motherhood, Labor Markets, and Public Work Supports." Paper prepared for the Ford Foundation Economic Development Program, New York.

Alexander, Charlotte, and Anna Haley-Lock. 2014. "Not Enough Hours in the Day: Work Hour Insecurity and a New Approach to Wage and Hour Regulation." Paper presented to the meeting of the Labor and Employment Relations Association stream of the American Economic Association. Philadelphia (January 4).

Allison, Juliann, Joel Herrera, and Ellen Reese. 2015. "Why the City of Ontario Needs to Raise the Minimum Wage: Earnings Among Warehouse Workers in Inland Southern California." Research and Policy Brief 36. Los Angeles: UCLA Institute for Research on Labor and Employment (July). Available at: http://www.irle.ucla.edu/publica tions/documents/ResearchBrief_Reese36.pdf (accessed July 2017).

Álvarez-Galván, José Luis, and Chris Tilly. 2011. "Wal-Mart and Local Markets: A Review of the Mexican and Chilean Experiences." Report to the Economic Development Department, Republic of South Africa. Los Angeles: UCLA Institute for Research on Labor and Employment (April).

Andersson, Fredrik, Harry J. Holzer, and Julia I. Lane. 2005. *Moving Up or Moving On: Who Advances in the Low-Wage Labor Market?* New York: Russell Sage Foundation.

Anner, Mark S. 2011. *Solidarity Transformed: Labor Responses to Globalization and Crisis in Latin America.* Ithaca, N.Y.: Cornell University Press, 2011.

Anner, Mark, and Peter Evans. 2004. "Building Bridges Across a Double Divide: Alliances Between U.S. and Latin American Labour and NGOs." *Development in Practice* 14(1/2, February).

Aoyama, Yuko, and Guido Schwarz. 2006. "The Myth of Wal-Martization: Retail Globalization and Local Competition in Japan and Germany." In *Wal-Mart World: The World's Biggest Corporation in the Global Economy,* edited by Stanley Brunn. New York: Routledge/ Taylor & Francis.

Appelbaum, Eileen, and Rosemary Batt. 1994. *The New American Workplace: Transforming Work Systems in the United States.* Ithaca, N.Y.: ILR Press.

———. 2014. *Private Equity at Work: When Wall Street Manages Main Street.* New York: Russell Sage Foundation.

Appelbaum, Eileen, Annette Bernhardt, Richard J. Murnane, eds. 2003a. *Low-Wage America: How Employers Are Reshaping Opportunity in the Workplace.* New York: Russell Sage Foundation.

———. 2003b. "Introduction." In *Low-Wage America: How Employers Are Reshaping Opportunity in the Workplace,* edited by Eileen Appelbaum, Annette Bernhardt, and Richard J. Murnane. New York: Russell Sage Foundation.

Askenazy, Philippe, Jean-Baptiste Berry, Françoise Carré, Sophie Prunier-Poulmaire, and Chris Tilly. 2012. "Working in Large Food Retailers: A France–United States Comparison." *Work, Employment and Society* 26(4): 588–605.

Askenazy, Philippe, Jean-Baptiste Berry, and Sophie Prunier-Poulmaire. 2008. "Working Hard for Large French Retailers." In *Low-Wage Work in France,* edited by Eve Caroli and Jérôme Gautié. New York: Russell Sage Foundation.

Autor, David H., Frank Levy, and Richard J. Murnane. 2003. "Computer-Based Technological Change and Skill Demands: Reconciling the Perspectives of Economists and Sociologists." In *Low-Wage America: How Employers Are Reshaping Opportunity in the Workplace,* edited by Eileen Appelbaum, Annette Bernhardt, and Richard J. Murnane. New York: Russell Sage Foundation.

Bailey, Thomas R., and Annette D. Bernhardt. 1997. "In Search of the High Road in a Low-Wage Industry." *Politics and Society* 25(2): 179–201.

Baker, Chris, and Jaqui Martinez. 2015. "Online Grocery: The Race Has Already Begun." Webinar, December 2. Oliver Wyman (Consultants).

Banjo, Shelly. 2013. "Wal-Mart Toughens Supplier Policies." *Wall Street Journal,* January 21.

———. 2016. "Amazon Finds Grocers Are Hard to Kill." Bloomberg-Gadfly, September 28. Available at: https://www.bloomberg.com /gadfly/articles/2016-09-27/amazon-fresh-grocery-delivery-is-in -for-a-fight (accessed September 2016).

Bank Muñoz, Carolina. 2011. "Labor at Wal-Mart Chile." Work in Progress, November 15. Available at: http://workinprogress.oowsection .org/2011/11/15/labor-at-wal-mart-chile/ (accessed May 2014).

Barbaro, Michael, and Reed Abelson. 2007. "A Health Plan for Wal-Mart: Less Stinginess." *New York Times,* November 13.

Barclay, Eliza. 2015. "Grocery Stores Are Losing You. Here's How They Plan to Win You Back." National Public Radio, March 30. Available at: http://www.npr.org/blogs/thesalt/2015/03/30/395774725 /grocery-stores-are-losing-you-heres-how-they-plan-to-win-you -back (accessed April 2015).

Bardacke, Frank. 2011. *Trampling Out the Vintage: Cesar Chavez and the Two Souls of the United Farm Workers.* London: Verso.

Baret, Christophe, Steffen Lehndorff, and Leigh Sparks, eds. 2000. *Flexible Working in Food Retailing: A Comparison Between France, Germany, the United Kingdom, and Japan.* London: Routledge.

Barr, Alistair, and Rolfe Winkler. 2014. "Google Adopts Delivery-Service Model, Targets Amazon." *Wall Street Journal,* October 14.

Barstow, David. 2012. "Wal-Mart Hushed Up a Vast Mexican Bribery Case." *New York Times,* April 21.

Bates, Jason. 1998. "Whole Foods Fight." *Santa Cruz Metro,* September 3–9.

Batt, Rosemary. 2000. "Strategic Segmentation in Front-Line Services: Matching Customers, Employees, and Human Resource Systems." *International Journal of Human Resource Management* 11(3): 540–61.

Belman, Dale, and Paul J. Wolfson. 2014. *What Does the Minimum Wage Do?* Kalamazoo, Mich.: W. E. Upjohn Institute for Employment Research.

Bensinger, Greg. 2016. "Amazon Plans Hundreds of Brick-and-Mortar Bookstores, Mall CEO Says." *Wall Street Journal*, February 2.

Bensinger, Greg, and Keiko Morris. 2014. "Amazon to Open First Brick-and-Mortar Site." *Wall Street Journal*, October 9.

Bensinger, Greg, and Laura Stevens. 2016a. "Amazon's Newest Ambition: Competing Directly with UPS and FedEx." *Wall Street Journal*, September 27.

———. 2016b. "Amazon to Expand Grocery Business with New Convenience Stores." *Wall Street Journal*, October 11.

Berfield, Susan. 2013. "Where Wal-Mart Isn't: Four Countries the Retailer Can't Conquer." *Bloomberg Business Week*, October 10. Available at: http://www.businessweek.com/articles/2013-10-10/where-walmart-isnt-four-countries-the-retailer-cant-conquer (accessed October 2013).

Berman, Jillian. 2011. "NLRB Accuses Target of Intimidating Workers Before Valley Stream Union Vote." *Huffington Post*, November 2. Available at: http://www.huffingtonpost.com/2011/11/02/valley-stream-target-union-dispute_n_1071255.html (accessed November 2011).

Berner, Robert. 2005. "Can Wal-Mart Wear a White Hat?" *Bloomberg Business Week*, September 22. Available at: http://www.business week.com/stories/2005-09-21/can-wal-mart-wear-a-white-hat (accessed May 2014).

Bernhardt, Annette, Ruth Milkman, Nik Theodore, et al. 2009. *Broken Laws, Unprotected Workers: Violations of Employment and Labor Laws in America's Cities*. Los Angeles: UCLA Institute for Research on Labor and Employment.

Birchall, Jonathan, and Kevin Allison. 2008. "Dell and Wal-Mart Test Tech Services." *Financial Times*, July 16.

Bortz, Jeffrey, and Marcos Aguila. 2006. "Earning a Living: A History of Real Wage Studies in Twentieth-Century Mexico." *Latin American Research Review* 41(2): 112–38.

Bosch, Gerhard, and Steffen Lehndorff, eds. 2005. *Working in the Service Sector: A Tale from Different Worlds*. London: Routledge.

Bosch, Gerhard, Ken Mayhew, and Jérôme Gautié. 2010. "Industrial Relations, Legal Regulations, and Wage Setting." In *Low-Wage Work in the Wealthy World*, edited by Jérôme Gautié and John Schmitt. New York: Russell Sage Foundation.

Boylaud, Olivier, and Giuseppi Nicoletti. 2001. "Regulatory Reform in Retail Distribution." *OECD Economic Studies* 1(32): 254–72.

Braine, Theresa. 2004. "Good Things in Mexico Come in Small Formats." *DSN Retailing Today*, December 13, 43–44.

Brunn, Stanley D., ed. 2006. *Wal-Mart World: The World's Biggest Corporation in the Global Economy*. New York: Routledge/Taylor & Francis.

Bundesagentur für Arbeit (BA). 2005. *Beschaeftigungsstatistik der Bundesagentur für Arbeit* (Employment Statistics of the Federal Employment Agency). Nuremberg, Germany: BA.

Burns, William. 1982. "Changing Corporate Structure and Technology in Retail Food." In *Labor and Technology: Union Response to Changing Environments*, edited by Donald Kennedy, Charles Craypo, and Mary Lehman. State College: Pennsylvania State University, Department of Labor Studies.

Burt, Steve, and Leigh Sparks. 2006. "Wal-Mart's World." In *Wal-Mart World: The World's Biggest Corporation in the Global Economy*, edited by Stanley Brunn. New York: Routledge/Taylor & Francis.

Business Week. 2006. "Best Buy: How to Break Out of Commodity Hell." *Bloomberg Business Week*, March 27, 76.

Bustillo, Miguel. 2010. "Wal-Mart Plans Small, Urban Stores." *Wall Street Journal*, October 14, B1.

Campaña Internacional contra los Contratos Colectivos de Protección Patronal en México (International Campaign Against Protection Contracts in Mexico). 2012. "Corrupción Laboral en Walmart" ("Labor Corruption at Wal-Mart"). *Boletín CCPP* (special issue) 25(4, May).

Campolieti, Michele, Rafael Gomez, and Morley Gunderson. 2013. "Does Non-Union Employee Representation Act as a Complement or Substitute to Union Voice? Evidence from Canada and the United States." *Industrial Relations* 52(supp. 1): 378–96.

Cappelli, Peter, and Anne Crocker-Hefter. 1996. "Distinctive Human Resources Are Firms' Core Competencies." *Organizational Dynamics* 24(3): 7–22.

Carbajal, Mariana. 2007. "Wal Mart, la empresa que odia los gremios" ("Wal-Mart, the Company That Hates Unions"). *Pagina 12* (Buenos Aires), May 27. Available at: http://www.pagina12.com.ar/diario/elpais/1-85594-2007-05-27.html (accessed April 2014).

Carew, Rick, Alyssa Abkowitz, and Sarah Nassauer. 2016. "Wal-Mart to Sell Chinese E-Commerce Business to JD.com." *Wall Street Journal,* June 20.

Carré, Françoise, Patricia Findlay, Chris Tilly, and Chris Warhurst. 2012. "Job Quality: Scenarios, Analysis, and Interventions." In *Are Bad Jobs Inevitable? Trends, Determinants, and Responses to Job Quality in the Twenty-First Century,* edited by Chris Warhurst, Françoise Carré, Patricia Findlay, and Chris Tilly. Basingstoke, U.K.: Palgrave Macmillan.

Carré, Françoise, Brandynn Holgate, and Chris Tilly. 2006. "What's Happening to Retail Jobs? Wages, Gender, and Corporate Strategy." Paper presented to the annual meeting of the International Association for Feminist Economics and the Labor and Employment Relations Association. Boston (January 5–8).

———. 2009. "Competitive Strategies in the U.S. Retail Industry: Consequences for Jobs in Food and Consumer Electronics Stores." Paper presented to the annual conference of the Industry Studies Association. Chicago (May 27–29). Industry Studies Association working paper WP-2009-5. Available at: http://isapapers.pitt.edu/169/ (accessed July 2017).

Carré, Françoise, and Chris Tilly. 2008. "America's Biggest Low-Wage Industry: Continuity and Change in Retail Jobs." Paper prepared for the Ford Foundation Economic Development Program, New York.

Carré, Françoise, and Chris Tilly, with Diana Denham. 2011. "Explaining Variation in the Quality of U.S. Retail Jobs." Paper presented to the annual meeting of the Labor and Employment Relations Association. Denver, Colo. (January 6–9).

Carré, Françoise, and Chris Tilly, with Brandynn Holgate. 2007. *Continuity and Change in U.S. Retail Trade: A Set of Company Case Studies.* Report to the Russell Sage Foundation, New York.

Carré, Françoise, Chris Tilly, Maarten van Klaveren, and Dorothea Voss-Dahm. 2010. "Retail Jobs in Comparative Perspective." In *Low-Wage Work in the Wealthy World,* edited by Jérôme Gautié and John Schmitt. New York: Russell Sage Foundation.

Carrefour Group. N.d. "Key Figures," available at: http://www.carre four.com/content/key-figures; "Net Sales," available at: http://www.carrefour.com/content/net-sales (accessed July 2014).

Center for Law and Social Policy, Retail Action Project, and Women Employed. 2014. "Tackling Unstable and Unpredictable Work Schedules." Policy brief. Washington, D.C., New York, and Chicago: Center for Law and Social Policy, Retail Action Project, and Women Employed. Available at: http://www.clasp.org/resources-and-publi cations/publication-1/Tackling-Unstable-and-Unpredictable-Work -Schedules-3-7-2014-FINAL-1.pdf (accessed July 2017).

Centraal Bureau voor de Statistiek (CBS, Statistics Netherlands). 2003. *Structure of Earnings Survey—Microdata.* Voorburg, Netherlands: CBS.

Chan, Anita, ed. 2011a. *Walmart in China.* Ithaca, N.Y.: Cornell University Press.

———. 2011b. "Introduction: When the World's Largest Company Encounters the World's Biggest Country." In *Walmart in China*, edited by Anita Chan. Ithaca, N.Y.: Cornell University Press.

Chandler, Adam. 2016. "Predictable Schedules Are the New $15 Minimum Wage." *The Atlantic*, September 22.

Chao, Loretta, and Steven Norton. 2016. "Retailers Bet Big on Retooling Their Supply Chains for E-commerce." *Wall Street Journal*, January 28.

Chaudhuri, Saabira, and Rick Carew. 2015. "MBK Partners Clinches Deal for Tesco's Korean Operations." *Wall Street Journal*, September 7.

Chirino, Fernando Cortés. 2015. "The 'Raise the Wage' Coalition in Los Angeles: Framing Opportunity Against Corporate Power." Research and Policy Brief 37. Los Angeles: University of California, Institute for Research on Labor and Employment (August). Available at: http://www.irle.ucla.edu/publications/documents/Research Brief37_Chirino.pdf (accessed September 2016).

Christopherson, Susan. 2006. "Challenges Facing Wal-Mart in the German Market." In *Wal-Mart World: The World's Biggest Corporation in the Global Economy*, edited by Stanley Brunn. New York: Routledge/ Taylor & Francis.

Chubb, Catherine, Simone Melis, Louia Potter, and Raymond Storry. 2008. *The Global Gender Pay Gap.* Brussels: International Trade Union Confederation (ITUC).

Clawson, Dan, and Naomi Gerstel. 2002. "Caring for Our Young: Child Care in Europe and the United States." *Contexts* 1(4): 28–35.

Clean Clothes Campaign. N.d. "Frequently Asked Questions (FAQ) About the Bangladesh Safety Accord." Available at: http://www .cleanclothes.org/issues/faq-safety-accord (accessed April 2014).

Clifford, Stephanie. 2011. "Where Wal-Mart Failed, Aldi Succeeds." *New York Times*, March 29.

Cognizant Reports. 2011. "Understanding U.S. Consumer Electronics Retailing." Cognizant Reports, December. Available at: http://www

.cognizant.com/InsightsWhitepapers/Understanding-US-Consumer
-Electronics-Retailing.pdf (accessed July 2017).

Cohen, Patricia. 2017. "Steady Jobs, but With Pay and Hours That Are Anything But." *New York Times*, May 31.

Coiling, Trevor, and Ian Clark. 2002. "Looking for 'Americanness': Home-Country, Sector, and Firm Effects on Employment Systems in an Engineering Services Company." *European Journal of Industrial Relations* 8(3): 301–24.

Conlin, Michelle. 2009. "Look Who's Stalking Wal-Mart." *Bloomberg Business Week*, December 7. Available at: http://www.bloomberg .com/bw/magazine/content/09_49/b4158030745931.htm (accessed December 2009).

Costco. 2015. *2015 Annual Report.* Available at: http://www.annual reportowl.com/Costco/2014/Annual%20Report?p=1 (accessed July 2017).

———. N.d. "Company Profile." Available at: http://phx.corporate-ir .net/phoenix.zhtml?c=83830&p=irol-homeprofile (accessed July 2017).

Coulter, Kendra. 2013. "Raising Retail: Organizing Retail Workers in Canada and the United States." *Labor Studies Journal* 38(1): 47–65.

De la Garza Toledo, Ernesto, ed. 2012. *La Situación del trabajo en México, 2012: El Trabajo en la crisis.* Mexico City: Plaza y Valdés.

De la Merced, Michael J., and William Alden. 2014. "Cerberus in $9 Billion Deal for the Safeway Grocery Chain." *New York Times*, March 6.

Depillis, Lydia. 2014. "Under Pressure, Wal-Mart Upgrades Its Policy for Helping Pregnant Workers." *Washington Post*, April 5.

———. 2016. "Walmart Is Rolling Out Big Changes to Worker Schedules This Year." *Washington Post*, February 17.

Dicker, John. 2005. *The United States of Wal-Mart.* New York: Jeremy P. Tarcher/Penguin.

Digital Home. 2008. "Wal-Mart Canada to Offer Extended Warranties for Electronics." *Digital Home*, March 17. Available at: http://www .digitalhome.ca/content/view/2380/206/ (accessed May 2009).

Dillender, Marcus, and Susan Houseman. 2015. "Effects of the Affordable Care Act on Employee Arrangements: Early Evidence." Presentation at the MIT Sloan School of Management, Institute for Work and Employment Research (October 6).

Dillender, Marcus, Susan Houseman, and Carol Heinrich. 2015. "The Potential Effects of Federal Health Insurance Reforms on Employment Arrangements and Compensation." Working Paper 15-228.

Kalamazoo, Mich.: W. E. Upjohn Institute for Employment Research.

D'Innocenzio, Anne. 2015. "Next Up for Wal-Mart Pay Raises: Department Managers." Associated Press, June 2.

Discount Store News. 1998. "Service." *Discount Store News* 37(21, November 9): 25.

Dollar General. N.d. "Company Facts." Available at: http://newscenter .dollargeneral.com/company+facts/ (accessed November 2015).

Dollar Tree. N.d. "The Story of Dollar Tree." Available at: https://www .dollartree.com/custserv/custserv.jsp?pageName=History&parent Name=About (accessed November 2015).

Donato-Weinstein, Nathan. 2015. "Amazon Planning Drive-Up Grocery Stores with the First Likely Coming to Sunnyvale—Sources." *Silicon Valley Business Journal,* July 23. Available at: http://www .bizjournals.com/sanjose/news/2015/07/23/exclusive-amazon -planning-drive-up-grocery-stores.html (accessed January 2015).

Doucouliagos, Hristos, and Tom D. Stanley. 2009. "Publication Selection Bias in Minimum-Wage Research? A Meta-Regression Analysis." *British Journal of Industrial Relations* 47(2): 406–28.

Doussard, Marc. 2013. *Degraded Work: The Struggle at the Bottom of the Labor Market.* Minneapolis: University of Minnesota Press.

Dribbusch, Heiner. 2003. *Gewerkschaftliche Mitgliedergewinnung im Dienstleistungssektor: Ein Drei-Laender-Vergleich im Einzelhandel (Trade Union Membership in the Service Sector: A Three-Country Comparison in Retail).* Berlin: Ed. Sigma.

DSN Retailing Today. 2001. "Wal-Mart International: Resilience and Format Diversity Keep First International Entry Excelente." *DSN Retailing Today,* June 1, 26.

Dube, Arindrajit, T. William Lester, and Barry Eidlin. 2007. "A Downward Push: The Impact of Wal-Mart Stores on Retail Wages and Benefits." Research brief. Berkeley: University of California, Center for Labor Research and Education (December). Available at: http:// laborcenter.berkeley.edu/retail/walmart_downward_push07.pdf. Consulted May 2014.

Dube Arindrajit, T. William Lester, and Michael Reich. 2010. "Minimum Wage Effects Across State Borders: Estimates Using Contiguous Counties." *Review of Economics and Statistics* 92(4): 945–64.

Dwoskin, Elizabeth. 2012. "Wal-Mart Workers' Black Friday Strike." *Business Week,* November 16. Available at: http://www.businessweek .com/articles/2012-11-16/wal-mart-workers-black-friday-strike (accessed November 2012).

Eaton, Leslie, and Anne Zimmerman. 2010. "Dollar Stores Keep Truck-ing—Low-Cost Retailers Hold on to Trade-Down Set Even as Econ-omy Recovers." *Wall Street Journal,* December 21.

The Economist. 2009. "Dollar Stores: Many a Mickle." *The Economist,* March 5.

———. 2013. "Sometimes on Sunday." *The Economist,* December 2.

Eidelson, Josh. 2012. "The Great Walmart Walkout." *The Nation,* Decem-ber 19.

Esbjerg, Lars, Klaus G. Grunert, Nuka Buck, and Anne-Mette Sonne An-dersen. 2008. "Working in Danish Retailing: Transitional Workers Go-ing Elsewhere, Core Employees Going Nowhere, and Career Seekers Striving to Go Somewhere." In *Low-Wage Work in Denmark,* edited by Niels Westergaard-Nielsen. New York: Russell Sage Foundation.

Esbjerg, Lars, Maarten van Klaveren, and Dorothea Voss-Dahm. Forth-coming. "Form Follows Function: Part-Time Pattern in Compari-son." *Travail et emploi.*

Esposito, Anthony, and Alexandra Ulmer. 2012. "Carrefour Sells Co-lombia Assets to Chile's Cencosud for $2.6 Billion." *Reuters,* October 18.

Euromonitor International. 2013. *World Retail Data and Statistics 2014.* London: Euromonitor PLC.

Europaeisches Einzelhandelsinstitut (European Retail Institute) (EHI). 2006. "Handel aktuell 2005–2006: Strukturen, Kennzahlen und Pro-file des deutschen und internationalen Handels" ("Trading Current, 2005–2006: Structures, Key Figures, and Profiles of German and In-ternational Trade"). Köln: EHI.

European Commission. 2007. *Employment in Europe* (database). Luxem-bourg: Office for Official Publications of the European Commission.

Evans, Peter. 2010. "Is It Labor's Turn to Globalize? Twenty-First-Century Opportunities and Strategic Responses." *Global Labour Jour-nal* 1(3): 352–79.

Evans, Peter, and Chris Tilly. 2015. "The Future of Work: Escaping the Current Dystopian Trajectory and Building Better Alternatives." In *Sage Handbook of the Sociology of Work and Employment,* edited by Ste-phen Edgell, Heidi Gottfried, and Edward Granter. Thousand Oaks, Calif.: Sage Publications.

Facchini, Claudia. 2005. "Sindicatos farão protesto contra a venda do Sonae" ("Unions Protest Against Sale of Sonae"). *Sindicato Mercosul,* November 21. Available at: http://www.sindicatomercosul.com.br /noticia02.asp?noticia=28023 (accessed April 2014).

Family Dollar. N.d. "2010 and Beyond." Available at: http://corporate .familydollar.com/pages/history---2010s.aspx (accessed November 2015).

Family Values at Work. N.d. "Paid Sick Days Wins." Available at: http://familyvaluesatwork.org/media-center/paid-sick-days-wins (accessed December 2015).

Featherstone, Liza. 2004. "Will Labor Take the Wal-Mart Challenge?" *The Nation*, June 28.

———. 2009. "Wal-Mart's Great Fight North." Global Research, January 2. Available at: http://www.globalresearch.ca/wal-mart-s-great -fight-north/11576 (accessed February 2014).

Fédération du Commerce et de la Distribution (FCD, French Food Retail Employers' Federation). 2007 and 2008. *Rapports de branche.* Available at: http://www.fcd.asso.fr (accessed January 2009).

Feintzeig, Rachel. 2016. "Full-Time Hires Buck the Trend at Fast-Food, Retail Chains." *Wall Street Journal*, April 26.

Fernández Milmanda, Belén, and Enzo Benes. 2009. "Moderación reivindicativa en el nuevo contexto macroeconómico post 2001: El caso del sindicato de comercio (Argentina 2003–2007)" ("Moderation of Demands in the New Macroeconomic Context Post-2001: The Case of the Retail Trade Union [Argentina 2003–2007]"). Paper presented to the Ninth Congreso Nacional de Ciencia Política, "Centros y Periferias: Equilibrios y Asimetrías en las Relaciones de Poder" ("Centers and Peripheries: Equilibria and Asymmetries in Power Relationships"). Santa Fe, Argentina (August 19–22).

Ferner, Anthony. 1997. "Country of Origin Effects and HRM in Multinational Companies." *Human Resource Management Journal* 7(1): 19–37.

Figueroa Cerda, Francisco. 2009. "Wal-Mart Chile haciendo de las suyas: Se lleva de viaje al sindicato "blanco" de Líder" ("Wal-Mart Chile Takes Care of Its Own: Takes Líder's 'White' Union on a Trip"). *El Ciudadano*, February 25. Available at: http://www.elciudadano .cl/2009/02/25/wal-mart-chile-haciendo-de-las-suyas-se-lleva-de -viaje-al-sindicato-%E2%80%9Cblanco%E2%80%9D-de-lider/ (accessed November 2015).

Fine, Janice, and Jennifer Gordon. 2010. "Strengthening Labor Standards Enforcement Through Partnerships with Workers' Organizations." *Politics and Society* 38(4): 552–85.

Fishman, Charles. 2003. "The Wal-Mart You Don't Know." FastCompany, December 1. Available at: http://www.fastcompany.com/47593 /wal-mart-you-dont-know (accessed May 2014).

FitzGerald, Drew. 2015. "Some Retailers Step Back from Black Friday Frenzy." *Wall Street Journal,* October 29.

FitzGerald, Drew, and Suzanne Kapner. 2016. "Staples Finds New Use for Its Stores: Office Space." *Wall Street Journal,* April 3.

Food Marketing Institute. N.d. "Supermarket Facts." Available at: http://fmi.org/facts_figs/?fuseaction=superfact (accessed January 2009).

Frazis, Harley, Maury Gittleman, Michael Horrigan, and Mary Joyce. 1998. "Results from the 1995 Survey of Employer-Provided Training." *Monthly Labor Review* (June): 3–13.

Freeman, Richard. 2007a. "The Challenge of Growing Globalization of Labor Markets to Economic and Social Policy." In *Global Capitalism Unbound,* edited by Eva Paus. New York: Palgrave Macmillan.

———. 2007b. *America Works: Critical Thoughts on the Exceptional U.S. Labor Market.* New York: Russell Sage Foundation.

Frege, Carola, and John Godard. 2014. "Varieties of Capitalism and Job Quality: The Attainment of Civic Principles at Work in the United States and Germany." *American Sociological Review* 79(5): 942–65.

Friedman, Thomas L. 2005. *The World Is Flat: A Brief History of the Twenty-First Century.* New York: Farrar, Straus and Giroux.

Frontline. 2004. "Is Wal-Mart Good for America?" PBS, *Frontline,* November 16. Available at: http://www.pbs.org/wgbh/pages/front line/shows/walmart/ (accessed May 2014).

Gadrey, Jean, and Florence Jany-Catrice. 2000. "The Retail Sector: Why So Many Jobs in America and So Few in France?" *Service Industries Journal* 20(4): 21–32.

Gadrey, Jean, and Steffen Lehndorff, with Thierry Ribault. 2000. "A Societal Interpretation of the Differences and Similarities in Working Time Practices." In *Flexible Working in Food Retailing: A Comparison Between France, Germany, the United Kingdom, and Japan,* edited by Christophe Baret, Steffen Lehndorff, and Leigh Sparks. London: Routledge.

Ganz, Marshall. 2009. *Why David Sometimes Wins: Leadership, Organization, and Strategy in the California Farm Worker Movement.* New York: Oxford University Press.

Gault, Barbara, Heidi Hartmann, Ariane Hegewisch, Jessica Milli, and Lindsey Reichlin. 2014. *Paid Parental Leave in the United States.* Washington, D.C.: Institute for Women's Policy Research.

Gautié, Jérôme, and John Schmitt, eds. 2010. *Low-Wage Work in the Wealthy World.* New York: Russell Sage Foundation.

Gautié, Jérôme, Niels Westergaard-Nielsen, and John Schmitt, with Ken Mayhew. 2009. "The Impact of Institutions on the Supply Side of the Low-Wage Labor Market." In *Low-Wage Work in the Wealthy World,* edited by Jérôme Gautié and Schmitt. New York: Russell Sage Foundation.

Gedye, Lloyd. 2013. "Walmart Job Talks Deadlock." *City Press* (Johannesburg), October 20. Available at: http://www.citypress.co.za /business/walmart-job-talks-deadlock/ (accessed April 2014).

Gelles, David, and Barney Jopson in New York and Anne-Sylvaine Chassany in London. 2013. "Buyout Groups Target U.S. Retailers." *The Financial Times,* May 23.

Gerstel, Naomi, Dan Clawson, and Robert Zussman, eds. 2002. *Families at Work: Expanding the Bounds.* Nashville: Vanderbilt University Press.

Ghemawat, Pankaj, and Ken A. Mark. 2006. "The Real Wal-Mart Effect." Boston: Harvard Business School (August 23). Available at: http://hbswk.hbs.edu/item/5474.html (accessed September 2006).

Goldberg, Jeffrey. 2007. "Selling Wal-Mart: Can the Company Co-opt Liberals?" *The New Yorker,* April 2.

Goldstein, Marianne. 2007. "Are Extended Warranties Worth the Money?" *CBS News,* August 11. Available at: http://www.cbsnews .com/stories/2007/08/10/earlyshow/contributors/raymartin /main3156565.shtml?source=RSS&attr=_3156565 (accessed May 2009).

González Amador, Roberto. 2008. "Pierde la *Cómer* oportunidad de renegociar deuda y salvar bienes" ("Comercial Mexicana Chain Misses Opportunity to Renegotiate Debt and Save Assets"). *La Jornada* (Mexico City), December 6. Available at: http://www.jornada.unam .mx/2008/12/06/index.php?section=economia&article=025n1eco (accessed December 2008).

Greenhouse, Steven. 2005. "How Costco Became the Anti-Walmart." *New York Times,* July 17.

———. 2011a. "Wal-Mart Workers Try the Nonunion Route." *New York Times,* June 14.

———. 2011b. "Workers Reject Union at Target Store." *New York Times,* June 18.

———. 2014. "A Push to Give Steadier Shifts to Part-Time Workers." *New York Times,* July 15.

Greenhouse, Steven, and Reed Abelson. 2011. "Wal-Mart Cuts Some Health Care Benefits." *New York Times,* October 21.

Greenhouse, Steven, and Stephanie Clifford. 2011. "Protests Backed by Union Get Wal-Mart's Attention." *New York Times,* November 18.

Grimshaw, Damian, and Jill Rubery. 1998. "Integrating the Internal and External Labour Markets." *Cambridge Journal of Economics* 28: 199–220.

Grugulis, Irena, and Odul Bozkurt, eds. 2009. *Retail Work.* Basingstoke, U.K.: Palgrave Macmillan.

Guthrie, Amy. 2012. "More Questions Raised on Wal-Mart's Mexican Affiliate." *Wall Street Journal,* August 15.

H&M (Hennes & Mauritz AB). 2013. *Annual Report 2012.* Available at: http://about.hm.com/content/dam/hmgroup/groupsite/documents/masterlanguage/Annual%20Report/Annual-Report-2012.pdf (accessed July 2017).

———. 2014. "About the H&M Group." Available at: http://about.hm.com/en/About/facts-about-hm.html (accessed July 2014).

Halvorsen, Jesse. 2015. "Driven to Poverty: Misclassification and Wage Theft in Southern California's Short Haul Trucking Industry." Research and Policy Brief 33. Los Angeles: UCLA Institute for Research on Labor and Employment (May). Available at: http://www.irle.ucla.edu/publications/documents/ResearchBrief_Halvorsen33.pdf (accessed July 2017).

Hamstra, Mark. 2014. "Retail Groups Urge 40-Hour Full-Time Definition in ACA." *Supermarket News,* January 28. Available at: http://supermarketnews.com/laws-regulations/retail-groups-urge-40-hour-full-time-definition-aca (accessed January 2014).

Harrup, Anthony. 2016. "E-commerce in Mexico Takes Coaxing." *Wall Street Journal,* January 1.

Harvey, David, 2007. *A Brief History of Neoliberalism.* Oxford: Oxford University Press.

Henly, Julia R., and Susan J. Lambert. 2014. "Unpredictable Working Time in Retail Jobs: Consequences for Employee Work-Life Conflict." *Industrial and Labor Relations Review* 67(3, July): 986–1016.

Hernández Castro, Juan José. 2008. "Abuso Corporativo Laboral: El Caso Wal-Mart" ("Corporate Labor Abuse: The Wal-Mart Case"). Master's thesis, Universidad Autónoma Metropolitana-Iztapalapa, Mexico City.

Herzenberg, Stephen A., John A. Alic, and Howard Wial. 1998. *New Rules for a New Economy: Employment and Opportunity in Postindustrial America.* Ithaca, N.Y.: Cornell University Press.

Hetland, Gabriel. 2015. "The Labour of Learning: Overcoming the Obstacles Facing Union–Worker Centre Collaborations." *Work, Employment and Society* 29(6): 932–49.

Hitt, Jack. 2011. "The Dollar Store Economy." *New York Times Magazine,* August 21.

Hocquelet, Mathieu, Marlène Bencquet, Cédric Durand, and Stéphanie Laguérodie. 2016. "Les Crises de la grande distribution." *Revue Française de Socio-Economie* 16(1): 5–20.

Holtgrewe, Ursula, Christian Kerst, and Karen Shire, eds. 2002. *Reorganising Service Work: Call Centres in Germany and Britain.* Burlington, Vt.: Ashgate.

Holzer, Harry J., Julia I. Lane, David B. Rosenblum, and Fredrik Andersson. 2011. *Where Are All the Good Jobs Going? What National and Local Job Quality and Dynamics Mean for U.S. Workers.* New York: Russell Sage Foundation.

Howoritz, Julia. 2017. "Oregon Is Now the First State to Mandate When Workers Get Their Schedules." *CNN Money.* August 9. Available at: http://money.cnn.com/2017/08/09/news/economy/oregon-advance-scheduling-law/index.html (accessed September 2017).

Horovitz, Bruce. 2015. "Millennials Crave Convenience Stores Most of All." *USA Today,* February 4.

Hortaçsu, Ali, and Chad Syverson. 2015. "The Ongoing Evolution of U.S. Retail: A Format Tug of War." Working Paper 21464. Cambridge, Mass.: National Bureau of Economic Research (August).

Hufford, Austen, Annie Gasparro, and Laura Stevens. 2017. "Amazon to Buy Whole Foods for $13.7 Billion." *Wall Street Journal,* June 16.

Human Rights Watch. 2007. *Discounting Rights: Wal-Mart's Violation of U.S. Workers' Right to Freedom of Association.* Washington, D.C.: Human Rights Watch. Available at: http://www.hrw.org/sites/default/files/reports/us0507webwcover.pdf (accessed April 2014).

Hyde, Phil. N.d. "Americans Have the Shortest Vacation in the Developed World." *The Timesizing Wire.* Available at: http://www.timesizing.com/1vacatns.htm (accessed November 2007).

IKEA. 2013. *IKEA Group Yearly Summary 2012.* Available at: http://www.ikea.com/ms/en_US/pdf/yearly_summary/ys_welcome_inside_2012.pdf (accessed January 2014).

Inditex Group. 2013. *Annual Report 2012.* Available at: http://static.inditex.com/annual_report/en/ (accessed July 2017).

———. N.d. "International Presence." Available at: http://www.inditex.com/en/our_group/international_presence (accessed July 2014).

Industrial Board for Retail Trades (IHBD). 2005. *Arbeidsmarkt in de detailhandel 2005 (The Labor Market in Retailing).* The Hague: IHBD.

Inman, Philip. 2016. "More Than 900,000 U.K. Workers Now on Zero-Hours Contracts." *The Guardian,* September 9.

Institut National de la Statistique et des Études Économiques (INSEE, National Institute of Statistics and Economic Studies). 2003. Trade database. Paris: INSEE. Available at: http://www.insee.fr/en (accessed August 2009).

———. 2008a. "Caractéristiques de l'emploi en 2008-Bases de Données" ("Employment characteristics in 2008-Databases"). Available at: https://www.insee.fr/fr/statistiques/2044668 (accessed August 2009).

———. 2008b. "Caractéristiques de l'emploi en 2008-Chiffres Détaillés" ("Employment characteristics in 2008-Detailed Figures"). Available at: https://www.insee.fr/fr/statistiques/zones/2132304 (accessed August 2009).

———. 2009a. "Monthly Household Consumption of Goods." Paris: FCD. Available at: http://www.bdm.insee.fr/bdm2/affichageSeries .action?idbank=001613500&codeGroupe=1309 (accessed January 2009).

———. 2009b. *Le Commerce en 2008: Rapport sur les comptes (Retail Trade in 2008: Report on Accounts)*. Paris: Commission des Comptes Commerciaux de la Nation (December 18). Available at: http://www .insee.fr/fr/publications-et-services/docs_doc_travail/E0910.pdf (accessed January 2009).

———. 2016. "Les Salaires dans le secteur privé et les entreprises publiques en 2013" ("Wages in the Private and Public Sectors in 2013"). Paris: INSEE (April 19). Available at: http://www.insee.fr/fr /themes/detail.asp?reg_id=0&ref_id=ir-irsocdads2013 (accessed September 2016).

———. Various years. *Annual Declaration of Social Data (DADS)*. Paris: INSEE. Available at: http://www.insee.fr/en/methodes/default .asp?page=sources/ope-adm-dads.htm (accessed August 2009).

Instituto Nacional de Estadística e Informática (INEGI). 2010. "2009 Censo Económico" ("Economic Census 2009") via Automated Census Information System [SAIC]. Available at: http://www.beta .inegi.org.mx/app/saic/default.aspx (accessed January 2014).

Inter IKEA Systems B.V. N.d. *IKEA Retailing Facts and Figures*. Available at: http://franchisor.ikea.com/ikea-retailing-facts-and-figures-new/ (accessed July 2014).

Jacobius, Arlene. 2014. "Private Equity Only Part of Safeway Merger Story." Pensions&Investments, March 31. Available at: http://www .pionline.com/article/20140331/PRINT/303319982/private-equity -only-part-of-safeway-merger-story (accessed March 2014).

Jacoby, Sanford. 1997. *Modern Manors: Welfare Capitalism Since the New Deal*. Princeton, N.J.: Princeton University Press.

Jaehrling, Karen, and Philippe Méhaut. 2013. "'Varieties of Institutional Avoidance': Employers' Strategies in Low-Waged Service Sector Occupations in France and Germany." *Socio-Economic Review* 11: 687–710.

Jany-Catrice, Florence, and Steffen Lehndorff. 2005. "Work Organization and the Importance of Labour Markets in the European Retail Trade." In *Working in the Service Sector: Tales from Different Worlds,* edited by Gerhard Bosch and Steffen Lehndorff. London: Routledge.

Jargon, Julie, Annie Gasparro, and Heather Haddon. 2017. "For Amazon, Now Comes the Hard Part." *Wall Street Journal,* June 18.

Jarley, Paul, and Cheryl L. Maranto. 1990. "Union Corporate Campaigns: An Assessment." *Industrial and Labor Relations Review* 43(5): 505–24.

Jayaraman, Saru, and Food Labor Research Center. 2014. *Shelved: How Wages and Working Conditions for California's Food Retail Workers Have Declined as the Industry Has Thrived.* Berkeley: University of California, Food Labor Research Center.

Johansson, Erin. 2007. "Fed Up with FedEx: How FedEx Ground Tramples Workers' Rights and Civil Rights." Washington, D.C.: American Rights At Work (ARAW) and Leadership Conference on Civil Rights (LCCR) (October). Available at: http://www.civilrights.org/publica tions/fedex/fedupwithfedex.pdf (accessed July 2017).

Johnson, Bradford C. 2002. "Retail: The Wal-Mart Effect." *McKinsey Quarterly* (Winter): 40–43.

Joyce, Amy. 2006. "Critics Say Wal-Mart Grows Part-Timers to Cut Benefits." *Washington Post,* May 26, D02.

Kadet, Anne. 2011. "What's the Allure of Dollar Stores?" MarketWatch, January 20. Available at: http://www.smartmoney.com/spend /family-money/whats-the-allure-of-dollar-stores-1326832110390 (accessed July 2017).

Kainer, Jan. 1999. "Not Quite What They Bargained For: Female Labour in Canadian Supermarkets." In *Women Working for the NAFTA Food Chain: Women, Food, and Globalization,* edited by Deborah Barndt. Toronto: Second Story Press.

———. 2002. *Cashing in on Pay Equity? Supermarket Restructuring and Gender Equality.* Toronto: Sumach Press.

Kalleberg, Arne L. 2011. *Good Jobs, Bad Jobs: The Rise of Polarized and Precarious Employment Systems in the United States, 1970s to 2000s.* New York: Russell Sage Foundation.

Kamerman, Sheila B., Michelle Neuman, Jane Waldfogel, and Jeanne Brooks-Gunn. 2003. "Social Policies, Family Types, and Child Outcomes in Selected OECD Countries." OECD Social, Employment and Migration Working Papers 2003:6. Paris: OECD. Available at: http://www.oecd.org/dataoecd/26/46/2955844.pdf (accessed June 2008).

Kapner, Suzanne. 2015. "Web Retailers, Now with Stores, Teach New Tricks." *Wall Street Journal*, August 11.

———. 2016. "Retailers Push Early Start to Black Friday Sales." *Wall Street Journal*, November 25.

Kary, Tiffany, and Alexander Deslongchamps. 2009. "Walmart Wins Canada High Court Ruling on Union Suit." *Bloomberg News*, November 27.

Kiselyova, Maria. 2012. "Analysis: Cautious Wal-Mart Missing Out on Russia's Retail Boom." *Reuters*, April 5.

Kitroeff, Natalie. 2016. "Warehouses Promised Lots of Jobs, but Robot Workforce Slows Hiring." *Los Angeles Times*, December 4.

Kolben, Kevin. 2007. "Wal-Mart Is Coming, but It's Not All Bad: Wal-Mart and Labor Rights in Its International Subsidiaries." *UCLA Journal of International Law and Foreign Affairs* 275: 275–332.

Kowitt, Beth. 2010. "Inside the Secret World of Trader Joe's." *Fortune*, August 23.

Kuruvilla, Sarosh, Ching Kwan Lee, and Mary E. Gallagher, eds. 2011. *From Iron Rice Bowl to Informalization: Markets, Workers, and the State in a Changing China*. Ithaca, N.Y.: Cornell University Press.

Lague, David. 2006. "Official Union in China Says All Wal-Marts Are Organized." *New York Times*, October 13.

Lambert, Susan. 2015. "Precarious Work Schedules in the U.S.: Prevalence and Possibilities for Change." Unpublished paper. Chicago: University of Chicago, School of Social Welfare.

Lambert, Susan J., Anna Haley-Lock, and Julia R. Henly. 2012. "Schedule Flexibility in Hourly Jobs: Unanticipated Consequences and Promising Directions." *Community, Work, and Family* 15(3): 293–315.

Lambert, Susan J., and Julia R. Henly. 2009. "Scheduling in Hourly Jobs: Promising Practices for the Twenty-First Century Economy." Washington, D.C.: The Mobility Agenda (May). Available at: http://www.mobilityagenda.org/home/file.axd?file=2009%2f5%2fscheduling.pdf (accessed July 2017).

———. 2010. "Work Scheduling Study: Managers' Strategies for Balancing Business Requirements with Employee Needs." Chicago: University of Chicago, School of Social Service Administration (May). Available at: https://ssascholars.uchicago.edu/sites/default/files/work-scheduling-study/files/univ_of_chicago_work_scheduling_manager_report_6_25_0.pdf (accessed July 2017).

Lancaster House. 2012. "Target Not Successor to Zellers' Union Obligations, B.C. Board Rules." Lancaster House, December 6. Available at: http://lancasterhouse.com/headlines/article/id/14168/tkn/92xc48jz (accessed February 2014).

Landler, Mark. 2006. "Wal-Mart Pulling Out of Germany." *New York Times*, July 28.

Landler, Mark, and Michael Barbaro. 2006. "Wal-Mart Finds That Its Formula Doesn't Fit Every Culture." *New York Times*, August 2.

Lane, Julia, Philip Moss, Hal Salzman, and Chris Tilly. 2003. "Too Many Cooks? Tracking Internal Labor Market Dynamics in Food Service with Case Studies and Quantitative Data." In *Low-Wage America: How Employers Are Reshaping Opportunity in the Workplace*, edited by Eileen Appelbaum, Annette Bernhardt, and Richard Murnane. New York: Russell Sage Foundation.

Lauer, Stéphane. 2016. "Chez Walmart, une hausse des salaires en trompe-lœil" ("At Wal-Mart, an Increase in Trompe-l'oeil Salaries"). *Le Monde*, February 20.

Lazo, Alejandro. 2016. "Oregon Governor Signs Landmark Minimum-Wage Law." *Wall Street Journal*, March 2.

Lebhar, Godfrey M. 1952. *Chain Stores in America: 1859–1950*. New York: Chain Store Publishing.

Lee, Annie. 2015. "Showrooms Usurp Stores in China Olympic Hero's Retail Push." *Bloomberg Business*, September 21. Available at: http://www.bloomberg.com/news/articles/2015-09-21/showrooms-usurp-stores-in-china-olympic-hero-s-retail-revolution (accessed July 2017).

Lehman, K. R., Jennie P. Psihogios, and Ruud G. J. Meulenbroek. 2001. "The Effects of Sitting vs. Standing and Scanner Type on Cashiers." *Ergonomics* 44(7): 719–38.

Lehndorff, Steffen, and Dorothea Voss-Dahm. 2005. "The Delegation of Uncertainty: Flexibility and the Role of the Market in Service Work." In *Working in the Service Sector: Tales from Different Worlds*, edited by Gerhard Bosch and Steffen Lehndorff. London and New York: Routledge.

Levey, Noam. 2016. "Despite GOP Efforts, Obama's Safety Net Expansion Is Historic." *Los Angeles Times*, January 17.

Levitt, Martin Jay. 1993. *Confessions of a Union Buster*. New York: Crown Publishers.

Lewis, Bill, Angelique Augereau, Mike Cho, Brad Johnson, Brent Neiman, Gabriela Olazabal, Matt Sandler, Sandra Schrauf, Kevin Stange, Andrew Tilton, Eric Xin, Baudouin Regout, Allen Webb, Mike Nevens, Lenny Mendonca, Vincent Palmade, Greg Hughes, and James Manyika. 2001. "U.S. Productivity Growth, 1995–2000." New

York: McKinsey Global Institute (October). Available at: http://www.mckinsey.com/insights/americas/us_productivity_growth_1995-2000 (accessed May 2014).

Leyva, Connie. 2016. "Workers, Labor Leaders, Legislators Call for Passage of Reliable Scheduling Bill." State Senator Connie Leyva website, May 18. Available at: http://sd20.senate.ca.gov/news/2016-05-18-workers-labor-leaders-legislators-call-passage-reliable-scheduling-bill (accessed October 2016).

Li, Shan. 2014. "Food-Delivery Start-Ups Are Fattening Up on Technology." *Los Angeles Times*, October 10.

Lichtenstein, Nelson, ed. 2004. *Wal-Mart: Template for Twenty-First Century Capitalism?* New York: New Press.

———. 2009. *The Retail Revolution: How Wal-Mart Created a Brave New World of Business.* New York: Metropolitan Books.

Lieber, Ethan, and Chad Syverson. 2012. "Online vs. Offline Competition." In *Oxford Handbook of the Digital Economy*, edited by Martin Peitz and Joel Waldfogel. New York: Oxford University Press.

Lincoln, James, and Arne Kalleberg. 1985. "Work Organization and Workforce Commitment: A Study of Plants and Employees in the U.S. and Japan." *American Sociological Review* 50(6): 738–60.

Lloyd, Caroline, and Jonathan Payne. 2016. *Skills in the Age of Over-Qualification: Comparing Service Sector Work in Europe.* Oxford: Oxford University Press.

Lo, Lucia, and Lu Wang, with Wei Li. 2006. "Consuming Wal-Mart: A Case Study in Shenzen." In *Wal-Mart World: The World's Biggest Corporation in the Global Economy*, edited by Stanley Brunn. New York: Routledge/Taylor & Francis.

Loeb, Walter. 2013. "How Walmart Will Fight to Be Successful in China." *Forbes*, November 6.

Logan, John. 2006. "The Union Avoidance Industry in the United States." *British Journal of Industrial Relations* 44(4): 651–75.

———. 2012. "Walmart's Poor Labor Record." *San Francisco Chronicle*, November 29.

———. 2013. "The Mounting Guerilla War Against the Reign of Walmart." *New Labor Forum* 23(1): 22–29.

Luce, Stephanie, and Naoki Fujita. 2012. "Discounted Jobs: How Retailers Sell Workers Short." New York: Retail Action Project.

Luhnow, David. 2001. "Crossover Success: How NAFTA Helped Wal-Mart Reshape the Mexican Market." *Wall Street Journal*, August 31, A1.

Maher, Kris. 2007. "Wal-Mart Joins Health-Care Call: Unlikely Coalition Of Labor, Business Pushes for Overhaul." *Wall Street Journal,* February 8.

Manatt Phelps & Phillips LLP. 2017. "Employers Halt On-Call Scheduling After AGs Send Letters." Lexology, January 18. Available at: http://www.lexology.com/library/detail.aspx?g=561ce72a-f8d7 -4c7c-af2c-b24545a55c39 (accessed January 2017).

Marsden, David. 1999. *A Theory of Employment Systems: Micro-Foundations of Societal Diversity.* Oxford: Oxford University Press.

———. 2000. "A Theory of Job Regulation, the Employment Relationship, and the Organization of Labour Institutions." *Industrielle Beziehungen/Industrial Relations* 7(4): 320–47.

Marshall, John. 2012. "Wal-Mart's Labor Problem: Limits to the Low-Road Business Model." Washington, D.C.: United Food and Commercial Workers, Capital Stewardship Program. Available at: http://makingchangeatwalmart.org/files/2012/10/WalmartsLabor Problem.pdf (accessed December 2015).

Martin, Timothy W. 2009. "May I Help You? Publix Super Markets Is Finding Success Where Rivals Aren't. Its Main Weapon: Customer Service." *Wall Street Journal,* April 23, R4.

Mason, Geoff, and Matthew Osborne. 2008. "Business Strategies, Work Organization, and Low Pay in U.K. Retailing." In *Low-Paid Work in the United Kingdom,* edited by Caroline Lloyd, Geoff Mason, and Ken Mayhew. New York: Russell Sage Foundation.

Massey, Daniel. 2011. "NYC Workers Fight for 40-Hour Week: Cash-Strapped Retailers Using Part-Time Models Are Cutting Back Hours, Leaving Workers to Scramble." Crain's New York Business, August 28. Available at: http://www.crainsnewyork.com/article/20110828 /SMALLBIZ/308289978 (accessed August 2011).

Matsa, David. 2010. "Capital Structure as a Strategic Variable: Evidence from Collective Bargaining." *Journal of Finance* 65(3): 1197–1232.

Maume, David J., Rachel A. Sebastian, and Anthony A. Bardo. 2009. "Gender Differences in Sleep Disruption Among Retail Food Workers." *American Sociological Review* 77(December): 989–1007.

Maurice, Marc, François Sellier, and Jean-Jacques Silvestre. 1986. *The Social Foundations of Industrial Power.* Cambridge, Mass.: MIT Press.

McCormick, Janice. 1986. "Introduction." In *The Social Foundations of Industrial Power,* edited by Marc Maurice, François Sellier, and Jean-Jacques Silvestre. Cambridge, Mass.: MIT Press.

McKinley, Jesse. 2015. "Cuomo to Raise Minimum Wage to $15 for All New York State Employees." *New York Times,* November 10.

Meardi, Guglielmo, Paul Marginson, Michael Fichter, Marcin Frybes, Miroslav Stanojević, and András Tóth. 2009. "Varieties of Multinationals: Adapting Employment Practices in Central Eastern Europe." *Industrial Relations* 48(3): 489–511.

Medina, Paula Abal. 2009. "Delegados en doble confrontación" ("Delegates in Double Confrontation"). Argentina Indymedia. (Originally published in *Diario Crítico de la Argentina,* November 15, 2009.) Available at: http://argentina.indymedia.org/news/2009/11/705533.php (accessed December 2015).

Meyerson, Harold. 2014. "Labor's New Reality: It's Easier to Raise Wages for 100,000 Than Unionize 4,000." *Los Angeles Times,* December 8.

Milkman, Ruth, Stephanie Luce, and Penny Lewis. 2013. *Changing the Subject: A Bottom-Up Account of Occupy Wall Street in New York City.* New York: City University of New York, Murphy Institute (September). Available at: http://sps.cuny.edu/filestore/1/5/7/1_a05051d2 117901d/1571_92f562221b8041e.pdf (accessed July 2017).

Miller, Claire Cain. 2014. "How a Part-Time Pay Penalty Hits Working Mothers." *New York Times,* August 21.

Milne, Richard. 2015. "Ikea Thinks Outside the Big Box." *Financial Times,* December 4.

Mishel, Lawrence, Jared Bernstein, and Sylvia Alegretto. 2007. *The State of Working America, 2007.* Ithaca, N.Y.: Cornell University Press.

Mishel, Lawrence, Jared Bernstein, and Heather Boushey. 2003. *The State of Working America, 2003.* Ithaca, N.Y.: Cornell University Press.

Mishel, Lawrence, Josh Bivens, Elise Gould, and Heidi Shierholz. 2012. *The State of Working America, 2012.* Ithaca, N.Y.: Cornell University Press.

Moberg, David. 2015. "The Union Behind the Biggest Campaign Against Walmart in History May Be Throwing in the Towel. Why?" *In These Times,* August 11.

Mochizuki, Takashi. 2016. "Panasonic Takes Item Out of Bagging Area: Human." *Wall Street Journal,* December 12.

Molyneux, Guy. 2015. "Support for a Federal Minimum Wage of $12.50 or Above." Washington, D.C.: Hart Research Associates (January 14). Available at: http://www.nelp.org/content/uploads/2015/03 /Minimum-Wage-Poll-Memo-Jan-2015.pdf (accessed March 2016).

Mosley, Layna. 2011. *Labor Rights and Multinational Production.* Cambridge: Cambridge University Press.

Moss, Philip, and Chris Tilly. 2001. *Stories Employers Tell: Race, Skill, and Hiring in America.* New York: Russell Sage Foundation.

Moss, Philip, Hal Salzman, and Chris Tilly. 2008. "Under Construction: The Continuing Evolution of Job Structures in Call Centers." *Industrial Relations* 47(2, April): 173–208.

Mui, Ylan Q. 2006. "Wal-Mart Shows Shareholders a New Face." *Washington Post,* June 3, D01.

———. 2008. "Quebec Wal-Mart Workers Unionize." *Washington Post,* August 16.

———. 2011. "Wal-Mart Works with Unions Abroad, but Not at Home." *Washington Post,* June 7.

Murphy, Maxwell. 2011. "Family Dollar Profit Rises, Plans Store Expansion." *Wall Street Journal,* September 28.

Nash, Kim S. 2016. "Wal-Mart's CIO on the Retailer's Push into Online Grocery Shopping." *Wall Street Journal,* September 27.

Nassauer, Sarah. 2015. "Wal-Mart Shrinks the Big Box, Vexing Vendors." *Wall Street Journal,* October 26.

———. 2016a. "Costco to Raise Its Minimum Wage." *Wall Street Journal,* March 3.

———. 2016b. "Wal-Mart to Boost Wages for Most U.S. Store Workers." *Wall Street Journal,* January 20.

Nassauer, Sarah, and Jack Nicas. 2015. "Wal-Mart Plans Outdoor Drone Tests." *Wall Street Journal,* October 26.

Nathans, Aaron. 2003. "Love the Worker, Not the Union, a Store Says." *New York Times,* May 24, C1.

National Employment Law Project (NELP). 2015. "City Minimum Wage Laws: Recent Trends and Economic Evidence Fact Sheet." New York: NELP (May).

National Institute of Standards and Technology (NIST). 2010. "A Guide to U.S. Retail Pricing Laws and Regulations." Gaithersburg, Md.: NIST (September 30). Available at: https://www.nist.gov/pml/weights-and-measures/laws-and-regulations/retail-and-unit-pricing-laws (updated August 25, 2016, accessed November 2016).

Natunewicz, Ann. 2011. "Dollar Days: How Dollar Stores Are Growing in a Weak Economy." Seattle: Colliers International (December 5). Available at: http://www.drugstorenews.com/sites/drugstorenews.com/files/Colliers_Whitepaper_DollarDays_20111201.pdf (accessed July 2017).

Neiswanger, Robbie. 2017. "Wal-Mart Tests Convenience Store: Sites in Rogers and Texas Offer Gas, Expanded Food Options." *Northwest Arkansas Democrat Gazette,* February 1.

Nesius, Steve. 2005. "Wal-Mart Workers Organize Without Union." *USA Today,* September 30.

Neumark, David, J. M. Ian Salas, and William Wascher. 2014, "Revisiting the Minimum Wage–Employment Debate: Throwing Out the Baby with the Bathwater?" *Industrial and Labor Relations Review* 67(3): 608–48.

NewsmaxFinance. 2015. "Wal-Mart Cost-Cutting Options Seen Including Sam's Club Spinoff." *NewsmaxFinance*, October 16. Available at: http://www.newsmax.com/Finance/Companies/walmart-stores -profit-sams-club/2015/10/16/id/696563/ (accessed December 2015).

Norman, Al. 2004. *The Case Against Wal-Mart.* Atlantic City, N.J.: Raphel Marketing.

Observatorio Social. 2000. *Relatório Geral da ObservaçãoWal-Mart Brasil Ltda* (*General Observation Report: Wal-Mart Brazil*). São Paulo: Observatorio Social. Available at: http://www.observatoriosocial.org.br /site/sites/default/files/relatoriogeral_walmart_jun2000.pdf (accessed April 2014).

O'Connell, Jonathan 2013. "Walmart Brings More Than Its Store to D.C., It Brings Lessons." *Washington Post,* December 6.

O'Donnell, Jayne. 2011. "Target CEO Talks Prices, Products, and Plans." *USA Today,* June 27.

Olney, Peter. 2015. "Where Did the OUR Walmart Campaign Go Wrong?" *In These Times,* December 14.

Olson-Kenney, Caitlin. 2014. "Policy Brief: An Innovative Policy for Labor Force Development." Unpublished paper. Los Angeles: UCLA, Department of Urban Planning (June).

Organization for Economic Cooperation and Development (OECD). 2003. *Employment Outlook.* Paris: OECD.

———. 2007. *Education at a Glance 2007.* Paris: OECD. Available at: http://www.oecd.org/document/30/0,3343,en_2825_495609 _39251550_1_1_1_1,00.html (accessed June 2008).

———. 2008. "Prices and Purchasing Power Parities." Paris: OECD. Available at: http://www.oecd.org/topicstatsportal/0,3398,en_2825 _495691_1_1_1_1_1,00.html#500300 (accessed June 2008).

Osterman, Paul. 1982. "Employment Structures Within Firms." *British Journal of Industrial Relations* 20(3): 349–61.

———. 2012. "Job Quality in America: The Myths That Block Action." In *Are Bad Jobs Inevitable? Trends, Determinants, and Responses to Job Quality in the Twenty-First Century,* edited by Chris Warhurst, Françoise Carré, Patricia Findlay, and Chris Tilly. Basingstoke, U.K.: Palgrave Macmillan.

OUR Walmart. N.d. Website. Available at: http://forrespect.org/ (accessed May 2014).

———. 2014. "Winning Access to More Hours." Available at: http://forrespect.org/more-hours (accessed May 2014).

Paumgarten, Nick. 2010. "Food Fighter: Does Whole Foods' CEO Know What's Best for You?" *The New Yorker,* January 4.

Peapod. N.d. "Peapod Facts." Available at: https://www.peapod.com/site/companyPages/our-company-overview.jsp (accessed March 2016).

Pearson, Samantha, and Sarah Nassauer. 2017. "Wal-Mart Doubles Down in Brazil Despite Sluggish Sales." *Wall Street Journal,* March 12.

Peltz, James F. 2016. "See Which Stores Will Be Open Thanksgiving Day—and Why Others Are Waiting Until Black Friday." *Los Angeles Times,* November 10.

Peterson, Hayley. 2015. "This German Store That Is a Cross Between Walmart and Trader Joe's Is Planning to Take over America." *Business Insider,* November 5. Available at: http://www.businessinsider.in/This-German-store-that-is-a-cross-between-Walmart-and-Trader-Joes-is-planning-to-take-over-America/articleshow/49650463.cms (accessed November 2015).

Piketty, Thomas. 2014. *Capital in the Twenty-First Century.* Cambridge, Mass.: Belknap Press of Harvard University Press.

Pires, Roberto. 2008. "Promoting Sustainable Compliance: Styles of Labour Inspection and Compliance Outcomes in Brazil." *International Labour Review* 147(2/3): 199–229.

Planet Retail. 2010a. "Tesco Lotus CEO Commits to Long-Term Investment in Thailand." Planet Retail, November 16. Available at: http://www.planetretail.net/NewsAndInsight (accessed November 2010).

———. 2010b. "AEON to Triple Capital Investment in Asia." Planet Retail, October 27. Available at: http://www.planetretail.net/NewsAndInsight (accessed October 2010).

———. 2010c. "Comercial Mexicana to Restructure Debt." Planet Retail, "News and Insight," May 31. Available at: http://www.planetretail.net/NewsAndInsight (accessed May 2010).

———. 2011. "Wal-Mart Restructures Online Operations." Planet Retail, August 15. Available at: http://www.planetretail.net/NewsAndInsight (accessed August 2015).

———. 2012. "Comercial Mexicana Pays Off Restructured Debt." Planet

Retail, "News and Insight," November 23. Available at: http://www.planetretail.net/NewsAndInsight (accessed November 2012).

———. 2013. "Carrefour Spins Off MENA to Franchisee." Planet Retail, May 23. Available at: http://www.planetretail.net/NewsAndInsight (accessed May 2013).

———. 2014. "Carrefour to Exit India." Planet Retail, July 8. Available at: http://www.planetretail.net/NewsAndInsight (accessed July 2014).

Proyecto de Derechos Económicos, Sociales, y Culturales (ProDESC). 2008. *Lo barato sale caro: Violaciones a los derechos humanos laborales en Wal-Mart México (Selling Cheaply Has Costs: Human Rights Violations at Wal-Mart Mexico)*. Mexico City: ProDESC.

Przeworski, Adam, and Henry Teune. 1970. *The Logic of Comparative Social Inquiry.* London: Cambridge University Press.

Quinn, Bill. 2004. *How Wal-Mart Is Destroying America (and the World) and What You Can Do About It.* Berkeley, Calif.: Ten Speed Press.

Raines, Laura. 2007. "All Work and No Play?" *Atlanta Journal Constitution,* May 18.

Ramakrishnan, Sruthi. 2014. "Best Buy Says Sales to Fall as More Shoppers Buy Online." *Reuters,* August 26.

Rampell, Catherine. 2013. "Part-Time Job Becomes Full-Time Wait for a Better Job." *New York Times,* April 19.

Ramstad, Evan. 2006. "Wal-Mart Leaves South Korea by Selling Stores to Local Rival; Sale to Shinsegae Follows April Pullout by Carrefour as Domestic Firms Prevail." *Wall Street Journal,* May 23, A2.

Ray, Rebecca, Milla Sanes, and John Schmitt. 2013. *No-Vacation Nation Revisited.* Washington, D.C.: Center for Economic Policy Research.

Reardon, Thomas, and Julio A. Berdegue. 2002. "The Rapid Rise of Supermarkets in Latin America: Challenges and Opportunities for Development." *Development Policy Review* 20(4): 371–88.

Reich, Michael, Ken Jacobs, Annette Bernhardt, and Ian Perry. 2015. "The Proposed Minimum Wage Law for Los Angeles: Economic Impacts and Policy Options." Policy brief. Berkeley: UC Berkeley Institute for Research on Labor and Employment (March).

Restaurant Opportunities Centers United (ROC-U). N.d. "Restaurants Advancing Industry Standards in Employment (RAISE)." Available at: http://www.raiserestaurants.org (accessed July 2017).

Retail Action Project (RAP). N.d. Available at: http://retailactionproject.org/ (accessed December 2015).

Reuters. 2012. "Timeline: Wal-Mart Eyeing the Russian Market." *Reuters*, April 5.

Richardson, Charley. 2005. "What's Happening to Retail Jobs?" Talk delivered at the conference "Sustainable Jobs, Sustainable Workplaces." University of Massachusetts Lowell (October 27–28).

Ritzer, George. 1998. *The McDonaldization Thesis: Explorations and Extensions*. Thousand Oaks, Calif.: Pine Forge.

Roberts, Anthony. 2015. "Wal-Mart's Limited Growth in Urban Retail Markets: The Cost of Low Labor Investment." Los Angeles: UCLA Institute for Research on Labor and Employment (July). Available at: http://www.irle.ucla.edu/publications/documents/Anthony Robert_WalMartReport_July2015.pdf (accessed January 2016).

Roberts, B. 2009. "Wal Mart: Where, How, and What Next." Planet Retail.

Robinson, Nick. 2006. "Even Without a Union, Florida Wal-Mart Workers Use Collective Action to Enforce Rights." *Labor Notes*, January 15. Available at: http://labornotes.org/2006/01/even-without-union -florida-wal-mart-workers-use-collective-action-enforce-rights (accessed May 2014).

Rosen, Ellen. 2006. "Wal-Mart: The New Retail Colossus." In *Wal-Mart World: The World's Biggest Corporation in the Global Economy*, edited by Stanley Brunn. New York: Routledge/Taylor & Francis.

———. 2008. "Adding Insult to Injury: Wal-Mart's Workers' Compensation Scam." *New Labor Forum* 17(1): 56–64.

Royle, Tony. 2006. "The Dominance Effect? Multinational Corporations in the Italian Quick Food Service Sector." *British Journal of Industrial Relations* 44(4): 757–59.

Ruan, Nantiya, and Nancy Reichman. 2014. "Hours Equity Is the New Pay Equity." *Villanova Law Review* 59(1): 35–82.

Ruetschlin, Catherine. 2014. *Retail's Hidden Potential: How Raising Wages Would Benefit Workers, the Industry, and the Overall Economy*. Washington, D.C.: Demos.

Russolillo, Steven. 2016. "No Comfort for Bed Bath & Beyond." *Wall Street Journal*, January 6.

Safdar, Khadeesha. 2017. "Best Buy Defies Retail Doldrums, Posting Higher Sales." *Wall Street Journal*, May 25.

Samuel, Henry. 2015. "Paris to Extend Opening Hours for Stores in 12 'International Tourist Zones.'" *The Telegraph* (London), September 24.

Satterthwaite, Ann. 2001. *Going Shopping: Consumer Choices and Community Consequences*. New Haven, Conn.: Yale University Press.

Scheiber, Naomi. 2015. "Starbucks Falls Short After Pledging Better Labor Practices." *New York Times,* September 23.

———. 2016. "Reporter to Trader Joe's: Are We Having Fun Yet?" *New York Times,* November 16.

Schmitt, John. 2013. "Why Does the Minimum Wage Have No Discernible Effect on Employment?" Washington, D.C.: Center for Economic and Policy Research. Available at: http://www.cepr.net/documents /publications/minwage-2013-02.pdf (accessed January 2015).

Schneider, Daniel, and Kristen Harknett. 2017. "How Work Schedules Affect Health and Well-Being: The Mediating Roles of Economic Insecurity and Work-Life Conflict." Working paper. Berkeley and Philadelphia: University of California and University of Pennsylvania.

Schnitzer, Yael. 2011. "Huelga de trabajadores de Ekono: Malas prácticas laborales de Wal-Mart aterrizan en Chile" ("Ekono Workers Strike: Wal-Mart's Bad Labor Practices Land in Chile"). *El Mostrador,* March 25. Available at: http://www.elmostrador.cl/noticias/pais /2011/03/25/malas-practicas-laborales-de-wal-mart-aterrizan-en -chile/ (accessed July 2017).

Schrank, Andrew, and Michael Piore. 2007. "Norms, Standards, and Labor Market Regulation in Latin America." Mexico City: CEPAL/ ECLAC (Economic Conference on Latin America and the Caribbean). Available at: http://www.eclac.cl/publicaciones/xml/3 /28113/Serie%2077.pdf (accessed December 2014).

Schwentesius, Rita, and Manuel Ángel Gómez. 2002. "The Rise of Supermarkets in Mexico: Impacts on Horticulture Chains." *Development Policy Review* 20(4): 487–502.

Sen, Aditi, and Carrie Gleason. 2015. *The Grind: Striving for Schedule Fairness at Starbucks.* New York: Center for Popular Democracy, Fair Workweek Initiative, and coworker.org (September).

Senén González, and Cecilia y Julieta Haidar. 2009. "El debate sobre la revitalización sindical: Un aporte al análisis sectorial en Argentina" ("The Debate on Trade Union Revitalization: A Contribution to Sectoral Analysis in Argentina"). Paper presented to the Ninth Congreso Nacional de Ciencia Política, "Centros y Periferias: Equilibrios y Asimetrías en las Relaciones de Poder" ("Centers and Peripheries: Equilibria and Asymmetries in Power Relationships"). Santa Fe, Argentina (August 19–22).

Silva, Elena. 2007. "On the Clock: Rethinking the Way Schools Use Time." Washington, D.C.: Education Sector (January). Available at: https://www.naesp.org/resources/1/A_New_Day_for_Learning _Resources/Making_the_Case/On_the_Clock_Rethinking_the _Way_Schools_Use_Time.pdf (accessed April 2016).

Silva, Jorge. 2016. "Licenciée pour avoir oublié de scanner un pack de bières et deux sacs plastiques." ("Sanctioned for Forgetting to Scan a Pack of Beer and Two Plastic Bags"). *Le Monde,* January 28.

Smith, Chris, and Peter Meiksins. 1995. "Systems, Society, and Dominance Effects in Cross-National Organisational Analysis." *Work, Employment and Society* 9(2): 241–67.

Smith, Rebecca, David Bensman, and Paul Marvey. 2012. "The Big Rig: Poverty, Pollution, and the Misclassification of Truck Drivers at America's Ports." New York: National Employment Law Project. Available at: http://nelp.3cdn.net/000beaf922628dfea1_cum6b0fab .pdf (accessed July 2017).

Society for Human Resource Management. 2015. "State Call-In/Call-Back/Reporting Pay Laws." Online fact sheet. Available at: http:// www.shrm.org/LegalIssues/StateandLocalResources/StateandLoc alStatutesandRegulations/Documents/Callbackcallinreportingpay .pdf (accessed December 2015).

Solow, Robert M. 1990. *The Labor Market as a Social Institution.* Oxford: Blackwell.

Soper, Spencer. 2015. "The Robots Chasing Amazon." *Bloomberg Business Week,* October 22. Available at: http://www.bloomberg.com/news /articles/2015-10-22/the-robots-chasing-amazon (accessed November 2015).

Soper, Spencer, and Olivia Zaleski. 2017. "Inside Amazon's Battle to Break into the $800 Billion Grocery Market." *Bloomberg Business Week,* March 20. Available at: https://www.bloomberg.com/news /features/2017-03-20/inside-amazon-s-battle-to-break-into-the-800 -billion-grocery-market (accessed March 2017).

Springer, Jon. 2016a. "Albertsons Pleased as It Bucks Self-Checkout Trend." *Supermarket News,* November 21. Available at: http://www .supermarketnews.com/online-retail/online-shoppers-view-super markets-stock-ups (accessed November 2016).

———. 2016b. "Online Shoppers View Supermarkets for Stock-Ups." *Supermarket News,* December 13. Available at: http://www.super marketnews.com/online-retail/online-shoppers-view-supermar kets-stock-ups (accessed December 2016).

Statbank Denmark. 2007. "Labor Market Table ATR1." Available at: www.statbank.dk accessed September 2007).

Statista. 2015. "The World's 50 Largest Companies Based on Number of Employees in 2015." Available at: http://www.statista.com /statistics/264671/top-20-companies-based-on-number-of -employees/ (accessed August 2015).

Statistics Denmark (Danmark Statistik). 2002. Database. Copenhagen: Statistics Denmark. Available at: http://www.dst.dk/HomeUK.aspx (accessed April 2004).

Statistisches Bundesamt (Federal Statistical Office). 2001. Fachserie 6. Reihe 4. Jahreserhebung.

Stevens, Laura, and Khadeeja Safdar. 2016. "Amazon Working on Several Grocery-Store Formats, Could Open More Than 2,000 Locations." *Wall Street Journal,* December 5.

Strauss, Maria. 2011. "Target Digs in Heels as Labour Union Applies to Keep Unionized Status." *Toronto Globe and Mail,* November 28.

Streeck, Wolfgang, and Kathleen Thelen. 2005. "Introduction: Institutional Change in Advanced Political Economies." In *Beyond Continuity: Institutional Change in Advanced Political Economies,* edited by Wolfgang Streeck and Kathleen Thelen. Oxford: Oxford University Press.

Supermarket News. 2014. "Walmart Joins Farm Workers' Rights Program." *Supermarket News,* January 17. Available at: http://super marketnews.com/produce/walmart-joins-farm-workers-rights -program (accessed April 2014).

Sykes, Jennifer, Kathryn Edin, Katrin Kriz, and Sarah Halpern-Meekin. 2015. "Dignity and Dreams: What the Earned Income Tax Credit (EITC) Means to Low-Income Families." *American Sociological Review* 80(2): 243–67.

Taal, Michelle. 2012. "Massmart: Wal-Mart into Africa." Cape Town: Labour Research Service, with Friedrich Ebert Stiftung and UNI Global Union (November). Available at: http://www.fes-southafrica.org /media/2013%20Massmart%20UNI%20Alliance%20final%20 report.pdf (accessed January 2016).

Target Sucks. N.d. Website. Available at: http://www.ihatetarget.net/ (accessed March 2014).

Taylor, Kate. 2015. "Kroger Is Building the Grocery Store of the Future." *Business Insider,* November 8. Available at: http://www.business insider.com/krogers-grocery-store-of-the-future-2015-11 (accessed November 2015).

Tesco PLC. 2013. *Annual Report 2013.* Available at: https://www.tesco plc.com/media/1456/tesco_annual_report_2013.pdf (accessed July 2017).

Tijdens, Kea 1998. *Zeggenschap over arbeidstijden: De samenhang tussen bedrijfstijden, arbeidstijden en flexibilisering van de personeelsbezetting* (*Control over Working Hours: The Relationship Between Opening Hours, Working Hours, and Flexible Staffing*). Amsterdam: Welboom.

Tijdens, Kea, Reinhard Bispinck, Heiner Dribbusch, and Maarten van Klaveren. 2007. "Exploring the Impact of High and Low Bargaining Coverage Across Eight EU Member States." Paper presented to the International Industrial Relations Association Eighth European Congress. Manchester, U.K. (September 3–7).

Tilly, Chris. 1996. *Half a Job: Bad and Good Part-Time Jobs in a Changing Labor Market.* Philadelphia: Temple University Press.

———. 2007. "Wal-Mart and Its Workers: Not the Same All Over the World." *Connecticut Law Review* 39(4): 1–19.

———. 2014. "Beyond 'Contratos de Protección': Strong and Weak Unionism in Mexican Retail Enterprises." *Latin American Research Review* 49(3): 176–98.

Tilly, Chris, Rina Agarwala, Sarah Mosoetsa, Pun Ngai, Carlos Salas, and Hina Sheikh. 2013. *Informal Worker Organizing as a Strategy for Improving Subcontracted Work in the Textile and Apparel Industries.* Los Angeles: UCLA Institute for Research on Labor and Employment. Available at: http://www.irle.ucla.edu/publications/documents /Informalworkerorganizingintextilesandgarments-UCLAReport -9-2013.pdf (accessed July 2017).

Tilly, Chris, and José Luis Álvarez Galván. 2006. "The Mexican Retail Sector in the Age of Globalization: Lousy Jobs, Invisible Unions." *International Labor and Working Class History* 70(1): 1–25.

Tilly, Chris, and Marie Kennedy. 2010. "On Strike in China." *Dollars and Sense* (September/October): 19–23.

Tilly, Chris, and Charles Tilly. 1998. *Work Under Capitalism.* Denver, Colo.: Westview Press.

Timmons, Heather. 2006. "Wal-Mart's British Unit Agrees to a Union Contract." *New York Times,* June 30.

Ton, Zeynep. 2012. "Why 'Good' Jobs Are Good for Retailers." *Harvard Business Review* (January/February): 127–31.

Toys "R" Us. N.d. "About Toys 'R' Us, Inc." Available at: http://www .toysrusinc.com/about-us/ (accessed January 2014).

Trigona, Marie. 2007. "Wal-Mart Faces Accusations of Anti-Union Practices in Argentina." Washington, D.C.: Center for International Policy, Americas Program (November 17). Available at: http://www .cipamericas.org/archives/888# (accessed April 2014).

Tuttle, Brad. 2012. "Why Shoppers and Shopping Centers Alike Now Embrace the Dollar Store." *Time,* January 27.

U.K. Office for National Statistics (ONS). 2005. *Annual Survey of Hours and Earnings.* London: ONS. Available at: https://www.ons.gov.uk /employmentandlabourmarket/peopleinwork/earningsandwork inghours/datasets/ashe1997to2015selectedestimates (accessed December 2007).

———. 2006. *Annual Survey of Hours and Earnings*. London: ONS.

Unger, Jonathan, Diana Beaumont, and Anita Chan. 2011. "Did Unionization Make a Difference? Work Conditions and Trade Union Activities at Chinese Walmart Stores." In *Walmart in China*, edited by Anita Chan. Ithaca, N.Y.: Cornell University Press.

UNI Global Union. 2005. "Wal-Mart Stores, Inc.: UNI Commerce Company Overview." Available at: http://www.unionnetwork.org/unisite/Sectors/Commerce/Multinationals/Wal-Mart_Report_UNI_Commerce_Dec_2005.pdf (accessed December 2015).

———. 2011. "UNI Meets Walmart Workers Union of Japan." UNI Global Union, June 29. Available at: http://www.uniglobalunion.org/news/uni-meets-walmart-workers-union-japan (accessed March 2014).

———. 2014. "Walmart Putting Female Workers at Risk." UNI Global Union, August 27. Available at: http://www.uniglobalunion.org/news/walmart-putting-female-workers-risk (accessed January 2016).

Unionstats.com. N.d. "Union Membership and Coverage Database from the CPS." Available at: http://unionstats.com/ (accessed August 2015).

United Food and Commercial Workers (UFCW) Canada. N.d. "Issues: Walmart Workers Canada." Available at: http://www.ufcw.ca/index.php?option=com_content&view=article&id=51&Itemid=90&lang=en (accessed February 2014).

U.S. Bureau of Labor Statistics. 2003. "Labor Force Statistics from the Current Population Survey (CPS): 2003 Annual Averages." Washington: U.S. Department of Labor, BLS. Available at: https://www.bls.gov/cps/cps_aa2003.htm (accessed July 2017).

———. 2005. "Labor Force Statistics from the Current Population Survey (CPS): 2005 Annual Averages." Washington: U.S. Department of Labor, BLS. Available at: https://www.bls.gov/cps/cps_aa2005.htm (accessed July 2017).

———. 2007. "Labor Force Statistics from the Current Population Survey (CPS): 2007 Annual Averages." Washington: U.S. Department of Labor, BLS. Available at: https://www.bls.gov/cps/cps_aa2007.htm (accessed July 2017).

———. 2008. *Quarterly Census of Employment and Wages*. Washington: U.S. Department of Labor, BLS. Available at: http://www.bls.gov/cew/ (accessed June 2008).

———. 2014a. *Occupational Outlook Handbook 2014.* Washington: U.S. Department of Labor, BLS. Available at: http://www.bls.gov/ooh/home.htm (accessed August 2015).

———. 2014b. "Table 21: Persons at Work in Nonagricultural Industries by Class of Worker and Usual Full- or Part-time Status." In *Labor Force Statistics from the Current Population Survey.* Washington: U.S. Department of Labor, BLS. Available at: https://www.bls.gov/cps/aa2014/cpsaat21.htm (accessed August 2015).

———. 2015a. *Job Openings and Labor Turnover Survey.* Washington: U.S. Department of Labor, BLS. Available at: http://www.bls.gov/jlt/ (accessed August 2015).

———. 2015b. *May 2014 National Occupational Employment and Wage Estimates: United States.* Washington: U.S. Department of Labor, BLS. Available at: https://stats.bls.gov/oes/2014/may/oes_nat.htm (accessed May 2017).

———. 2015c. "Labor Force Statistics from the Current Population Survey (CPS): 2015 Annual Averages." Washington: U.S. Department of Labor, BLS. Available at: https://stats.bls.gov/cps/cps_aa2015.htm (accesed February 2016).

———. 2016a. *Current Employment Statistics—CES (National).* Washington: U.S. Department of Labor, BLS. Available at: http://www.bls.gov/ces/ (accessed September 2016).

———. 2016b. "May 2016 National Industry-Specific Occupational Employment and Wage Estimates" (sectors 44–45, retail), *Occupational Employment Statistics.* Washington: U.S. Department of Labor, BLS. Available at: http://www.bls.gov/oes/current/oessrci.htm#44-45 (accessed September 2016).

———. 2016c. "Characteristics of Minimum Wage Workers, 2015." BLS Report 1061. Washington: U.S. Department of Labor, BLS (April). Available at: http://www.bls.gov/opub/reports/minimum-wage/2015/home.htm (accessed September 2016).

U.S. Census Bureau. 2005a. *Product Lines: 2002.* 2002 Economic Census, Retail Trade, Subject Series. EC02-44SL-LS. Washington: U.S. Government Printing Office (October). Available at: http://www.census.gov/prod/ec02/ec0244slls.pdf (accessed June 2008).

———. 2005b. *Miscellaneous Subjects: 2002.* 2002 Economic Census, Retail Trade, Subject Series. EC02-44SX-SB. Washington: U.S. Government Printing Office (December). Available at: http://www.census.gov/prod/ec02/ec0244sxsb.pdf (accessed June 2008).

———. 2014. *Monthly and Annual Retail Trade Survey—2011.* Available at: http://www.census.gov/retail/index.html#arts (accessed January 2014).

———. 2015. "American FactFinder: Retail Trade: Subject Series—Miscellaneous Subjects: Floor Space by Selected Kind of Business: 2007." EC0744SXSB1. Available at: https://factfinder.census.gov/faces/tableservices/jsf/pages/productview.xhtml?src=bkmk (accessed August 2015).

U.S. Department of Agriculture. Foreign Agricultural Service. 2013. "Canada: Retail Foods: Retail Food Sector Report." GAIN Report CA13001. Washington: USDA (January 23). Available at: https://gain.fas.usda.gov/Recent%20GAIN%20Publications/Retail%20Foods_Ottawa_Canada_1-22-2013.pdf (accessed February 2012).

U.S. Department of Labor. N.d. "Apprenticeship USA." Available at: http://www.dol.gov/apprenticeship/ (accessed December 2015).

———. N.d. "History of Federal Minimum Wage Rates Under the Fair Labor Standards Act, 1938–2009." Washington: U.S. Department of Labor, Wage and Hour Division. Available at: https://www.dol.gov/whd/minwage/chart.htm#content (accessed April 2016).

U.S. Federal Reserve Board. 2009. "Foreign Exchange Rates (Annual)." Available at: http://www.federalreserve.gov/releases/g5a/current/ (accessed February 2009).

Van der Horst, Linda. 2015. "Wal-Mart Uprising: The Battle for Labor Rights in China." *The Diplomat*, November 14. Available at: http://thediplomat.com/2015/11/wal-mart-uprising-the-battle-for-labor-rights-in-china/ (accessed December 2015).

Van Grove, Jennifer, and Shan Li. 2016. "Amazon to Open 2nd Physical Bookstore, This One in Southern California." *Los Angeles Times*, March 8.

Van Klaveren, Maarten. 2008. "Retail Industry: The Contrast of Supermarkets and Consumer Electronics." In *The Dutch Model of Low-Wage Work,* edited by Wiemer Salverda, Maarten van Klaveren, and Marc van der Meer. New York: Russell Sage Foundation.

———. 2009. "Low Wages in the Retail Industry in the Netherlands." Working paper. Amsterdam: Amsterdam Institute for Advanced Labor Studies (AIAS).

Van Klaveren, Maarten, Kea Tijdens, and Wim Sprenger. 2007. *Dicht de loonkloof! Verslag van het CLOSE-onderzoek (Close the Gender Pay Gap! Report of the CLOSE Research Project).* Eindhoven and Amsterdam: STZ Consultancy and Research and the Amsterdam Institute for Advanced Labor Studies.

Vega, Joel. 2005. "Retail Ergonomics." *Elsevier Food International* 8(3, September).

Vidalon, Dominique. 2010. "Casino to Buy Carrefour's Thai Assets for $1.2 Billion." *Reuters*, November 15.

Viswanatha, Aruna, and Devlin Barrett. 2015. "Wal-Mart Bribery Probe Finds Few Signs of Major Misconduct in Mexico." *Wall Street Journal,* October 19.

Vorley, Bill. 2007. "Supermarkets—Global Trends and Implications." PowerPoint presentation to the International Institute for Environment and Development. London (March 1).

Voss-Dahm, Dorothea. 2000. "'Service-Sector Taylorism' and Changes in the Demands on Working-Time Organization: The Example of the Retail Trade." Paper presented to the international conference "The Economics and Socioeconomics of Services: International Perspectives." Lille/Roubaix, France (June 22–23).

———. 2003. "Zwischen Kunden und Kennziffern: Leistungspolitik in der Verkaufsarbeit des Einzelhandels" ["Between Customers and Indicators: Performance Policy in Retail Sales Work"]. In *Dienstleistungsarbeit: Auf dem Boden der Tatsachen: Befunde aus Handel, Industrie, Medien und IT-Branche (Service Work: Grounded in Fact: Findings from Retailing, Manufacturing, the Media, and the IT Industry),* edited by Markus Pohlmann, Dieter Sauer, Gudrun Trautwein-Kalms, and Alexandra Wagner. Berlin: Ed. Sigma.

———. 2008. "Low-Paid but Committed to the Industry." In *Low-Wage Work in Germany,* edited by Gerhard Bosch and Claudia Weinkopf. New York: Russell Sage Foundation.

Wall Street Journal. 2000. "Overdue Overtime Is Set to Be Paid, Answering Suit." *Wall Street Journal,* January 26.

———. 2012. "Year in Review: Year of the Oops: Firms Spent in Reverse." *Wall Street Journal,* January 3, B1.

Wal-Mart. 2011. *2011 Annual Report.* Available at: http://s2.q4cdn .com/056532643/files/doc_financials/2011/Annual/2011-annual -report-for-walmart-stores-inc_130221022810084579.pdf (accessed July 2017).

———. 2013. *2013 Annual Report.* Available at: http://s2.q4cdn.com /056532643/files/doc_financials/2013/Annual/2013-annual-re port-for-walmart-stores-inc_130221024708579502.pdf (accessed July 2017).

———. 2015. *2015 Annual Report.* Available at: http://s2.q4cdn.com/05 6532643/files/doc_financials/2015/annual/2015-annual-report.pdf (accessed July 2017).

———. N.d. "Our Business." Available at: http://corporate.walmart .com/our-story/our-business/sams-club (accessed January 2014).

———. N.d. "Company Facts." Available at: http://news.walmart.com /walmart-facts.

Wal-Mart México. 2009. "Informe Anual 2009" ("2009 Annual Report"). Available at: http://walmex.mx/es/informacion-financiera/anual .html (accessed January 2014).

Wang, Shuguang, and Yongchang Zhang. 2006. "Penetrating the Great Wall, Conquering the Middle Kingdom: Wal-Mart in China." In *Wal-Mart World: The World's Biggest Corporation in the Global Economy*, edited by Stanley Brunn. New York: Routledge/Taylor & Francis.

Warhurst, Chris, Françoise Carré, Patricia Findlay, and Chris Tilly, eds. 2012. *Are Bad Jobs Inevitable?* London: Palgrave Macmillan.

Warhurst, Chris, Chris Tilly, and Mary Gatta. 2017. "A New Social Construction of Skill." In *Handbook of Skills and Training*, edited by John Buchanan, David Finegold, Ken Mayhew, and Chris Warhurst. Oxford: Oxford University Press.

Warren, Dorian. 2005. "Wal-Mart Surrounded: Community Alliances and Labor Politics in Chicago." *New Labor Forum* 14(3): 8–15.

Weil, David. 2008. "Mighty Monolith or Fractured Federation? Business Opposition and the Enactment of Workplace Legislation." In *The Gloves-Off Economy: Workplace Standards at the Bottom of America's Labor Market*, edited by Annette Bernhardt, Heather Boushey, Laura Dresser, and Chris Tilly. Ithaca, N.Y.: Cornell University Press.

Westergaard-Nielsen, Niels. 2008. "Statistical Analysis and History of Low-Wage Work in Denmark." In *Low-Wage Work in Denmark*, edited by Niels Westergaard-Nielsen. New York: Russell Sage Foundation.

Whitley, Richard. 1999. *Divergent Capitalisms: The Social Structuring and Change of Business Systems*. Oxford: Oxford University Press.

Wingfield, Nick. 2017. "Amazon's Ambitions Unboxed: Stores for Furniture, Appliances, and More." *New York Times*, March 25.

Wonacott, Peter. 2003. "Wilting Plants: Behind China's Export Boom Heated Battle Among Factories; As Wal-Mart, Others Demand Lowest Prices, Managers Scramble to Slash Costs; Rising Concerns About Safety." *Wall Street Journal*, November 13.

World Bank. N.d. "Databank." Available at: http://databank.worldbank .org/data/home.aspx (accessed July 2017).

Zhao, Kate. 2009. "Family Dollar Gets Boost from Food Subsidy Plan." *Wall Street Journal*, August 19, B5A.

Zimmerman, Ann. 2005. "Wal-Mart Urges Congress to Raise Minimum Wage." *Wall Street Journal*, October 25, A2.

———. 2008. "Home Depot Learns to Go Local." *Wall Street Journal*, October 7.

———. 2011. "Dollar Stores Find Splurges Drying Up." *Wall Street Journal*, July 11.

———. 2012. "Selling TVs at Full Price." *Wall Street Journal,* May 23.

Ziobro, Paul. 2015. "Target to Increase Wages to at Least $9/Hour by April." *Wall Street Journal,* March 19.

Ziobro, Paul, and Eric Morath. 2015. "Wal-Mart Raising Wages as Market Gets Tighter." *Wall Street Journal,* February 19.

Index

Boldface numbers refer to figures and tables.

accidents, 161–163
Accord in Fire and Building Safety, 188
ACFTU (All-China Federation of Trade Unions), 183
acquisitions and mergers: corporate take-overs, 179, 182–183, 249n13; in electronics retail, 62–64, 66, 200; private equity investment and, 199
Affordable Care Act (2010), 140, 210–211, 233, 241n25, 255nn61–64, 255–256n67
African Americans, 29, 30, 239n34
age: of food retail workers, 28; French-U.S. comparisons, 1, 168; part-time jobs and, 7–8, 28, 30, 73–74, 103, 119, **121**, 122; turnover rates, 135–136; wages and, 125–126, 142–144, 149, 152
agency of employers, 34–35, 50–54, **52–55**
Aldi, 128, 179, 185, 186, 202
All-China Federation of Trade Unions (ACFTU), 183
Amazon: book stores of, 208, 254n46; competition with, 49, 200, 208, 217; convenience stores of, 209; effect on retail, 8; electronics sales of, 254n48; food sales of, 206–207, 216; Whole Foods, purchase of, 206–207, 217
Andersson, Fredrik, 31, 33, 134
Apple, competition with, 200, 208
Argentina, Wal-Mart in, 176, 180–183, 190–191, 231
Askenazy, Philippe, 246–247
autonomy: of companies, 90, 102; of managers, 195, 227; of workers, 110

axes of comparisons, **11**, 11–12

baggers, 1, 2, 126–127, 134, 160–161, 253n19
Bailey, Thomas R., 7, 38, 116, 152, 219
bankruptcy, 39–40, 185–186, 200, 249n7
Baret, Christophe, 116
Bargain Warehouse, **43**, 68–71, 99–102, 109–110, 241n22
barriers to entry, 128, 167, 179–180, 186, 201–202
benefits: cross-national comparisons, 140, 246n47; cross-sector comparisons, 20; French-U.S. comparisons, 164; for full-time jobs, 210–211, 255nn62–64; health insurance, 20, 82–83, 140, 161–162, 212, 224; lack of, 35; in Mexico, 154; for part-time jobs, 60, 167, 187, 210–211, 255n62; policy improvements for, 224; union membership and, 82–83; of Wal-Mart, 83–84, 177, **178**, 187; for warehouse store employees, 69–70. *See also* Affordable Care Act
Bernhardt, Annette D., 7, 38, 116, 152, 219
Berry, Jean-Baptiste, 246–247
Best Buy, 61, 200, 209, 217, 254n48
big box stores. *See* warehouse stores
Black Friday, 225, 257n111
blue laws, 224–225
bonuses, 50, 60, 89, 95, 98, 164
book stores, 8, 208, 254n46
Bosch, Gerhard, 116
boycotts, 229